MW01039400

An Orphan Has
Many Parents

An Orphan Has Many Parents

by Phil Craft and Stan Friedland

Foreword by Father Val J. Peter
Executive Director, Boys Town
Omaha, Nebraska

KTAV Publishing House, Inc.

1998

Copyright © 1998
Phil Craft and Stan Friedland

Library of Congress Cataloging-in-Publication Data

Craft, Phil, 1927–
       An orphan has many parents / by Phil Craft and Stan Friedland: Foreword
by Val J. Peter.
       p.   cm.
       ISBN 0-88125-650-1
       1. Pride of Judea Children's Home—History. 2. Orphans—New York
(State)—New York —Biography 3. Brooklyn (New York, N.Y.)

I. Friedland, Stan, 1931–   .   II.Title.
HV995.N52P753   1998
362.73'—DC21   98-21915
                                                                        CIP

Manufactured in United States of America
KTAV Publishing House, Inc.
900 Jefferson St.
Hoboken, NJ 07030

Dedicated to the host of caring friends
who helped me along the way.

—Phil Craft

Dedicated to the loves of my life: my family.

—Stan Friedland

Contents

Foreword

What a wonderful group of recollections! The authors of *An Orphan Has Many Parents* have captured not only the history of the Pride of Judea, but have recaptured many of the real "feelings" that were generated there. And almost all were positive feelings—fond memories now viewed from afar.

Back then orphanages were a part of the fabric of society. Some kids had no parents, or only one, and needed good care. It was a fact of life. They weren't "emotionally disturbed," "Attention Deficit Disorder," "delinquent," or "mentally ill"—they were just kids who needed a warm place to stay and caring supervision, adequate food, etc.

When I finished this book, I felt I really knew orphanage life at Pride of Judea, and I respected the work that was done there. It was a safe place, a good place to grow up, considering that few skilled, caring foster families could be found for children back then.

If it weren't for the problematic backgrounds of the children—both boys and girls—and the fact that some children came to the orphanage at a very early age, life at the Pride of Judea Children's Home could almost have passed for life at an upper-class English boys school. The difference, obviously, is the lack of emotional support from a caring family at home, and the self-confidence that springs from children who have a strong, supportive network of family and friends.

The idea of generating a permanent "history" and record of the times is prudent, inspiring, and fun to read. So much good was done in such orphanages. But virtually no record exists about what life was like there. What a wonderful legacy for the alumni authors to leave behind—what a wonderful way to "pay back" the Pride of Judea—for the helpful things it did for children.

It was a simpler time then—kids could safely walk to the public schools, and adults were helpful and sensitive to the needs of these children. Especially people in the neighborhood. No NIMBY (not in my back yard) reactions here just help and support for the "orphans"—a sharp contrast with the present.

These days there are few orphanages, even though there are many children without good homes. Many kids today have parents, but they often receive little parenting. They're sometimes called social orphans. The girls—and even many of the boys—have been sexually and physically abused by the very persons who are supposed to treat them as the wonderful gifts they are. In some ways, it is easier if a parent is dead. In those cases children can let fantasy and history combine to create "would be" memories of caring parents.

The trend away from orphanages toward developing permanent and semi-permanent foster families is a natural outflow of our realization that a relatively high number of today's single (and other) parents cannot or will not provide what their children need. We know the reasons— substance abuse, preoccupation with their own needs, an inability to relate to others, mental illness, poverty and a concomitant inability to deal with the resulting stresses, fragmented family life, missing support systems—the list could go on and on.

But the good news is that children are children. They are resilient. Most learn quickly, and if we as adults become knowledgeable enough, skilled enough and wise enough, we can compensate— sometimes almost fully—for the lack of love, caring, and parenting these children have experienced.

There were many caring adults in the lives of the children at the Pride of Judea Children's Home but we have since learned of the need for children to bond with persons who love them over the long haul. Orphanages did a wonderful job of providing the necessities of life and for many of the emotional needs of children. But ever present low salaries for workers in the orphanage, combined with other factors, such as shift work, made a more permanent placement with an intact family a more attractive alternative.

A number of references were made to the poor quality of foster homes generated by the social workers of the time, in New York City; however, many adoptive and foster families provided outstanding care and parenting for these children. Then, of course, there were some foster parents who took in children only "for the money."

Today, placing children in inadequate settings is unnecessary. The sad reality, however, is that even though I believe many families are "out there" who possess the skills, knowledge, and willingness to provide good quality parenting for children, no real priority has been given to finding them.

It's almost as if governmental leaders and average citizens simply don't care to help these children. In my view the "homeless" children of today are more in need of help than those in "The Pride," and yet little is done to help them—compared with what we now know they need.

We now know that many children's problems have a physiological base sometimes exacerbated by inappropriate adult reactions to such situations. We have developed pharmacological interventions that truly help children with certain problems, and genetic therapies are coming across the horizon. Moreover, other "psychological" interventions are much more reliable than in the past.

But how often do we see them used? Not often. Such remedies cost money, and sometimes a lot. The United States has never been a country in which primary preventative measures have been given priority. Indeed, the history of children's services in the United States is one of allowing problems to fester until they become so visible and embarrassing that politicians finally "invest" a few taxpayer dollars to "solve" the current crisis (or forestall it until the media lose interest and move on).

The United States as a society has perfected the bad habits of (1) not funding preventative programs that would keep problems from escalating, (2) not funding early intervention strategies that hold at least some promise of "salvaging" the future of a child or a family that's in trouble, and (3) only reluctantly and belatedly providing legislation (for example, legislation for child support, child abuse, spouse abuse and other family violence) so that life for disadvantaged children and families can get better in a sensible planned way.

The Pride of Judea Children's Home was an outstanding program for children of that time. What would an outstanding program for today's children look like? Today's troubled children need to be in a caring family setting. The "family" is nature's way of rearing the young. Moreover, research shows us that children need to "bond" with adults. They need loving role models to teach and discipline them so that they will develop the ability to take personal responsibility for their own actions. Children need parents. For children whose families are non existent or permanently disabled, quality substitute families must be found. Of course the children need to maintain relationships with important relatives, and "parents," when and where they exist; but the bottom line is that they need full time parents.

But what about children who are mentally ill, emotionally disturbed, badly neglected and abused, and showing clear reactions to that neglect and abuse? They need special places like Boys Town. Some children have such severe problems that for a time we need to create "artificial families" that can love them, care for them, teach them, model quality parenting for them, and reshape them through love and thoughtful therapy and discipline so that they can regain emotional stability. Sometimes it is not possible to bring them all the way back especially when society has ignored their problems until they have reached crisis proportions. But it is possible to do this for most children. We now have the means to do this.

There truly are reliable ways to efficiently and effectively assess the needs of such children, and to intervene effectively so that the children grow and "flower" into responsible adults. Unfortunately, the public, the media, and even some professionals seem to be in denial about many of the helpful things that can be done for these children.

At Boys Town we know how to motivate unmotivated children. We know how to break through the anger and defiance these children show us when they arrive. There are reliable and effective ways to break through to these often frightened, troubled children. Even though these children almost always want help, they often do not know how to get it, or even ask for it. But they need it.

We need to do today what the wonderful founders, benefactors, and staff at the Pride of Judea did for the children of their time. They gave them what they needed then; we need to give our troubled children what they need now. Life in the twenty-first century will not be kind to children who grow up without strong, positive family relationships, emotional supports, teaching, skills development, and parenting. Today's children "cycle back home" time and again, until they are sometimes 30 years old before they become truly independent. What of those children who have never bonded with parents, who have experienced terrible, punishing parenting and have no families to "cycle back to"? The answer is that unless we do what we know works with these children, and do it in a timely way, and continue to be actively supportive of them for a long period of time, many will not flower. In fact, research shows that most will wither on the vine But do we do that today? Not often. We do things—as a society—like push kids out of high school. We "emancipate them" when they are still children, emotionally, and then we watch as the jails, mental hospitals, and homeless shelters "help" them. We end up paying the price financially, they pay the price in other ways. The sad news is that these children—our children—who need parenting and love and someone to care for them, often find their troubled counterparts, and in their desperate search for love conceive new babies, who in their turn begin an unrequited search for true parenting.

When will it stop? It will stop when responsible citizens choose to give their time and other resources to make change happen. That's not as remote a possibility as it might seem. People are now learning the limits of accumulating "things," and relearning the importance of relationships. There are vast human and financial resources now accumulating in the hearts and bank accounts of many persons and groups: older Americans, synagogues, churches, wisely managed human service organizations, foundations, and many others. What we need now is leadership in the literally dozens of areas that need to combine to bring forceful commitment and change to the parenting of our nation's parent-less children.

The founders of the Pride of Judea did what was needed in their day—they cared for those who were less fortunate than they—they shared their talents wisely—and they did it in a responsible, thoughtful way. They did what was needed at that time. We, too, must act responsibly in this time of stormy change. The good news is that we have the resources—both human and financial—to do it. What we need most of all is what the Pride of Judea had—mature, intelligent, kind, committed leaders who understood their times and responded with thoughtful sacrifice.

It is we, the lucky ones, who must now take the reins. We did not earn our good health, our good parenting, our good intelligence, education, skin color, values, aspirations, and country of birth. These were happenstance; they were given to us; we did not earn them. We were lucky. We were in the right place at the right time.

There are hundreds of thousands of children who are as unlucky as we were lucky. The lucky ones need to help the unlucky ones—it's as simple as that. The good news is that we now know what children need, and how to help them. It's time to act. I hope and ask everyone who reads this statement to make a personal, lasting commitment to help those unlucky children. They need us now, not later.

Father Val J. Peter

Father Val J. Peter has served since 1985 as Executive Director of Father Flanagan's Boys' Home, known popularly as Boys Town. This famous nonsectarian organization was founded in Omaha, Nebraska in 1917 by Father Edward J. Flanagan, and its headquarters are a National Historic Landmark. Directly caring for more than 30,000 abused, abandoned, neglected or otherwise at-risk children each year. Its mission is to change the way America cares for youngsters and families in crisis. Boys Town is national in its scope, with numerous youth care and family programs in cities and towns across the United States. Through its national hotline and many training programs, Boys Town assists hundreds of thousands of children and parents annually. During the last ten years, Boys Town has undertaken one of the greatest expansions of a private youth care program in U.S. history, and expects to serve many thousands more in the years to come.

Acknowledgments

With deep appreciation, we'd like to thank Sam Arcus, not only for his excellent memoir, but also for his editorial guidance and wisdom with specific book segments. Heartfelt thanks to Charlie Vladimer and Harry Koval for their enthusiasm, encouragement, and their own fine memoir accounts. Thanks to Adele Arcus, Lou Kaplan, Bernie Friedland, Morrie Sloop, Allen Schwartz, Manny Fineberg, and Roy Lachman for their important contributions. We are grateful to those members of our alumni organization who responded fully to our questionnaire so that their thoughts and experiences could provide a wider view of our "Home". We are also most thankful to Paula Held Scharf, director of the outstanding Pride of Judea Mental Health Center, for her many contributions to this project. Finally, we'd like to recognize and thank all the men and women who worked at or lived in the Pride of Judea Children's Home during its thirty-six-year lifespan, all of whom are represented in this book.

Chapter 1

My Dark Legacy

Phil Craft

For much of my early life, I earnestly wished that I could be someone else, with an altogether different family background. The hand that fate had dealt me was full of awful cards, ordaining a life of misery, guilt, resentment, and distrust. Few have been born in more adverse circumstances. I was the unfortunate harvest of an unwanted and lethal pregnancy, which transformed a husband into an angry widower and a happy, loving son into a bereaved, resentful orphan and older brother. I was the tragic product of a disaster which, before I was aware of it, had destroyed an intact family, taken the life of a beautiful woman, and irretrievably damaged the lives of those closest to her. Although I had never asked to be born, my birth, and the consequent death of my mother in giving birth to me, was to be my mantle of guilt and punishment, a dark legacy indeed.

In this unfriendly soil, I was planted into the scarred remains of a family which did not want me, ignored my wants, and grudgingly met only my most basic and primitive needs. In fact, there was an almost total rejection right from the beginning. I went directly from the hospital to an infant home, where my first five years were filled with such indescribable terror and misery that a merciful unconscious, even today, continues to conceal most of the details.

Of course, I did not come out of such a formative period unscathed. I emerged with a chronic learning disability in the form of an error-prone slowness of comprehension and response, which plagued me throughout my school years. I had a lingering inner turmoil symptomized by rage and vindictiveness, especially in response to perceived injustices or brutality to myself or to others. I

1

often sought refuge in solitude and self-analysis, searching for rational solutions, and engaging in a self-protective "exorcism" in the struggle for a life filled with loving thoughts and deeds. These contradictory feelings often rendered me conflicted, distracted, and indecisive, and may explain why I never married or even learned how to drive a car.

The upward path in my life began at age five, with my transfer to the Pride of Judea Children's Home, located on Dumont Avenue in the East New York section of Brooklyn, New York. It was 1932. Since I had been rejected overtly by the man who I thought was my real father, and by my older brother, Bernie, I was intent on developing badly needed friendships with youngsters and supervisors who were totally unaware of my hidden legacy of shame, which I concealed from everyone. Despite my continuing inner turmoil, I tried to subordinate my hostile and destructive impulses, and to carry the outward persona of a compliant, mild-mannered, and inoffensive little boy, fearful of rejection and eager to please.

As I deliberately built a new life apart from the family to which I had never really belonged, their scheduled weekly visits, which were obligatory for my stay there, became a bothersome and unpleasant intrusion into my new life. On these occasions, the dialogue between father and older son was warm, cheerful, and delightfully animated. My own compulsory role was to be present, to be silent, and to be ignored. Any attempts to participate were rebuffed instantly by the stern command, "Be still. This doesn't concern you!"

In payment for my part in this weekly ritual, I received a nickel, which I accepted each time with mixed feelings. Although I liked and looked forward to the good things it could buy, it was never given with an iota of love, but only as a token of my presence, and most grudgingly. Only years later, when I learned the meaning of the term "prostitute," did I truly understand the basis of my ambivalent feelings.

Apart from these weekly ordeals, Bernie, who was five years older, persistently brushed off my repeated efforts to get closer. This was not done with any violence or cruelty, but with an almost regretful determination and implacability, as though he could not help how he felt. At times, there were even slight traces of sympathy and regret in his manner. I grew to believe, at last, that it would be best for each of us if I just stopped trying to force my presence into his life. I was unaware then of the resentment and even hatred building up within me, like a molten stream deep underground, fed by his rejection.

One day, when I was about ten years old and eagerly looking forward to a class trip to a movie about the Civil War and Abraham Lincoln (whom I admired greatly and had "adopted" as my secret father), I was informed by my supervisor (a kindly woman named Mrs. Weingust) that I could not go to school because my father had died and I had to go to his funeral with my brother and the now-separated wife he had married after my mother's death.

My feelings were jumbled and confused. I was very disappointed that I had to give up this long-awaited good time just for him! Not wanting to be seen as selfish and heartless, I suppressed my angry feelings. At the same time, I felt a tremendous but inexpressible sense of relief that I would no longer have to see him. Nevertheless, I felt intense guilt for harboring such unacceptable, though hidden, feelings about my own father.

The ordeal of the funeral was terrible. Confused and guilt-ridden, I first had to go to the hospital for the body; then accompany it on the ferry to Staten Island, and on to the cemetery, where we waited interminably for the grave to be dug, and for the delayed presence of a strange rabbi to pray over it, while always pretending to feel grief that I did not feel at all. It developed into the most agonizing and traumatic day I have ever lived through.

For many years, I was haunted by guilt about the vile feelings that had consumed me on that awful day. It gave further credence and validity to my long-felt conclusion that there was no justification for my being alive; that indeed, I had no right even to have been born, particularly when so many others had suffered from that tragic event!

It was not until years later that I gained some resolution with my brother. During World War II, just before he went into overseas combat, I received a package from him containing a small cardboard-framed picture of our mother, accompanied by a long handwritten letter.

This was the very first time I had seen what my mother really looked like, and I was in awe. But the letter from my brother was even more revealing and shocking. In it, Bernie reviewed in detail the circumstances of my birth, as he had learned of it from his father and from close relatives. After his own difficult birth, five years prior to mine, our mother had been warned that she would not survive another childbirth. Her relationship with her husband, Bernie's father, had steadily deteriorated after his birth until it became, in his words, "a living hell" for her. Legal, economic, and social factors, plus her deep love for Bernie, had prevented her from leaving this misery-laden situation. Seeking love elsewhere, or perhaps actually attempting in some roundabout way to end her unhappy existence via suicide, she conceived me with another man, whose identity she never revealed.

Bernie proceeded to explain that he had loved her so dearly that he was never able to conceal, or get past, his deep resentment of me for causing her death, for depriving him of the central person in his young life, and for breaking up the family, thus forcing his own placement in an orphanage, which he had never been able to accept. His sending our mother's photo and this lengthy letter to me, he added, was an overdue attempt to shed light on many of my unanswered questions, to reduce my confusion and pain, and to make peace with me, and with himself, before going into combat.

The letter and photograph shocked and exhilarated me. I pored over both items again and again. My feelings were a strange mixture of relief and sadness. In that era, the worst epithet that could be hurled at anyone was the word "bastard." I had learned to resent the term, and even to fight when challenged with it. Now, although my brother had tactfully omitted the word in his letter, his meaning was perfectly clear.

Instead of cringing inside and shriveling up at this belated testament to my own illegitimacy, I felt strangely relieved, even elated, to realize for the very first time that the man toward whom I had felt so much hatred, and later so much guilt, was not my father after all! It made his terrible attitude and behavior toward me more understandable and even reasonable. And, most importantly, this revelation enabled me to reduce my self-imposed stigma of being so worthless that even my own father had rejected me.

Bernie's letter, to a considerable extent, liberated me. It took me off the hook for all of the venomous thoughts I had directed toward the man I previously had known as my father. Even his name, "Weinberg", was not really mine (I would change it, years later, to my mother's maiden name, Craft). At last, I was free! Ironically, although my brother Bernie had never given me anything before, his letter and the photo of our mother, whom I was seeing for the very first time, were the most precious and most enduring gifts he could have bestowed!

Bernie survived the war, and a few years later he tried, during one sudden and brief encounter, to establish a new relationship with me, based on our sharing the same mother. It almost broke my heart to reject his overtures, because he obviously was sincere and genuinely seeking to make amends, with offers to help me, both materially and fraternally. But my longstanding bitterness regrettably had made him a virtual stranger to me, without any visible positive qualities that might have endeared him to me in other circumstances.

Bernie's visit, which came as a total surprise, was too emotionally confusing for me to deal with immediately and appropriately. My gratitude for his letter and the photo of my mother was not yet fully developed. Indeed, it was only years later, after considerable time in therapy, that I fully appreciated what he had done for me. Even then, my understanding of his own ordeal and my forgiveness toward him were operative solely on an intellectual level. I knew that he was not to blame; but I still could not feel it.

My "legacy" has permeated my entire existence, and even today it sometimes filters into important events and relationships. A few years ago, I passed through an ordeal that brought my whole life, and my feelings about it, into clearer focus. My goddaughter, Miriam Concepcion, has been especially dear to me since I became part of her life almost thirty years ago, when she was just a little girl. The years have brought us closer together in a relationship without obligation, whether imposed or implied. We give to each other freely and spontaneously out of love and concern for each other because the act of doing so brings constant pleasure to both of us.

These feelings extend to Miriam's husband, Willie, and to her young sons, Willis and Oshea. In the autumn of 1993, when Miriam was more than two weeks overdue for the birth of her third child, I became very worried. I had been surprised at her decision to have another child seven years after Oshea's birth, because she already had her hands full with her two active sons, and because she was now in her mid-thirties, which had been my mother's age when she gave birth to me. Of course, my alarm bells went off. I was frightened by the specter of a repetition of my own tragic experience.

The possibility of Miriam dying while giving birth to her third child haunted my daily thoughts and even invaded my sleep. I prayed passionately and fervently that such a possibility would not come to pass; but that if only one could survive, it would be Miriam and not the baby!

Fortunately, and thankfully, mother and new daughter came through okay, with both now thriving and well. Little Cassandra has crept into a special place in my heart, next to her brothers and her parents, even though I can still remember my misgivings before her birth.

As I write and contemplate these thoughts, I am struck by the realization that in the midst of this crisis, my attitudes and feelings toward the still-unborn baby must have been exactly how my brother felt about me, except that he was only five years old when confronted by his trauma! I suddenly realized, and now also felt, how unfair I had been toward him. And my bitterness and resentment, both emotional as well as intellectual, finally were gone!

Today, I know not whether or where my brother lives. I only know that if he is still alive and I could locate him, I would be more than ready to reach out to him as he once did to me. It is too late, of course, and I feel a tinge of regret. But now, with regard to him, I feel fully at peace because I have come to grips with my own life and the circumstances of my entry into this world.

My brother and I were both victims of this situation, each no less than the other. Indeed, in retrospect, I may have been far more fortunate than he, because with my entry into the Pride of Judea Children's Home for a fourteen-year stay, I encountered adults and peers who were so caring for me that they became the family I so desperately wanted and needed. This story is as much their story as it is mine because I owe them my life!

Chapter 2

Peewee Comes to the Pride

Stan Friedland

It was a cloudy, cold, unpleasant day in December of 1940 when I first saw the Pride of Judea Children's Home. I was with my older brother, Bernie, and a family friend we called Uncle Fred. We had been driven there by a New York City social worker, and when I stepped from the car, there was this huge, four-story, dark brick building in front of me. It took up the entire block, and I felt its ominous presence. It was surrounded by a tall wrought-iron gate and had all the physical charm of a . . . prison! I didn't like it, and a shudder ran through me. However, given what I had just come from, I adopted a wait-and-see attitude.

Bernie and I had just spent three months in a foster home on the other side of Brooklyn, awaiting entry to the Pride. We had rather liked the lady whose home it was, though we had known that it was only a temporary placement. We had been put there after running away from our long-term foster home, where, after three and one half years, we just couldn't take the abuse anymore. We were tired, yet, strangely enough, in decent mental shape. My life, so transient at that point, had begun well, and this undoubtedly helped me to weather the rough experience we had just come through.

My father was always in poor health, and my mother told me, some years after his death, that he had been gassed in World War I and was never the same again. He rarely was able to work, and we lived on his meager disability pension and his small income. However, we never felt poor, because my mother was an excellent homemaker and a source of unyielding love. But in May of 1935,

7

just before I turned four, my father suffered a fatal heart attack at the age of thirty-seven.

My mother was utterly devastated. One of my earliest, clearest, and most painful memories is of her cries of anguish as we sat *shivah*, the period of mourning. The life and spirit just seemed to go out of her, although she always dutifully took good care of us. Not long afterward she was diagnosed with the dread disease of multiple sclerosis and deteriorated so rapidly that she had to be confined to a wheelchair in a sanitarium where she spent the last thirteen years of her life. It was a major tragedy for all of us.

Bernie and I were placed in our first orphanage, the Brooklyn Hebrew Orphans' Home (BHOA), in the Atlantic Avenue section of our home borough of Brooklyn. I was four and a half; Bernie was eight. It wasn't a bad place. It wasn't a good place. We handled it. Bernie was a good brother. He looked after me. We both could handle things, and . . . we had each other. Then came the foster home from hell.

The BHOA wanted its children to be placed in foster homes. That was its policy and also that of its supporting New York City agency in the thirties. Yes, there was a depression. Foster parents were paid approximately $50 per month per child, providing clothing and medical services for each, and everyone would be happy; well, maybe not everyone. So Bernie and I were placed in a lineup on certain days while prospective foster parents came to look us over for possible selection. It was not long before we were taken by a family, and off we went for three and a half years.

The Kaplans (not their real name) were Jewish. Since the overseeing agency was the Jewish Board of Social Services, that was always the case. Mrs Kaplan ran the roost, dominating her husband and two daughters. Needless to say, she dominated us as well and did not tolerate misbehavior or any deviation from her rules and regulations. Mr. Kaplan was a nice guy, but a pussy cat, and he toed the line as well. The daughters were in their early twenties and hated having their home intruded upon by two strange kids, just for the money. They ignored us.

Mrs. Kaplan not only made the rules, she enforced them—and with a heavy hand. Or, better yet, with anything she could get her hands on at any given time. One of her rules was, once you got into bed, you could not go to the bathroom till morning. Perhaps it was because they had but one bathroom, but nonetheless, that was it. Well, I often could not make it through the night, and so I took to opening a window and "watering" the bushes. I simply wiped the window sill with the curtain, and all was well. Until I got sloppy. She found a puddle on the window sill one morning and flew into a rage. When I confessed to the "crime," she was so angry that she picked up a wooden hanger from the chair and cracked me right over the head with it! It immediately broke in half, which probably reduced its impact somewhat.

On another occasion, when they went out for an evening, Bernie and I swiped some apples from the fridge. Not wanting to throw them in the garbage can, we flushed the cores down the toilet. Only one went down. Well, this time it was the dog chain, right over my back, some three times or so. Fortunately, such beatings, while frequent enough, were not everyday occurrences. But the threat of them always hung over us. We were not wanted. We lived, if not in fear, then in anxiety. It was not a happy time.

We lived for the weekends when we could see our mother. My two aunts and uncles, while barely able to make a living for themselves, were very attentive to my mother and knew how much our visits meant to her. They rarely missed a Sunday, rotating the responsibility for picking us up and taking us to mom for a good two hours before bringing us back again, all by public transit. The Kaplans had a car, but they never took us even once.

Despite our efforts to put a bright face on things, it didn't take mom long to learn that our foster home was not too happy a place. But in those days, not much could be done about it. Unless there were visible signs of abuse or mistreatment, or consistent pressure from the right sources, placements remained unchanged.

So we persevered, and not everything was bad. Mom cared very much about our efforts in school. So I became a good student, mainly because it made her happy. I was able to tell her, each Sunday, of my good grades and achievements for the past week, and was delighted to bring a smile to her face.

Given her bleak prospects, we were the only bright spots in her existence. She never complained, and I mean never! She focused her attention, love, and compassion on us, and in those two measly hours per week, she probably did more to build up our self-esteem than any two grade-A parents could have done in a normal home setting. Her influence on me, then and now, is at the core of my being.

A number of other things helped as well. Bernie and I were good athletes, which always served us in good stead, socially. The pecking order favored good athletes, and we did well in many different sports. I often played with Bernie's friends, and because of my small size, they soon pinned the nickname of Peewee on me. It would last throughout my boyhood.

In addition, my brother was a major positive force in my life, especially in those years. My mother always reminded him to look after me. And he did, even when it meant occasionally giving me a gentle smack on the head if I did something stupid. More often, it was an attentiveness and protectiveness that made me more secure, just knowing that he was there. We shared our lives together, fully, and that helped greatly to dilute the negative atmosphere of our life in the foster home.

Finally, we decided to run away. It was a Sunday in September and I wasn't feeling well. Bernie had a chance to be taken by friends of our mother to see her and he jumped at it. He felt the same way about her as I did and always enjoyed the visits. So on this day, because I had to stay behind, I was more unhappy than usual. Bernie was told to come home by 6:00 p.m. because there was school the next day and there were preparations to be made.

Six o'clock came and went, and no Bernie. Seven, and still no Bernie. Sometime about 7:45 he came in and immediately said, "I can explain"—when boom! Mrs. Kaplan whacked him as hard as she could across his face, screaming at the top of her lungs, "How dare you disobey me like that! Get out. Get out. Stand in front of the house until I allow you back in!" Bernie again tried to explain, but she hit him hard one more time. He quickly left the house. Some ten minutes later, she told me to get him, "and be quick about it!" But when I got outside, Bernie took my hand and said, "Let's go; we're getting out of here!" I always had total trust in my brother, and without so much as a moment of hesitation, off we ran.

After several minutes of darting in and out of alleys, climbing over fences, and sprinting across streets, I asked him where we were going. "To the Gotleibs," he replied. "Mom wants it this way. We're not going back there again." I was astonished. We resumed running, and it wasn't long before we reached the sanctuary of the Gotleib home.

The Gotleibs were longstanding friends of our mother and had taken Bernie to visit her on this day. Mom knew a little about what we were going through, but we never gave her the full story in order to spare her any more frustration and unhappiness than she already had to bear, given her situation. That day Bernie may have said just enough for mom and the Gotleibs to conclude that we had to get out of there. The Gotleibs had car trouble on the way home, which explained Bernie's lateness. They had offered to come in and explain, but Bernie, familiar with Mrs. Kaplan's temperament, knew what she would do and saw it as the opportunity to make our exit. He had even told the Gotleibs not to be surprised if there was a knock on their door in the near future. Sure enough, they greeted us with open arms, and we both breathed big sighs of relief. We were out of there!

Later that evening, my uncle Sam, knowing full well where we were, called the Kaplans and asked to speak to us. They told him what had happened, sanitizing the account in their favor, and saying that they did not know our whereabouts. My uncle feigned anger and told them that if anything happened to us, he would sue them for all they had.

This possibility greatly frightened them, because they phoned the Gotleibs soon afterwards, inquiring as to our whereabouts. The Gotleibs explained about their earlier car trouble, and, knowing what had happened, rubbed the Kaplans' noses in it, without letting on that we were there. They also warned the Kaplans that they would be liable if anything happened to us. We were tickled pink! Not only were the Kaplans frightened witless, but we were really out of there!

Several days later, after Uncle Sam and the Gotleibs had gone to the appropriate authorities to give them a detailed report and formalize our placement elsewhere, my uncle went to the Kaplans and collected all of our things. He made a point of telling them what he thought of them, which brought a smile to our faces when he told us about it.

After about a week, we were placed in another foster home for three months while deliberations went on for our next placement. We did not want another foster home, for obvious reasons. Regrettably, our aunts and uncles still could not afford to move to bigger apartments to accommodate us, and so the question remained, where could we go?

Mom had become friendly with a man who did volunteer work at the sanitarium, and he had told her about the good reputation of a nearby orphanage that might be suitable for us. She asked him to see what he could do to get us into the place. "Uncle Fred," as we called him, was an aggressive guy, and when he knocked on doors, they usually opened wide. It wasn't long before we were accepted into the Pride of Judea Children's Home.

We weren't too happy at that point. We actually liked our new foster home, though we knew it was temporary. There were several other kids living there, and thanks to the nice lady whose home it was, we all got along quite well. We also had settled into a new school. I was in the fourth grade, and this was my first year of cursive writing. I happened to like my new teacher and classmates, especially a very cute girl in my class. But my good mother said that this would be best for us, and so we packed our bags once again, said our goodbyes, and got into the car for the ride to the Pride. It was going to be a three-school year for us, but so what? After life with the Kaplans, any change was welcome. It was December, 1940; Bernie was almost thirteen. I was nine. Looking at that forbidding building, we had no idea that our stay in the Pride of Judea Children's Home would play such an invaluable role in our lives.

Chapter 3

The Pride of Judea Children's Home

The Pride of Judea Children's Home, located on Dumont Avenue between Elton and Linwood Streets in the Brownsville–East New York section of Brooklyn, first opened its doors in April, 1923. However, it had its origins some seven years earlier, when some Jewish residents of the neighborhood became concerned about the increasing number of families that had to farm out their children because they were unable to care for them. At that time, there was only one Jewish orphanage in the borough, the Brooklyn Hebrew Orphan Asylum, located between Ralph and Howard Avenues, on the borderline between the neighborhoods of Brownsville and Williamsburg. Founded in 1878 and opened in 1892, the BHOA, in 1915, had about 700 Jewish orphans and was at peak capacity.

Some affluent Jewish businessmen felt that another orphanage was needed to care for the current group of indigent and orphaned Jewish children who could not be squeezed into the crowded BHOA. Virtually all of these Jewish business leaders were of Russian or East European ancestry, Orthodox in belief and practice, and very desirous of having all Jewish orphans brought up in a faithful Orthodox setting similar to that of the BHOA. Indeed, that was their major motivation.

Consequently, they organized the Jewish Orphan Asylum of Brownsville and East New York in 1915, establishing their headquarters at 512 Sutter Avenue, which was approximately a mile from where the Pride of Judea Children's Home ultimately would be built. In fundraising, they followed the Russian tradition of raising money by placing coin-boxes (*pushkes*) in all of the neighborhood stores. In this fashion, they collected pennies, nickels, and dimes steadily, along with larger donations from their more affluent friends, until they were able to purchase the land and then begin construction of the new orphanage.

As their efforts proceeded, they attracted several highly respected communal leaders. One of these was Max Blumberg, a successful merchant, who was beginning an impressive career as a generous and energetic philanthropist, and ultimately would open and maintain several Jewish charitable institutions. Mr. Blumberg, after having made sizable donations to the cause, was elected president of the board of the Jewish Orphan Asylum in 1920, and actively provided it with great leadership for almost twenty years.

Some three years later, on Monday, April 16, 1923, the Pride of Judea opened its doors on Dumont Avenue. Including land and all, this "commodious building," occupying a city block, 200 by 400 feet, cost $300,000 to build, and had a yearly maintenance budget of $115,000 for its expected capacity of 250 orphan children. The building was an architectural departure from its predecessors, the BHOA and the larger and older Hebrew Orphans' Asylum (HOA) in uptown Manhattan, each of which looked like a cross between a castle and a prison. The Pride, instead, was a regal and imposing square-shaped, dark brick building, with a pillared facade. The *New York Times*, in its account of the opening, reports the presence of a thousand people, including many political and religious dignitaries. Preceding the speeches of these officials and of Max Blumberg, the board president, a "pageant was given by the children of the home." The Pride of Judea was inaugurated and ready to open its doors for its interesting life as a Jewish orphanage.

The first board of trustees was a hands-on group that, from the outset, was directly involved in shaping the orphanage. They emphatically wanted the children who resided in the Home to be well-educated, including a traditional Jewish education, and to emerge from the orphanage well-developed in all respects and ready for the real world. Even as the Pride was being built physically, early accounts show, the board members began the search for "staff members who would be dedicated and caring, and show affection for their charges." Said one veteran trustee, "The staff that we ultimately hired, were men and women who went far beyond the call of duty to do their jobs. They believed as implicitly as did the founders that they were their 'brother's keepers' in every sense of the phrase."

With this set of values firmly established as criteria for the selection of staff, and with the board of trustees overseeing the selection process, it is easy to see why this philosophy permeated the people who worked at the Pride of Judea throughout its thirty-six-year lifetime. Both Max Blumberg and his wife played active roles in the management of the Pride during the twenty years of his board presidency. When he passed away in 1939, his successor was his good friend and longtime trustee Jacob H. Cohen. Mr. Cohen, a very strong-minded individual, made sure that the guiding beliefs of Max Blumberg, and the practices put in place to deliver them, were carried on.

All the boys had to go to Hebrew school after regular school, three days a week, to learn Hebrew to be prepared for their bar mitzvah at age twelve or thirteen. Synagogue services were mandatory on Friday evenings and Saturday mornings. A kosher kitchen was kept and all Jewish holidays were observed. Doing well in school was stressed, and there was a mandatory homework hour each evening, after supper. The children attended public schools so that they would be able to adjust to the outside world in all respects. When they were in eighth grade, their aptitudes were evaluated so as to select the high school most suited to their capabilities and interests. All of these contingencies were covered, and appropriate procedures put in place that would last for the full life of the Pride. The basis established by this founding group was a strong one that shaped the Pride totally and made it a highly effective institution throughout its lifetime.

The Pride opened its doors in 1923 and came out running. It soon had its peak enrollment of approximately 250 boys and girls, and ran smoothly for the first ten years. Then, in 1933, disaster struck!

Understanding the developmental needs of children quite well, the Pride often took its charges on a variety of field trips. This was especially true in the summertime. On August 8, 1933, the Pride took most of the kids to Edgemere Beach in the Rockaways—and then the unthinkable happened. As the *New York Times* reported in a front-page article,

> a heavy wave swept forty children off a sandbar at Edgemere Beach yesterday afternoon and turned an orphans' outing at the beach into one of the season's worst tragedies. Seven children, all [residents] of the Pride of Judea Home, in Brooklyn, were believed to have drowned, although only one body was recovered. Five others were

taken to the hospital for treatment for submersion and four were revived on the beach before panic-stricken throngs. All but one were less than sixteen years old.

Lifeguards at the scene were critical of the children's chaperonage, saying that a more treacherous stretch of beach could not be found anywhere along the Rockaway shore. That the loss of life was not greater was due to the heroism and efficiency of the city lifeguards at the scene. Working in teams, they piled the children on catamarans and ferried them to shore.

Four officers of the home and ten women, including the wife of the President of the Board of Directors [Mrs. Blumberg], who had volunteered to act as chaperones for the outing, were questioned by the police. Afterwards, a police spokesman said that "there is no evidence of criminal negligence and no arrests will be made." A total of 105 children had been on this outing.

Needless to say, this tragic occurrence blemished the fine reputation the Pride had earned for itself in its first decade. However, enrollment did not slacken, and the orphanage continued to operate at maximum capacity for many years to come. However, for the rest of the thirties, Pride summer outings were directed to swimming pools rather than the ocean. This changed in the early forties, when day trips to the beaches of Coney Island and Seagate were resumed under the tightest of supervision by the Pride's staff. Later on, around 1943, a generous philanthropist by the name of Martin Scharf donated two fine homes near the shore at Long Beach to the Pride, and they became the summer residence of the Pride's children from then on. Supervision and security in the water were always very strict, and but for the usual scares, there was no other loss of life of any Pride youngster ever again.

In 1950, another unpleasant incident occurred, less subject to headlines, and fortunately featuring no threat to life. The Pride had its first major labor problem, which resulted in the mass firing of its supervisory staff. Among them were some outstanding supervisors.

In the late forties, as the cost of living went up, Pride salaries and employment conditions remained essentially the same. Supervisors earned about $100 a month, worked a six-day week, had to reside in a room on site, and were given the same meals as the children. At this time in postwar America, the union movement was in full swing, and the supervisors felt that the only way they could improve their lot would be to unionize. They asked the highly regarded Harry Koval to be their first president, and while Harry accepted the post, he cautioned them that they should only proceed if they were willing to risk losing their jobs. When they agreed, Harry went to Jacob H. Cohen to inform him of their affiliation with a national union. Cohen, the longtime owner of a flourishing nonunion lumberyard, summarily fired all ten supervisors, saying, in effect, "I won't have any Communists working here!"

Harry Koval, a truly outstanding supervisor, his wife, Sarah, who was another fine supervisor, and eight other good staff members left the Pride. The board of directors and the executive director went into high gear and recruited a new staff as quickly as possible. Not much publicity was given to this occurrence, and it was smoothed over rapidly as a new group of supervisors was put in place. Eyewitness accounts, from people who were residents at the time, indicate that while they were puzzled and upset by the sudden departure of their well-liked supervisors, the interim was a short one because, as one said, "Mr. [then-executive director Julius] Nierow and his people made sure that we were well taken care of." Life at the Pride soon resumed its normalcy, and the orphanage moved into the fifties, which, unbeknownst to anyone, would be its last decade of existence.

When children applied to the Home for admission, the major criterion for acceptance by any of the agencies they went to was their need of a home rather than whether they had a parent or parents. In this regard, the definition of "orphan" often was rather loose. Indeed, according to the statistics kept for all Jewish orphanages in the entire country for the first half of the twentieth century, there were three categories of need reflected by the residents of these institutions. Around 10 percent of the children were full-orphans, meaning that they had no parents. Some 72 percent were half-orphans, with only one parent. Eighteen percent had two living parents, who, usually for reasons of sickness, divorce, or poverty, could not provide adequate care for them. The Pride of Judea Children's Home had a population of children during its lifetime that mirrored these categories pretty accurately. For those of us who lived there, it didn't make much difference. We were all "orphans." The Pride was our home, and surprisingly, most of us weren't ashamed of it!

Another interesting study of institutionalized children in this era had to do with how well they adjusted to outside life after departing their respective orphanages. Many, upon being reunited with their parents or to other family members, experienced adjustment problems so severe that they wanted to return to their institutions, space permitting. Or else they required immediate counseling to get them through the transition period.

The primary reason for these difficulties was the difference in routine, lifestyle, and overall culture between the orphanage and a one- or two-parent home. Institutional life often left residents quite shy with outside adults and peers, particularly members of the opposite sex. The Pride of Judea attempted to deal with these difficulties by having its children attend regular public schools and encouraging them to participate in extracurricular activities whenever possible. It also had social dances which were open to young people from the immediate neighborhood. Hardly any children, upon leaving the Home, came back to live there. But most did come back to visit frequently, and they often mentioned how much tougher it was on the outside.

In the 1950s, enrollments began to diminish. By that time, the Pride of Judea was the only orphanage in Brooklyn. As enrollment fell steadily from 200 to 150 to under 100, the decision was made to convert the orphanage into a children's counseling and service center. Given the burgeoning need for a fuller umbrella of counseling and social services for all members of the family, the Pride would be of greater value to the community with this new and more modern identity. In 1959, the Pride of Judea Children's Home closed its doors as an orphanage. In its thirty-six-year lifetime, it had housed some 2,000 Jewish orphan children, and had served them well.

Chapter 4

Daily Life in the Home

Stan Friedland

We never called it by its full name or, rarely, even the Pride. It was simply "the Home." In December of 1940, when Bernie and I came there, the Home had its regular population level of about 250 boys and girls, divided into four age groups, called Midgets, Juniors, Intermediates, and Seniors. With the age range of the population going from about six to eighteen, each group had a two- to three-year age span of its own. Even though I was nine, I initially was placed in the Midget group for a short time so the staff could evaluate me. Then, when they saw that I could handle myself, I was moved into the Juniors, where nine was a more appropriate placement.

The Home was a big place. It stretched a short block wide and a full block long, like a large rectangle. The interior of the building was comfortable and well maintained. The ground floor had a rather pleasant dining room, the kitchen, the staff dining room, and the laundry and linen rooms, where the clean clothes were stored. The first floor contained the administrative offices, the infirmary, the library, classrooms, and the auditorium, used for holiday services and special events. The boys' dorms and the playroom were on the second floor, and the girls had to hike up to the third floor for their dorms. There was a reason why the girls occupied the highest floor. The boys would not have the high ground from which to peek down into their rooms at night.

Entering the building from the street, one went right through it and came out into a large yard which served as a basketball court, playground, and site for punchball and stickball games. Then came a long, attractive gazebo called the Summerhouse which stretched out into the ballfield, where we played softball, football, and the like. Walk to homeplate and you were virtually a whole block away from the main building. It was a spacious place.

As for the dorms, where you slept each night, there were eight beds in each room, with a chair beside each bed and several dressers for clothing. I had one full drawer for my worldly possessions, which, for each of us, was more than adequate to contain them. We'd leave our toothbrushes in a slot on the bathroom sink and use a communal bar of soap for our washing needs. Of course, we kept our combs in our pockets, so we could comb our hair whenever we wanted to, which was the custom in those days. There also were some steel lockers in the halls for the older boys and girls.

Sleeping next to someone else was a mixed bag. If you liked the person, it was great because you could have his companionship from rise and shine to the quiet whispers that preceded your falling asleep each night. If you were lucky enough to have friends on both sides of your bed, then you felt quite secure and content because of your pleasant interactions with the two of them. But if you had someone in the next bed whom you disliked, then it was not a good feeling. If it became a hassle, you could arrange to trade beds with someone in your group who either was willing, could be coerced into it, or could be bartered with. Then you'd tell your supervisor about the change, and generally he would authorize it.

In my room, at one time or another, there was every conceivable type of sleeper. One of my good friends not only picked his smelly toes each night but snored something terrible as well. Although he was well liked, no one wanted to sleep anywhere near him. We used to plead with him to give us a headstart in falling asleep so that we wouldn't have to contend with the strange gurgling sounds that came from him when he slept. We'd sometimes use a "designated talker" to keep him awake for this purpose, but it rarely helped. It was a good thing that he was well liked.

Another problem was body odor. When someone's aroma began to reach us from lack of washing, we'd make him an offer he couldn't refuse, and ultimately he would take a much-needed shower. With living conditions this close, there was little subtlety between us, and yet we got along remarkably well. Chalk that up to basically good leadership from our supervisors, as well as generally decent kids.

The dorms were also used for horseplay, more organized games like Johnny on a Pony, chicken fights, and quiet games such as cards, checkers, and for the more sophisticated, chess. I received a serious injury in my dorm during one vigorous chicken fight. The heavier guys carried the lighter guys on their shoulders in a free-for-all to see which team could knock down every other team and remain standing. We were doing quite well until we got blind-sided. Down went my anchorman right over a bed, flinging me over the next one with such force that I hit the back of my head on the sharp part of the bed's underframe. The sound of the contact was a loud crack, and while I didn't black out, I saw the entire galaxy. The blood came gushing out and my head became a bloody mess. Fortunately, it looked worse than it really was. The blood flow was easily stopped with a wet towel, and I was carried to the infirmary for an overnight stay. I pleaded a headache the next morning in order to miss school. After that cushiony day, I was fine.

At its best, sleeping in the dorms at the Pride gave one instant and continuous family. At its worst, one had a loss of privacy. The former was a far greater need for most of us, and we were the better for it. I usually liked dorm life and remember many of my dorm-mates and some of our good times to this day.

Clothes in the Home were neat and simple. Before each change of season, we'd go down to Mrs. Gatner's supply room to get the appropriate clothing. The clothes we were issued were replenished on an as-needed basis, and while not stylish, were remarkably adequate for the lives we led. But you had to follow the rules and take care of your stuff. For example, no playing in your school clothes, and you had to fold everything neatly over your chair.

For play, we had to wear a one-piece khaki jump suit called, accurately enough, overalls. These received the wear-and-tear of our varied activities, but they could be turned in for a clean pair almost on a per-need basis. Oddly enough, during my seven-year stint in the Home, I never felt poorly dressed, even later on in high school when I tried to flirt with some of the pretty girls.

The food in the Home wasn't too bad either, especially since I wasn't a fussy eater. Come to think of it, not too many orphans are. We're mainly quantity, not quality, eaters, and for us having a lot of food was the criterion of a good meal. While that did not always happen, it was more the norm than not. We'd have hot and cold cereals in the morning, occasionally eggs or pancakes, plus toast, hot chocolate, milk, and juice. Then, on a school day, we'd grab a bag lunch and a penny for milk, and off we'd go to school. The bag lunch always had a sandwich (peanut butter and jelly, of course), a fruit, and maybe a cookie. It was more than adequate. After school, back to the Pride, and waiting for us was always an enticing batch of cookies and milk. End of the school day, ready for play, and milk and cookies; what could be bad?

Dinner was the big meal, and again, it usually was more than adequate. The dining room was a nice spacious room, and no one could be served until every group was in place. The head supervisor stood in the middle as a signal for silence, and the blessing of the bread was said, along with some other announcements. Then, on to the attack of the voracious! Eight kids at a table, served platter style, and well supervised so that the strong could not victimize the weak. We usually bartered food with our table-mates, and wheedled some from the supervisors. I was good at both, and by the time I finished a meal, I usually had my fill. Food, to an orphan, is more than just nourishment, as you will see later on.

We walked to our elementary school, P.S. 202, which was about four long blocks away. The younger kids were chaperoned on the round-trip walk by a security person. The older kids were permitted to walk on their own, but could lose the privilege if they broke the rules. For high school, public bus or subway got you there. The change to public transportation was beneficial, for two reasons. It compelled you to fend for yourself in getting places, whether you were comfortable or not. Dealing with the subway required you to be alert, to think rapidly, and to be resourceful. Secondly, if you went to a moderately close high school, as I did, then you could save your dime-a-day carfare for something truly important, such as a delicious kosher hot dog from the neighborhood delicatessen. The Home was located just three blocks from the New Lots Avenue station, which was the last stop on the subway line. I went to Thomas Jefferson High School, which was only two subway stops away, on Pennsylvania Avenue. I often walked the round trip, especially in good weather, because that dime gave me spending money, which we didn't get otherwise. It was a good deal.

I loved the sports activities, both indoor and outdoor, and that's what I did with every free moment. Basketball was my favorite, and the two baskets on either end of the yard were always in play. The physical configuration of our facilities shaped our play and taxed our creativity. For example, the baskets were hung on a solid brick wall. Drive to the basket and you would lose your face and your teeth. So I developed a running hook shot, which enabled me to drive, stop, and extend my arm away from my opponent, in an almost unblockable way. With only two baskets, we played winners stay on, and so we often had very intense competition that would spill over into temper displays, foul language, and occasional fights.

But our punchball rules really challenged our imagination. Factoring in a deep alcove between building wings, we developed a playing field that truly favored lefties (which was me), and when I was on my game, I could slice that "spaldeen" right into the alcove so that the fielders were not seen again until I was rounding third, heading exultantly toward home.

We had a small but adequate-sized baseball field, only big enough to play softball, which I also liked a great deal. The field had a short right-field fence, and hitting the ball over it was an automatic double. However, on the other side of the fence were the backyard and gardens of one Joseph Randazzo, a crusty old man. Retrieving the ball, which the hitter often had to do, was not too pleasant, especially when Mr. Randazzo had his somewhat fierce dog doing guard duty. As a lefty, I often hit doubles over the fence, and so I had to develop my best negotiating skills to plead with Mr. Randazzo to either return the ball or let me climb over and get it. Eventually, when he got to know me, he wasn't so bad after all. I was a first-baseman because my cousin had given both Bernie and me first-baseman's gloves and we enjoyed that position. To this day, I have the crooked fingers on both hands to show for it. We had a shortstop with a rocketlike arm who was as wild as a March hare. Since I was fearless, I tried to catch everything thrown my way, whether my hand was gloved or bare, often resulting in broken or sprained fingers. Not too smart, but a lot of fun.

When the weather was bad or, in winter, too cold, it was ping-pong time, and that too was a sharply competitive activity. Lots of wagered desserts changed hands, and since I loved my desserts, I became a good ping-pong player. Knock-hockey, board games, and the like, also were in abundance in our playroom. We didn't lack for things to do in this pre-television era, nor for playmates to do them with.

The Home's daily schedule was a good one, allowing us to get in many worthwhile activities. During our pre-*bar mitzvah* years, we had Hebrew school right after our afternoon milk and cookies. After dinner, we went to a supervised homework classroom and could do our homework quietly or get help, if needed, from a homework teacher, specifically employed for this purpose. We then went to our music lessons, since most of us were encouraged to take up an instrument. I started with the "King" trumpet, partially because my brother played it well, and because it was the prestige instrument. However, I wasn't good at it. The band teacher, upon hearing my off-notes, would knock the trumpet from my mouth; he did it gently, but it hurt. He then put me on the French horn, which was a low-prestige instrument that I didn't like at all. Bernie continued on and became a good trumpeter, but, alas, I dropped out, much to my regret today.

There were other important activities as well. The Pride had a newspaper, completely put out by the children, with the help of an adult advisor. Obviously, this gave the participants a chance to develop their writing skills. Several editions from the early forties came to light recently, and they were fun to read.

We even had a Home Council, made up of representatives from each group, which was supposed to give us an advisory voice in the governance of the Home. As I recall, it didn't amount to much, which probably was due to our lack of attention to it.

Friday nights and Saturday mornings, we had services in the large room on the third floor that served as our synagogue. These sessions were tolerable—not too long, but not too interesting to me, especially on good-weather Saturdays, when I wanted to get out and play. Which is what we did, and it was fun. We played games all afternoon, stopping only for ice-cold milk and whatever else we could wheedle out of the kitchen.

We also were taken to the movies on Saturdays. We'd usually walk there in group formation unless the weather was bad, and then we might go by truck or, very occasionally, by bus. We went to either of our neighborhood movie theaters, the Biltmore or the Supreme, and had a great time. The Saturday program had two feature films and a serial. In the latter, the hero was left in a death-defying situation, and you wouldn't find out how he got out of it until the next week's installment. The theater was always full of noisy, loud children, and it was a hoot. The supervisors usually came back with headaches.

On Sundays, the most important thing for Bernie and me to do was to see mom. We got there more often than not, because the adults in our lives knew how important these visits were to us. They completed our week, and we looked forward to them. When we couldn't go, for some reason, the day felt incomplete, even though we had play activities before us. Mom was our wellspring, and I needed and wanted those visits. They lasted approximately two hours and were over too quickly. She would cut our fingernails lovingly, and we would discuss our respective activities for the week. It was a soft and loving time which sustained us considerably. She was so pleased that we liked the Home and relieved to have us out of our previous foster home from hell. I also would write to her at least once a week because I knew how much my postcards meant to her. She kept them wrapped in a rubber-band and would read them from time to time. She also wrote to me, and I, in turn, would keep her cards and letters.

Bernie left the Home in early 1946 to join the Navy. I stayed for an additional year and a half, and left against my will. A new executive director had just arrived in the fall of 1947 and, without even meeting any of us, he moved to oust the older kids as a costs-savings device. At sixteen, I was among them and was asked to leave. Just entering my senior year in high school, I was placed in another foster setting on the other side of Brooklyn. I had to take two different buses for over an hour just to get to school. It was not a good year, and I badly missed the Pride. My seven years there were good ones and extremely valuable in remedying the harsh treatment I had received in the foster home. When I left the Pride, premature as it was, I was in much better shape to take on the rest of my life.

But there was one additional element in our Pride years that made an invaluable contribution to our lives at that vulnerable time: the superb group of supervisors who served as our parent figures. If not for them, things might have been quite different.

Chapter 5

Key Parent Figures in My Life

Phil Craft

Mrs. Braverman: She Was My First

During my thirteen-plus years in the Home, I encountered many adults who, in differing ways and degrees, had strong effects on my daily life. The very first of them was my first supervisor, Mrs. Braverman. When I arrived at the Pride in 1932, she was already an institution in her own right, having been there for a good many years. Although I was in her group, the Midget Boys, less then a year, she is not someone that I'm likely to forget.

My first impression of this short, stout, formidable-looking lady was of the no-nonsense glare radiating through her thick, rimless glasses. It was more powerfully emphasized by her mean, stinging right hand to the face or rear end, which gave instant, ample, and lasting notice to transgressor and witness alike that she was not someone to be trifled with.

In that specific way, she reminded me, all too well, of the angry, vindictive, matronly authority figures in the infant home from whence I had come. Those caretakers had made the first five years of my life so terrifying and traumatic that I still have the mental and psychological scars from the oft-repeated threats, slaps, taunts, and beatings that I received there. For that reason, I not only was very fearful of Mrs. Braverman with her harsh discipline, I also couldn't respond to her attempts at affection. Whenever she reached out to me with maternal warmth, and she did try to do so, I was too fearful and distrustful to allow myself to warm up to her, even though I desperately wanted her affection. Instead, I hovered, at a safe distance, watching other little boys receive and embrace

26

her expressions of love, while I was torn by self-pity and helpless envy.

Nevertheless, whenever I saw Mrs. Braverman in that loving mood, I felt that I could relax, safe for the time being from the threat, or the fallout, of her irritation or anger. I longingly looked forward to such pleasant interludes as an agreeable, if momentary, reprieve from the lingering anxiety that made her a person to fear and avoid. For someone like me, who often was too slow to understand others and correctly size up situations, and who learned mainly from his own miscalculations and mistakes, the challenge to behave blamelessly in order to avoid her swift punishment seemed almost impossible.

As I later learned, however, Mrs. Braverman came to understand and secretly sympathize with my dilemma and obvious unhappiness, as she began to hit me quite rarely, if at all. Perhaps she realized that no one tried harder than I to obey her, and that the ordeal of witnessing others being punished was, in itself, enough to make me want to be a good little boy.

As the months went by, I became increasingly aware of Mrs. Braverman's tireless efforts to ensure that we were always clean, well-behaved, and properly cared for in every respect. She was here, there, and everywhere in order to accomplish this, because we, as young children, were all over the place in our habits, needs, and differences. That she accomplished her task so well enabled me to see that she had gained, for herself and for all of the boys in the group, widespread approval and respect. It felt quite good to share in that universal esteem, probably because I was experiencing it for the first time. Many years later, when I was in the Army, I had a drill sergeant who reminded me vividly of Mrs. Braverman. He had "whipped our asses" into such good shape that we had become the envy of other platoons. Mrs. Braverman did the same. I didn't like her at the time, but I felt better and better about being in her group.

Later that year, as more and more younger kids came in to join the group, I was transferred "sideways," to the other Midget group, under a softer, gentler lady, Mrs. Weingust. I was elated! I was being released at last from further threat or jeopardy, into a group that was easier-going and more relaxed. I enjoyed Mrs. Weingust a great deal, but I also noticed that we usually were second-best to Mrs. Braverman's group in just about everything.

While I didn't mind it then, I've been able to put things in a more mature perspective as the years have gone by. I now realize that my negativity toward Mrs. Braverman was as much a product of my own hangups and immediate background as it was of her authoritarian ways and the fear they aroused within me. Her style was quite common in those days, and, in fact, was the norm for those in charge of groups of children. As a true representative of her era, her best efforts were quite good, and her concern for her young boys was, in its own way, genuine and caring. She was, for me, an important bridge from my traumatic and harmful first five years to this next thirteen-year period in which more positive seeds were planted that would help my growth and development. In this regard, encountering her was quite valuable, because, tough as she was, her efforts were in my behalf, and I knew that she was on my side!

Trig: My First "Hall of Fame" Supervisor

After that brief stint in the two Midget Boys groups, I was transferred to the Junior Boys, where, after several nondescript supervisors, I met a positive adult in my life. His name was Mr. Abel, but everyone called him "Trig," short for "Trigger," because he was tall and rangy and resembled the cowboy stars then in vogue who were pictured on the lids of dixie cups from Horton's Ice Cream. More likely, though, it was because we in his group, who admired him as a square-shooter, had eagerly adopted this nickname for him as a token of our affection.

In refreshing contrast to earlier supervisors, whose control had come mainly from physical size and intimidation, Trig initiated a program of incentives which rewarded cooperative effort and good behavior with extra privileges. I cannot recall him ever resorting to corporal punishment. He just never had to, since we all liked him so much that we always sought his approval.

Early on, Trig installed a very effective pass-card system which monitored our conduct during the week and then provided "liberty" on weekend afternoons exclusively for those charged with fewer than five demerits. Possession of this card entitled us to either leave the grounds, with his permission and knowledge, or, if we stayed inside, to be exempt from any daily chores until the five o'clock bell. We used to leave, mainly in groups, with the clear directive that we behave ourselves and return punctually before dinnertime. Our favorite destinations included the candy store on the corner, Schneider's Jewish deli, two blocks away, the huge playground bordering the IRT's storage yards, the very attractive Highland Park, a half-mile away, or our two local movie theaters, also within walking distance.

I had never before experienced the sensation of such freedom. I had always been under some sort of supervision or control, which generally was of an unpleasant nature. So this was a brand-new feeling, which, initially, was not as agreeable as I thought it would be. My sense of uncertainty and insecurity overwhelmed me on the first few trips, and I returned early to the familiar sanctuary of the Home. But after several outings, always with people I regarded as friends, I began to relax and really experience the joy of being on my own—doing as I wished, with no other authority other than myself. It may have been a turning point in how I looked at myself.

Trig's pass-card was also good for during the week, for such times as after school, after Hebrew classes, and after our homework hour. With the aid of this pass, plus my increasing confidence in my ability to be on my own, I began to earn money for the very first time. I had become friendly with an old porter who liked his beer. He would give me a nickel if I returned his empty beer bottles to a near-by deli for a new six-pack. I didn't know then that this practice was illegal, even in those days. But the deli owner didn't care, probably because I always bought a delicious hot dog with my newly earned nickel each time that I bought the beer. Anyway, the pass-card became, for me, a symbol of freedom, maturity, and trust. My self-esteem and confidence increased sharply, and it became one of the first successful experiences in my life.

Trig also did a lot for us educationally. Given the way we always dawdled at bedtime, he encouraged promptness from us by reading aloud to us each night from the chapters of exciting books. He was a good reader, and soon no one in our group delayed in being ready for him to start a new and exciting chapter in whatever book he was reading at the time. My particular favorite was Tom Coe, the Pirate, which centered on a stalwart young cabin boy, whose engaging friendliness and sterling character helped him to gain the respect and affection of his pirate captors. This nightly activity and Trig's selection of inspiring stories helped to plant within me a powerful urge to read, to learn, and to get enjoyment from books. Despite a chronically slow reading rate, this love of books and reading, persists to this day and has enriched my life deeply.

Trig's stay at the Pride was all too brief. Within two years, after meeting and falling in love with a beautiful gal who also was a supervisor, he left the Pride, bearing our best wishes and heartfelt gratitude. Although I was very sorry to see him go, he had given me the hope that future supervisors might be straight-shooters like him, and fortunately this was what happened. Brief as was his involvement in my life, his contribution to my development was positive, strong, and lasting. I had found a worthy parent figure, and just in time. Thankfully, there were more to come.

One Boy's Hero

Supervisors didn't stay long at the Pride. The pay wasn't very good, their rooms were adequate but far from luxurious, and they had to sleep at the Home five or six nights a week. The job itself was stressful—having to put up with twenty-five or thirty demanding kids. When recruiting supervisors, the Pride asked for experience in working with children; it preferred college graduates but could not always get them. Many people came in, stayed a short while, and then went their own ways. To say the least, this was not too good for orphan children who, at best, had mainly transient adults in their lives. As for me, I had no caring adults in my life, with no family to speak of or to recognize as desirable. After Trig left, the supervisors who succeeded him were so mediocre as to be unremembered. I began to drift again, until I got lucky and a very memorable and significant supervisor stepped squarely into my life.

Lou Feigelson had two wonderful qualities, which forever endeared him to me. Like Trig, he too was a square-shooter who treated us as maturing, potential grown-ups rather than as little kids, as most supervisors did. Also, I never had cause to doubt that he really liked me and would do anything he could to help me whenever I needed it. Now, remember that caring adults of this type were in very short supply for me. While Trig was good to me as part of his positive attitude toward all of us, Mr. Feigelson brought that extra dimension of caring and regard for me personally, and let me know it. How great that made me feel!

Mr. Feigelson had poor eyes and wore glasses. But he was solidly and powerfully built and was a great athlete. So I simply associated his glasses with Superman's disguise as Clark Kent, and felt that I had my own personal legendary hero!

My rapport with Mr. Feigelson really intensified when he found out that I had no parents and had been a foundling orphan right from the beginning. On some Saturday afternoons, when other boys were visited by family members or were going to the movies, he sometimes would take me and two other lucky boys joy-riding in his car, either on a sightseeing jaunt or else on a visit to his home in Corona, Queens. There, his mother and his friendly kid brother would make us feel comfortable and especially welcome.

These visits marked several important firsts for me. My first time experiencing the luxury of riding in a private car, and on a pleasure trip no less! Next, and more important, my first exposure to a loving home and the mutual affection of two sons and their mother. Although these visits occurred only several times, I cherished each one. I came to regard his mother and brother with some of the affection and enthusiasm that I lavished on Mr. Feigelson. I still recall those visits with warmth and appreciation because they opened up yet another essential vista for me.

In time Mr. Feigelson was transferred to the Intermediate Boys group and I was very upset. Six months later, when I was transferred to the very same group, I almost blew it all in a silly frenzy of joyful but thoughtless behavior, which Mr. F. had never seen in me before. He hurriedly summoned me and another culprit to his small room to chew us out. He was very angry and upset. To control his anger, he began to peel an orange, literally tearing the skin off in large chunks. In an agitated voice, which he struggled to keep low, he solemnly warned us that this nonsense must stop immediately! I vaguely recall the word "probation" also being used, and for weeks after that I had nightmares about being sent back to the Juniors. Needless to say, I was on my best behavior after that and never got into trouble with him again.

There was another time though, when, from behind the wheel of his car, he spotted me walking home from high school in order to save the nickel carfare. Now, my school was fully one and a half miles from the Home, and we weren't allowed to walk that far. When he honked his horn and I saw who it was, I thought for sure that he'd bawl me out for this transgression and was prepared for the worst. Instead, he simply focused on how I was getting along in school, since he knew that school was never easy for me, even though I worked diligently at it. I also suspected that he secretly approved of my walking home, which was an industrious way of getting extra spending money, a commodity always in short supply for me.

Mr. Feigelson left the Home soon afterwards, to marry and go into the Army, where he became an officer. Once again, I was deeply shattered and angry. The repetitive pattern of loss of a loved parental figure was getting tougher rather than easier to take. I became somewhat hostile and cynical, believing that no one could ever fill Mr. Feigelson's shoes. Once more, to my great fortune and surprise, another "angel" came my way. But Lou Feigelson was and continued to be a memorable and invaluable adult in my life, and I will always remember him with great affection and deep gratitude.

Postscript: the adoption that might have been. One winter evening, when I was about sixteen years old, some of my more adventurous friends decided to break into the social workers' office at the Pride to see the records. Easily influenced and having nothing better to do, I decided to join them. I was only mildly curious to see the contents of my own file because I believed it to be mostly empty, since I earnestly and successfully tried to avoid contact with the Pride social workers. My aversion to them was self-protective. It seemed that every time one of my friends was called in to see one of them, he usually ended up being discharged to his own family, never to return. To me, that was a horrible thought to contemplate, since, with no family, I wanted only to stay at the Pride with my friends and good supervisors. So, I avoided the social workers and their office like a veritable plague.

When we gained entry into the office, I offered to serve as lookout while the others looked through their folders. They couldn't believe it when I told them, in response to their question, that I wasn't even interested in looking at my own file. One of my friends said, "Now you've really made me curious. I'm going to look for you!" When he began to read my file aloud but in a low voice, he revealed for the first time a surprising possibility that could have changed my entire life.

I was shocked! Four years earlier, Miss Predd, the social worker, had called me in to tell me that a family wanted to adopt me and asked whether I would be interested. Thinking of the terrible experience in a foster home of my good friend Bernie Friedland and his kid brother, Peewee, I reacted to her suggestion with visible panic and stark terror. It was such a grossly negative reaction that she dropped the idea immediately.

But now, as my friend read about it in my records, the identity of the family was revealed for the first time. It was the family of Lou Feigelson! On the few occasions that he had taken me to visit his mother and brother, they had always had been very friendly and welcoming toward me. Despite my innate shyness, I instantly was attracted to them, and we had gotten along extremely well. I was always sad to leave their home, but I basked in the aftermath because of the warmth and affection I had received. Mr. F. left for the service soon thereafter, and I never saw his mother and brother again.

For a long time thereafter, I remembered Miss Predd with bitterness as a bumbling figure. However, I was comforted by the belated realization that some people whom I had truly come to love had wanted me in their own family!

Only after years in therapy, when I came to have a clearer view and understanding of my own many hangups, did I finally realize that even with everyone's best intentions, this adoption would have been laden with considerable risk and probable disappointment. Was I actually ready to leave the Pride and move in with a family, even one as nice as Mr. F.'s? Probably not. Would I have caused aggravation to the wonderful Mrs. Feigelson? Possibly. And even the pressure to avoid being a problem to them might have been too much for me.

All of these thoughts, of course, came very much later. However, at the time of the "break-in," I was shocked and very confused to learn about this might-have-been. None of this diminished my love for Mr. Feigelson, nor my appreciation of what he had done for me. He continues to be one of the important heroes of my childhood, who brought something special, precious, and lasting into my life. Just think, though; he also could have been the loving, older brother I had always wanted! But fate ordained that it was not to be!

Charlie and Willie

When Sam Arcus and Charlie Vladimer succeeded Lou Feigelson as my co-supervisors, I greeted them with suspicion and detachment. Tired of this revolving door of adults in my life, I decided to keep my distance from the two newcomers. Fortunately, they were so caring and creative that it wasn't long before I was drawn fully into their orbit.

At first, Charlie Vladimer seemed to be the more influential and prominent member of the team. At the time, the two of them were in their early twenties. Later on, I would discover, much to my amazement, that they had both come directly from an orphanage setting of their own, where they had been fast friends for many years. Charlie was a real cheerleader, with an enthusiastic "rah-rah" approach to things, while Sam was the intellectual and deep thinker. In our eyes, he appeared to have a judicial manner in the way he resolved problems or conflicts, and it wasn't long before we nicknamed him "the Judge." He also liked to use big words when he addressed our weekly group meetings, inspiring in me a strong interest and respect for their beauty and power.

But Charlie was the guy out front. He always seemed to be initiating one type of activity or another, not unlike a camp counselor or cruise director. He was shamelessly gregarious, a person who, at the end of a trip or outing, would initiate, spontaneously and loudly, cheers for the bus driver, or, on a wild impulse, start a friendly snowball fight or touch-football game. He seemed to come up with one fun idea after another that soon would develop into an organized game or activity. If one attempt failed to catch on, he didn't just give up; he'd try a new one and see how that turned out. He had the energy and vitality of a whirling dervish; but it was his bubbling enthusiasm, combined with his genuine fondness for all of the kids, that endeared him to us. I had never before encountered a supervisor who would actually ask each of us how we felt about the Home and our groups in order to elicit ideas for change and improvement. He really cared how we felt about ourselves and our lives, and wanted to respond accordingly.

Charlie was very imaginative. He helped us to form the Pride's first social club in which each officer was elected by secret ballot rather than appointed by the supervisor. That was an interesting first for most of us. We planned and staged different activities, such as dances, contests, and tournaments, and he made us resolve ourselves whatever disputes and disagreements arose during these events. It was heady stuff for all of us—new frontiers, literally— and we loved the importance that we were experiencing for the very first time.

As our advisor, but not the club's chief officer, Charlie made us aware of our accountability, and of the hard work involved in doing things well. He broached new ideas to the club's officers, who often would get caught up in his enthusiasm and present them at our next meeting. We would usually adopt them and move them forward as an intended activity. For many of us, it was our first taste of the democratic process, and though a little suspicious and wary at first, we soon took to it, much to our considerable enjoyment and benefit.

Charlie's goodwill and genuine concern did not, however, eliminate conflict or misbehavior. The positive thrust of his beliefs and practices actually encouraged us to become more self-assertive, and since this was happening for the first time to virtually all of us, some unintentional collisions were bound to occur. I, for one, did not handle this new freedom too well, and when I didn't get my way, I used to explode, rebel, and then run out of the room, no matter who was there. Charlie would shout loudly, "Come back here, Willie Weinberg!" A bit stunned and annoyed, I would stop and heatedly remind him, "My name is Philly, not Willie!" He would smile patiently at my sense of outrage, and then tell me how long I was grounded for.

This sequence was repeated again and again. "Call me Philly!" I demanded. But he just couldn't help it. Finally, he told me that at his own orphanage, the Hebrew National Orphans' Home, in Yonkers, New York, there had been a kid named Willie Weinberg, and he thought that the name fit me as well. As I began to like him more and more, the new name didn't bother me so much. After all, whenever I got into trouble with other authority figures, they'd usually call me Philip, which I really hated. Furthermore, since only he called me that, it made for an even more special bond between us.

Then the inevitable happened. In December 1942, Charlie was drafted into the Army. It was World War II, and just as it had taken Lou Feigelson away, so too did it take Charlie Vladimer away. But this time I did something about it! I began an intense and lengthy correspondence with him that undoubtedly was the most important of my life. When I began to miss Charlie badly, I got his new address from the Judge and wrote him a letter, signing it "Willie."

Following this cue, Charlie would address his letters to me in that name. The more we wrote, the more we learned about one another, and our friendship deepened wonderfully during those war years. Charlie was only about ten years older than I, though to a fifteen-year-old, initially, that was enough to separate adult from child. But as I expressed my hopes, problems, and worries in my letters, Charlie responded like a concerned, helpful older brother. Since I had already rejected my own half-brother because of the way he had made me feel about "causing" our mother's death, I used to fantasize that Charlie was my real brother.

Once, when I expressed this thought to Charlie in a letter, he answered right away. He told me for the first time that indeed, he'd once had a little brother who would have been about my age, but that he had died when he was a child. He felt deeply touched that I wanted to be his kid brother, and said he had the same feelings about me. He suggested that, at least, in spirit and friendship, we could make this come true. He cautioned, however, that it would be best to keep this special bond between us to ourselves. He didn't want others at the Pride to think that he liked them less, or me, more. Knowing just how much he was loved, respected, and missed, I understood and honored this request. I never told anyone else at the time. I really didn't have to, because just realizing and feeling this special bond between us had made me quite happy, and that was more than enough.

Charlie and I have been brothers since then, and throughout our lives. This special kinship has been most treasured by me, and of such great value that it's far more than words can express. Later on, I would follow directly in his path, earning an undergraduate degree from CCNY as he had done, and then a master of social work degree from Columbia University.

Charlie's inspiration, advice, and ceaseless encouragement helped not only to make all of this possible, it also infused me with his own dedicated passion to help others. That sole criterion became my own bottom line! Neither of us ever gained great wealth, and I was too limited, mentally or emotionally, to seek prestigious positions or power. Yet we each gained a unique level and quality of genuine happiness which brightens and blesses each of our lives.

After losing several earlier parent figures in my life, not only did I not lose Charlie, but I actually gained the best of all possible big brothers!

Here Comes the Judge: Sam Arcus

Sam Arcus and Charlie Vladimer came to the Home together, during the High Holidays in 1942. Both wore glasses and were not particularly athletic, which stereotyped them to me immediately as intellectuals, or, in today's parlance, nerds. In the midst of my own adolescent revolt against religion, I shunned them as suspicious characters, probably plotting to pressure me into an unwilling return to Orthodoxy. This was typical thinking for me in those days, because I was rather paranoid and sullen in my approach to newcomers. With such negative vibrations shooting out from me toward these two jokers, it still seems totally improbable, even today, that they would both eventually influence and crucially shape the person I am today. Only a creative imagination, the likes of an O. Henry, could have conceived such an unlikely outcome.

Both Mr. Charles and Mr. Arcus, as they then were called, had served "hard time" together as youngsters at the Hebrew National Orphans' Home, located in Yonkers, New York. As orphans themselves, they had each had their own share of hard knocks and cruel people. Indeed, Mr. Arcus, only in his early twenties then, wore dentures because his teeth had been knocked out by a brutal supervisor when he was younger. He had vowed, thereafter, that if he ever became a supervisor, his own approach would be entirely different. Indeed it was.

As the weeks became months, and my foolish preconceptions vanished into the warm climate of their formidable deeds, these two stereotypes became real human beings, as well as unique individuals. Mr. Arcus was a more serious, articulate, and assertive person than his good buddy. He loved music, sports, history, and books, and sought to stimulate our interest in these areas in every way imaginable. He also had a focused and active concern for our well-being and the need to develop our potential so as to be able to cope in the outside world. He was emphatic about the latter, expressing this repeatedly.

As supervisors, Mr. Arcus and Mr. Vladimer were obliged to enforce institutional rules and policies, but they did so with our best welfare in mind. Both actively helped each of us, in many different ways, to deal with our problems successfully and to meet the challenges in our lives in a stronger fashion.

Mr. Arcus had a great vocabulary, and since he never talked down to us, he would always use big words that made us smile in our ignorance. To us, he sounded like a benevolent judge, and so we began to call him "Judge Arcus." He laughed when he heard it for the first time, and since it was a promotion for him on the social ladder of important positions, he readily accepted our calling him that. From then on it was "Charlie" and "the Judge," always said affectionately, for the two supervisors we had come to like so very much.

When Charlie went off to do his military service, as described earlier, we held our collective breath to see if the Judge would join him. Much to our relief and satisfaction, he was rejected because he had a potentially serious bone disease, osteomyelitis. Fortunately, it was a mild case which never really bothered him. Happily for us as well, we still had him with us to maintain a secure life-climate, and to stimulate our continued growth in many areas. As I think back, his profound influence would include music, literature, current events, sports, ethics, social relationships, and self-realization. He would initiate conversations or discussions in any of these categories, or we could approach him on any subject of interest for a pleasant discussion. Even today, I regard his stay at the Pride as the golden age of my long life, because he and Charlie, together, transformed a fearful, angry, suspicious little boy into an understanding, more confident, and competent man, who found his own happiness in a life devoted to helping others to become self-fulfilling individuals. This orphan was lucky indeed to have several important parent figures in his life. Charlie and the Judge were two of the best!

Postscript: The Judge, One More Time

I can't leave Judge Arcus without sharing a significant anecdote that reveals just why he was an important figure in many of our lives.

During World War II, when the country was caught up in a patriotic fervor, many of us held attitudes and stereotypes fostered by movies, radio, and comic books. Our Japanese foes, then called Japs or Nips, were always portrayed as short, bespectacled, buck-toothed, little savages who were sneaky, cowardly, and hatefully cruel. The images of the Germans were scarcely better. They were depicted as insensitive thugs, blindly obedient to a egomaniacal dictator with a funny mustache. They hated and murdered Jews, bombed helpless civilians, and wanted to take over the world. Given the media saturation promoting these extreme, villainous images, it was quite easy for someone as immature as I was to stereotype all Germans as Nazis, loathsome aggressors, whom we hated fiercely.

Such prejudices made me hostile and suspicious toward anyone with a German name or European accent. Hence, my negative attitude toward Fritz, the Pride's new wartime cook. He was a bald, heavy-set man with a pronounced German accent. Knowing nothing else about him, he became, for many of us, the personification of Erich von Stroheim, the cruel and sadistic Kraut officer in the movies. While his official status as the Home's head cook may have deterred us from making fun of him openly, it didn't prevent us from making Fritz the whispered butt of our strongly anti-German humor. Even his pleasant-mannered wife, Edith, came in for some of our barbs because of her heavy accent.

The ever-present and wise Judge soon became aware of the ridicule and sarcasm we directed at this couple, but, instead of saying anything to us in a preachy vein, he simply invited several of us to accompany him one Friday night to visit some "good friends." We walked to a near-by apartment house, and, with a sense of excitement and anticipation, looked forward to meeting our popu-

lar supervisor's "mystery" friends. When Fritz answered the door-
bell, my delight turned instantly to chagrin and confusion. What
was going on here?

Greeting each of us cordially, Fritz and Edith served us some
hot tea and delicious homemade cookies. Then, at the request of
Judge Arcus, they began to describe their past history. As prosper-
ous Jews in prewar Germany, they had done quite well until the
antisemitism of Adolf Hitler began to poison their town. After seeing their business destroyed, and suffering the humiliation of physical violence as well, they had packed up their possessions and were
lucky to be able to leave Germany while it was still possible.

We sat there in rapt silence, each of us feeling the shame of our
own stupid prejudice. By the time we left, our hearts had gone out
to both of them, and I, for one, viewed them as real people, blessed
with goodness and courage. It was easy to see them, indeed, as the
fine people they were, and they became cherished friends throughout my final years at the Pride. When I asked the Judge, the next
day, why he hadn't explained their background to us before, he
smiled at me and said, "Would it have been better coming from
me, or from them?" I smiled back because no answer was necessary. Once again, he had taught me an invaluable lesson, one I
would retain throughout my life!

Chapter 6

Memorable Supervisors, Good and Bad

Stan Friedland

There were two major things to adjust to if you lived in the Pride of Judea Children's Home: communal living, and the adults in your life. Fortunately for me, during my seven-year stay I had good experiences in both areas.

I rather liked communal life. Loving sports as I did, I always had numerous playmates in every choice of activity. We played outdoor sports in good weather, and when we couldn't go outside, we engaged in indoor activities, such as ping-pong, knock hockey, all kinds of board games, and different games of cards. There was constant companionship, and with enough kids in your group, if you fell out with any of them, there were plenty of others to hang around with.

I was a good athlete and also quite competitive in everything I did. I hated to lose, and usually did not. Of course, my competitive nature occasionally crossed the line into being a sorehead and poor loser. But, given the pecking order of what's important to kids, my all-around abilities made me a leader in my group, which, in turn, fostered a decent amount of confidence in myself. I had my food, clothing, and shelter; I had my friends and activities; my brother was close by, and I saw my mother each week. I was in pretty good shape, far better off than I had been in the foster home, and needing only some supervisors whom I could relate to on a positive basis. Fortunately, I came up smelling like roses in this important category, much to my life-long benefit. The following are the memorable supervisors that I had at the Pride, both good and bad, although the latter group is, happily enough, a very small one. My first three choices already have been written about by Phil. But he

41

and I, as two distinct individuals, "filtered" things quite differently, and our separate takes on each of these men are worth noting.

Lou Feigelson

Mr. Feigelson was a popular and nurturing figure to everyone who had him as a supervisor, and he was my first memorable one. He came to the Pride in 1941 and went into the service about a year later. He came back after the war for another short stint. In these two stays, he worked with three different age groups, and I was lucky enough to be in one of them.

Mr. F. was my first male role-model, meaning that I wanted to be like him. First of all, he was a very good-looking guy. Though his eyes were weak and he wore glasses, he had a handsome face, an excellent build, and he walked and ran gracefully. Why his physical appearance meant so much to me, I don't know, but it did. Perhaps it had something to do with the fact that my father, what little I remembered of him, had been a small man and rather sickly in our few years together.

I also liked Mr. F's manner and demeanor. You knew that he was not a pushover because he was quietly assertive without being authoritarian or controlling. He was even-tempered, slow to anger, and his voice was clear, firm, and calming. He was a strong male adult in my life, very unlike any other male adult I had encountered before. While I had several uncles with whom I was close, none of them had Mr. F.'s singular sense of masculinity, which I identified with and admired as an impressionable boy.

Given my leadership status in the group, Mr. F. took an interest in me which further solidified our relationship and added to his impact on me. He was a college graduate and therefore encouraged all of us to do as well as possible in school. He also was a good athlete and frequently played baseball with us. He was an excellent swimmer and pretty much directed the water safety and swim instruction part of our water activities during the summer. When we started summering in Long Beach, he did the same after he had returned from the service.

During that summer, I struggled through some of the Red Cross swim tests just to impress Mr. F. I had become a good diver by then and was beginning to dive competitively for my high-school swim team. So that summer I showed off for him on all three diving boards at the Long Beach Municipal Pool. The swan dive was my strong suit, and it usually felt good to have all eyes on me as I did my thing. Anyway, Mr. F. made it a point to express his appreciation of my skill, which came to mean a great deal to me.

But what really drew me to the man and enhanced our relationship forever was his taking my brother and me to visit our mom on several occasions. There were times when we couldn't get anyone else to take us, which, fortunately, was a rare occurrence. None of my aunts and uncles ever owned a car. When they took us out, it always was by public transportation. None of them had a well-paying job, and they often worked five and a half to six days a week. They tried their very best to take us to mom every week but couldn't quite do so. Lou Feigelson stepped into the breach.

He had a car, and the first time he took us, we were in seventh heaven. We could count on two hands the frequency of our car trips thus far in our lives. The first time that Mr. F. met my mom, they hit it off real well. He was in his early twenties then, and mom was about forty-two. Each recognized the other's strengths, and they both relayed their favorable impressions to us afterwards. Mr. F. extolled my mom on the way home in his car. She, in turn, sang his praises on a postcard she sent me almost immediately. I was ecstatic! Not only did I have a swell guy for a supervisor, but my mom had achieved some rare happiness also, in knowing that we really were in good hands.

Mr. F. subsequently took us to see mom several more times during his first stay at the Pride. As a result, he took an even stronger interest in Bernie and me, and we both enjoyed a really good relationship with a special guy.

After Mr. F. went into the service in 1942, we did not correspond with him too often. Consequently, we sort of lost touch with him until he came back to the Pride after the war ended. By that time, he had married, had a child, and just couldn't make it on the meager salary paid by the Pride. So he left in less than a year, to get his master's degree in social work and then to work in that field to support his family. We all said goodbye reluctantly to a special person, but it wasn't to be our last contact.

Some twenty years later, when I was a guidance counselor for the Great Neck schools, I went to a professional meeting that had about 200 people in attendance. As I casually walked to the nearest table to sit down for lunch, there was Lou Feigelson! The conference was on child abuse, and this fine social worker was in attendance, always looking to improve his professional skills. He was as astonished as I by our chance meeting, and we had such an animated and spirited conversation that I don't think we even tasted our lunch!

Mr. F. had a varied and successful career in social work, and pioneered some important programs. Except for a brief period, we've been in touch with each other since that chance luncheon meeting. He was a valuable male-parent figure in my life and in the lives of others residents at the Pride. In a recent conversation, he recalled his first "tour" at the Pride as being the most satisfying experience of his entire career. Needless to say, it was a great year for many of us as well!

Charlie Vladimer

Laughter is a precious commodity in our lives at any time. Charlie Vladimer was the very first adult in my life to make laughter an everyday occurrence that brightened all of our lives. That's probably the reason why he is loved and cherished by so many of us.

With my father dying very early in my life, and my mother becoming incapacitated soon after, there was only loss and deprivation in my formative years; certainly not much occasion to laugh. Then came a relatively unhappy interlude in an orphanage, followed by the miserable period in the foster home from hell. I really didn't have much to laugh about in my life, and also, I had little exposure to good-humored adults. My aunts and uncles, all well-meaning people whom I loved very much, were poor, and busy, for the most part, in taking care of their own lives. So when Charlie Vladimer entered my life, it was like a breath of fresh air!

Charlie did not consciously try to be funny. He did understand its value, however, and simply looked for the humor in any given situation. He also realized the power of being positive and complimentary, and this emphasis was typical of his approach to all of us. Nor was it insincere. Kids have a way of spotting insincerity very quickly, and it turns them off. Charlie was able to focus on the individual and his actions, and to look for the best in both.

When you're treated in such a manner, you tend to respond in kind. So Charlie generated great rapport with each of us, and he also created a positive atmosphere in which we were nicer to, and more cooperative with, one other. That's why he was able to introduce so many new wrinkles into our activities that turned out so successfully.

During his two stays at the Pride, Charlie was not my supervisor for any substantial length of time. He had been with my brother's and Philly's group for most of the time. In his second stay, the Pride was between directors, and for a time Charlie was our acting head supervisor. I had the pleasure and value of interacting with him on a daily basis and, needless to say, enjoyed him very much. He cared about me, and he made me laugh. When you stepped out of line, his approach was to ask you what was going on, which made you state the problem and explain why you were acting as you were. In this vein, he made us accept accountability for our actions, and yet he did so in a nonthreatening way that made you ready to "fess up" and then go on to correct your problems.

Charlie was not a good athlete, but he liked sports and often participated in our activities. He liked to coach us, and even though we realized that he often didn't know fully what was going on, we enjoyed being on his team because we knew that's where the fun was going to be. Always the cheerleader, loud and funny, he made the activity as much fun as possible. He also kept things light and in perspective, so that when someone didn't do well, he showed the way in laughing it off. That was new for me and for many other competitive-minded kids. In the same vein, he always had us shake hands, or acknowledge the other team, when the activity was over. Basically, he wanted us to extract enjoyment from an activity and not lose perspective about its importance. That, of course, was a valuable lesson.

Charlie used to enjoy taking us on trips so that we could widen our world. Since money was scarce, we didn't go to places requiring admission fees. But every trip he took us on was an enjoyable one, even the tedious bus rides. In the bus, Charlie would lead us in song, even when we didn't know the words. Laughter and frivolity were his targets, and he usually hit the bull's-eye. A mainstay of every trip was his leading us in a "For He's a Jolly Good Fellow" tribute to the bus driver, which humanized the drivers for us, especially when they smiled and thanked us for the attention. Another good lesson in human relations. Charlie, while not long in my life, taught me how to laugh. Can anything be more valuable?

Harry Koval

Harry was probably my favorite supervisor at the Pride. He came in the early part of 1946, and was there for four years, until 1950. Since I was expelled from the Pride in the fall of 1947, he was my supervisor for about a year and a half, making my relationship with him the longest, by far, that I had had with any supervisor in my seven-year Pride stint. Fortunately for me, he was a wonderful parent figure.

Harry was a soft-spoken, serious individual. Due to his own harsh family background (which I didn't learn about until much later), he didn't smile much and did not have a visible or overt sense of humor. What made him so effective, though, with virtually everyone, was his unerring interest in us, and his ability to communicate that. Even in a group setting, whatever he had to say to any of us was stated quietly and directly to the individual concerned, who felt that it was a private conversation even though others were around. He also stressed the positives of a situation and directed compliments and encouragement to all of us with such frequency that we each felt better about ourselves in that particular activity.

Harry was the straightest of straight-shooters. I felt like a favorite of his, yet he never played favorites. As I have learned when we sometimes reminisce about him, many others felt the same way. We each remember some positive affirmation directed to us individually that made us feel special. For example, as our basketball coach, he had entered us in a tough industrial league, with much older players. He told us not to worry about our record because it probably wouldn't be a strong one. "Let's just try to play as a team and see where it takes us." He took the pressure off, and, as I recall, we won at least half of our games, which was pretty darn good, considering that we were up against teams that were older, more experienced, and physically superior. I felt quite elated about being high scorer of the team, but here again, he kept it in perspective. He defined our roles and made sure that we each knew that everyone had an indispensable job to do if we were to perform up to our potential. And we did. We also had a good time in the process. Most importantly, we learned the real value of teamwork, which carried over beyond the court. Certainly, later on in my life, when I became a teacher and basketball coach, I patterned myself after Harry and didn't do too badly.

Harry was an excellent athlete himself. He ran very well and could more than hold his own in all of our activities. To give us the best softball sessions, he often pitched for both sides. He was a talented pitcher and could keep the score quite even by simply bearing down on the winning team while easing up on the losing one. Fancying myself a good hitter, I generally would challenge him to show me his best stuff. That would elicit a smile from him and a quiet nod of the head. Whoosh! More likely than not, I'd whiff, but once in awhile, either he'd let me get a hit or I'd get lucky and tag him for one. Either way, we all enjoyed competing with or against him, because of the way he conducted our games.

He also emphasized good sportsmanship, probably even more than Charlie, who was especially noted for this. It was reflected by the constant stream of compliments and encouragement he directed to both teams when we played our various games. Since he knew his stuff, his coaching comments were very helpful, especially since he applauded our best efforts and took note of our continuing progress. This clear, positive approach rubbed off on us and blunted our own single-minded emphasis on winning. He really was a fine sportsman, an excellent coach, and a great role model.

Fortunately for us, Harry and Charlie served in the Pride together, and made it a golden era for me. Both had been in military service during World War II and both came to the Pride afterwards, Harry for the first time, and Charlie, returning for his second. Harry was older, and already was a graduate of the University of Illinois, while Charlie was in the beginning stages of his college career. Since they were caring adults and very competent supervisors, they hit it off immediately and formed a strong partnership. They've been close personal friends ever since.

In choose-up activities, Harry and Charlie took opposite sides and tried, good-naturedly, to beat each other. Charlie rarely had much success, because Harry could outplay and outcoach him. Yet

Harry always made it seem that his side was lucky to win, emphasizing that we had all had a lot of fun. In other words, both kept the emphasis on the fun side of the activity rather than on the outcome. It was a win-win situation for all of us, rather than just for half of us. Again, this taught me a valuable lesson that I kept coming back to later on in my life and my career in education.

In 1947, disaster blind-sided me. I was expelled from the Pride, suddenly and without any warning, just for the cardinal sin of being sixteen years old. A new executive director had just been appointed, and one of his admonitions from the board of directors was to save money. The sixteen- and seventeen-year-olds, some eight to ten boys and girls at the time, needed the most money for carfare and the like. Also, as I later found out, in the eyes of the new director, the older kids were likely to be trouble-makers. So, without even meeting any of us, he arbitrarily directed the Pride's social workers to place us in foster homes if we had no family to take us in.

My brother had left the Pride in early 1946 to join the Navy. It was our first separation, but with Harry and Charlie at the Pride, I was quite happy and comfortable having two strong adults in my life. My brother was discharged from the Navy a year later because the government was reducing its forces in the aftermath of World War II. He then moved in with our aunt and uncle, sharing the last bedroom in their apartment with my other uncle. Therefore, there was no room for me with them, and I again was placed in a foster home. I was extremely unhappy and resentful.

Without so much as interviewing me to determine my actual needs or preference, the social worker placed me with a family clear on the other side of Brooklyn. I was in the early part of my senior year in high school, where I was doing well and wanted to graduate. I had to take two buses for over an hour each way in order to commute to school daily. I was uprooted, confused, and furious!

It was going to be a bad year. Harry sadly broke the news to me, explaining the new policy in which sixteen would now be the new age limit at the Pride, and that I, along with the other older kids, simply had the bad luck to be the first ones to kick off the new policy. He also told me that he had done everything he could to get them to phase it in gradually so that all of us could finish school first before having to depart. He said that if I cared to come back on weekends, he'd make sure that I was welcome to partici- pate in our normal weekend athletic activities. He was as support- ive and attentive as he could be, but my time was up. I had to leave, and I did.

I was still angry, and this immediately manifested itself in my relationship with my new foster adults. They were nice enough, but by now, with the bad taste of my previous foster home reawakened, I vowed that no one would ever mistreat me again. For the year that I lived with them, we had a distant relationship, at best. I didn't cause them any trouble, and when they realized that I was a law- abiding and self-sustaining person, they left me pretty much alone to lead my own life. However, I had my worst year in school. I was late a lot, inattentive, and sometimes, less than civil with my teach- ers, all of which was a departure from my prior spotless record. I even got to meet the dean of students on several occasions, and received my first detention.

Of course, when I visited my mother, I pretended that every- thing was okay, and she never picked up on my hurt feelings and sour morale. By that time, in 1947–48, she had developed adult diabetes along with her advancing multiple sclerosis, a deadly com- bination that would cause her death in July of 1949. She was only forty-nine.

I went back to the Pride virtually every Saturday of that year, and true to his word, Harry made me feel quite welcome. Not only did I enjoy whatever games we played, but I got milk and cookies, just as when I was a resident. After a strenuous session, cold milk was a favorite of mine, and this left me content for the time being. As I found out later on, the director usually took Saturday after- noons off, and so I didn't even have to fret or worry about him. Harry usually would be sure to ask me how things were going and he maintained his strong interest in me. I fully appreciated his decency and always felt that he was unswervingly in my corner. He was a very solid male parent-figure in my adolescence, when I most needed one, and as such, he did a great deal for me.

Other Supervisors

In 1992, the Pride Alumni Association decided to honor the best supervisors we had in the Home. Anyone could be nominated if it was felt that he or she had made a significant contribution to our lives during our stay there. The people selected for these Appreciation Plaques were Sam Arcus, Lou Feigelson, Harry Koval, Charlie Vladimer, and Andy Schreiber. Andy worked at the Pride in the late forties and early fifties, and was highly regarded by all who had him as their supervisor.

I was surprised by the noticeable absence of any female supervisors from this list and asked a number of women who had been in the Pride in the thirties, forties, and fifties why no female supervisors had been selected. All of them generally had the same thing to say. While they had liked many of their supervisors, there simply had been none that stood out as special. They named several as having been good, but not so good as to warrant a plaque of distinction. They also had another interesting observation to make. They couldn't think of anyone who had been very bad, either. While there had been many mediocre ones, the women felt, all in all, that their supervisors had been okay and had provided satisfactory care. When asked who the significant adults in their lives had been during their time in the Pride, the women mentioned family members, teachers in school, and only occasionally a supervisor.

The men were asked the same questions. Aside from the names mentioned above, they too talked about the revolving-door tenure of many supervisors, their short stays, and the subsequent lack of any impact on them. However, when asked about bad or destructive supervisors, one name invariably was given by those who had been in the Pride in the late thirties and early forties. To protect his identity, a fictitious name will be used in this account.

Sam "Tony" Arano

Sam Arano was a Sephardic Jew, meaning that his parents were not European and had come from a North African country or the Middle East. He was a short, swarthy, dark-complexioned man and looked very Italian, hence the nickname of "Tony." He didn't hesitate to tell anyone that he had once been a guard at Sing-Sing Prison in upstate New York. He certainly wanted to promote a tough-guy image because he believed in fear and intimidation, and wanted the kids to be afraid of him.

Mr. Arano came to the Pride as a supervisor in the late thirties, in the waning days of Max Blumberg's tenure as director of the board. A stern disciplinarian, he believed strongly in corporal punishment. The paddle was his favorite weapon, and when he became head supervisor, that was what he wanted used, especially on the boys. He was head supervisor when Bernie and I came into the Pride, and while neither of us ever was bad enough to warrant this punishment, I remember watching it inflicted on some of my group-mates.

Mr. Arano was a contentious guy with fast hands. If he saw something happening that he didn't like, he'd clout the culprit without even pausing for an excuse or explanation. Needless to say, he wasn't liked too well, but that's the way he wanted it. He'd stand in the front of the dining room before every meal and wait briefly for silence so that we could say the blessing. If it wasn't forthcoming quickly enough, some randomly selected kid would be sent outside, to be summoned much later for an isolated meal. Mr. Arano rarely smiled and gave no sense of caring for anyone. Fear was his stock in trade.

On one occasion, he caught my Junior Boys group (around nine to eleven years of age) in an after-lights-out pillow fight. All twenty-five of us were forced to get up and remake our beds. Then we had to strip them totally and make them up again. This was repeated about three times. After we did this to his satisfaction, we had to stand at the foot of our beds, backs to the center of the room, hands behind our heads, while he walked quietly behind us, from room to room. Naturally, some boys would grumble and curse, as quietly as possible, or so they thought. Suddenly, there'd be the loud sound of a hard smack to the head, or the more muffled sound of a kid being pushed very hard onto his bed. Occasionally, a boy would start crying, which brought a sneer to his face. Net result: we hated his guts!

A notable incident occurred in 1942, when some of the more aggressive Senior Boys who could no longer take his abuse decided to jump him as he made his night rounds to see if we were all in bed. Four of these boys hid by the lockers in the dark hallway and did just that. They jumped him, and a battle royal ensued which spilled over into the dorms. Surprised as Arano initially was, the boys got in some good licks and bloodied his face. When they realized, however, that he knew who they were, they deliberately eased up on him so that he could get his own licks in, which, they felt, was inevitable anyway. Everyone wound up pretty well bloodied, but they were the heroes of the year. No one had ever done anything like that before, and especially to a guy everyone hated and feared. Naturally they were punished pretty severely, but they reveled in our universal admiration and appreciation of what they had done.

Tony Arano left soon thereafter, and definitely was not missed. He was not the first supervisor who believed in this mode of dealing with the residents of the Home, because corporal punishment was an accepted method of discipline in those days. He was, however, its most severe advocate, and, with this along with the other negative features of his abrasive personality, he was a universally hated figure. He obviously did not care for kids, and that was communicated readily in everything that he did. A prison guard mentality describes him accurately, because that's how he came across. That his kind was rare at the Pride is strong testimony to the values established by the Home's founding fathers, back in 1915.

When Tony Arano left, we were quite happy to see him go; in fact, we were elated! Charlie Vladimer and Sam Arcus had just come on the scene, and the disciplinary methods would change dramatically for the better. A "bad" man had come and gone; we were relieved, and once again, we were free!

Chapter 7

The Impact of the Supervisors on Our Lives

As should be quite evident by now, the supervisors played an important parental role in the lives of the orphans who lived in the Home. Most of us were there because we had no parents; others had one or even two parents who were unable to take care of them, due to divorce, desertion, illness, or poverty. Generally, our views of our parents, and of family adults, were not happy ones. From our perspective, they had failed to provide adequate homes and had abandoned us to an orphanage. Now, here we were, in a group setting, being cared for and taking orders from adults who were virtual strangers. The odds for both a good relationship and a good experience were not too strong. Furthermore, given the minimal salaries and the mandatory requirement to live at the Pride on a full-time basis, the probability of getting quality supervisors who could provide good child care was also on the low side.

Supervisors sailed in and out of our lives with great frequency and rapidity. The faces and names of many of them are now quite blurred because they hardly made any impact on us, either good or bad. Yet, remarkably, for the most part the quality of the supervisors was surprisingly high. There was a reason for this. The original mandate of the Pride's founding fathers, "to hire staff members who would be dedicated and caring and would show warmth and affection for their charges," seems to have been followed as closely as possible in the hiring process.

From interviews with former supervisors, there is strong reason to believe that caring about kids was the priority for all supervisor applicants. While both authors are male, and reminisce about their male supervisors, there is much evidence that a decent quality of supervisory care existed for the girls as well. Whenever the Pride alumni get together, the women's remembrances about their supervisors, while not as enthusiastic as those of the men, generally are quite positive. Many interviews with alumni women bear this out. They all remember several good supervisors, have only fleeting memories of the ones who stayed for a short time, and hardly recall any who were really destructive, cruel, or bad.

Does this mean that there weren't any lemons? Probably not, as was detailed above. But the small number of unsuitable personnel does mean that the tradition of seeking people who cared for kids usually remained strong and essential. One of the primary founders of the Pride, Max Blumberg, was a strong individual who remained board chairman for some twenty years. He and his wife, Lena, who later served on the board, were known for their passionate commitment to young people. Their successor, Jacob H. Cohen, who was their good friend, made no bones about carrying on their high priority of getting the very best people to care for their charges with love and firmness, the combination of traits most sought after in those days. That this policy succeeded, as indicated by our positive recollections and profiles of our most memorable supervisors, is eloquent testimony to the uniqueness of the Pride of Judea Home, and that is why it was able to play such a positive role in all of our lives.

As we look at the revered supervisors whom we have singled out, it is easy to see how valuable and essential they were to our normal development. Just as orphaned infants need to be picked up frequently to be hugged and spoken to, so do orphan children need good adults in their lives to play the indispensable parental roles. An important requisite for our sustained growth was the presence of these people at central moments of our childhood and youth.

Philly could very easily have remained suspicious, confused, and self-destructive during his formative years, emerging inevitably as a wounded and fragile adult. Instead, the likes of Trig, Lou Feigelson, Charlie Vladimer, and Sam Arcus connected with him strongly and turned him around.

The same holds for Peewee Friedland. With a sickly father whom he could barely remember, the likes of Lou Feigelson, Charlie, and then Harry Koval all exerted a crucially strong and positive influence upon him.

Yet there is another side to the coin. Always straining to make financial ends meet, the Pride was constantly strapped for funds. Drawing its money from a combination of state and city funds,

Jewish welfare agencies, and private donors, the Home paid meager salaries to its staff members. Young people just out of college, and still without family responsibilities, usually worked there for a short time, picked up some experience, and then moved on.

Whether or not they were satisfactory supervisors certainly was a top priority in addressing our needs. But the transiency of their stays at the Pride was itself a negative factor which had a considerably adverse effect upon us. We were orphans because of parental departures due to death, divorce, or desertion. Now, here we were in the Home, experiencing similar but more frequent departures by substitute parents who continually passed into and out of our lives. This did not help already insecure kids to feel very worthy, and many of the children retained this fabric of insecurity as they were growing up.

The orphanage did not, of course, meet everyone's developmental needs, as you will read about later on. What is most amazing, however, is that the group whose needs were unmet was but a small minority, and that most of the Home's alumni can and do look back at the their years there with warmth and appreciation. They invariably recall, fondly and appreciatively, their supervisors and the other adults who provided the love, attention, and support so vitally needed by every child.

Yes, the role of the supervisor in our lives definitely was a key one. Through them, an orphan did indeed have many parents! We were lucky to get some great ones, regardless of how long they stayed with us, and they affected our lives decisively and favorably!

Chapter 8

Our True Alma Mater: P.S. 202

Stan Friedland

Talk to the alumni of the Pride about going to school, and they'll smile and say, "Oh, you mean 202?" That was our school! Different high schools came later for all of us; some of us made it through college and beyond; but P.S. 202 was our common school, our "roots" school, if you will, because it played an important role in our lives.

First of all, getting there was interesting. The Pride only occasionally owned a bus because it was expensive. So the older kids were permitted to walk to school unescorted. The younger kids, however, were escorted, often in formation, by a sort of security guard. Ben Karp, a burly man, assumed this role for many years. We'd walk the four blocks in a double line, but in a casual yet well-paced fashion. We didn't mind the showcase because most of us were not ashamed of being in the Pride. We each had a brown bag lunch, our books held in a strap, and we were ready to go.

Our assembling together this way every morning seemed to provide an impetus for attending school. Consequently, there was hardly any malingering while we went to 202. Later on, as we went our separate ways to high school, truancy was much more prevalent. Individually, it was easier to get away with cutting school because no one would know about it until report cards came out every eighth or tenth week, and by then, who remembered what had happened weeks ago? The street-smart people also knew not to cut school on successive days, or on days too close to one another because that pattern was likely to draw a call from the truant officer. But as younger kids going to P.S. 202, we weren't into that yet.

The 1940–41 school year was a screwed-up year for me. I started the year in fourth grade in P.S. 99, in the Midwood section of Brooklyn, where my foster home was located. I liked 99, and in the first three grades I had gotten off to a successful start. When my eventful fourth-grade year started, I very much liked my new teacher and even had won her contest that September for the student who had read the most books. I was ready for an enjoyable year.

Suddenly, I'm no longer there! That October, we ran away from our foster home, and one week later, I'm sitting in P.S. 210, in Flatbush. I had a new and strange class, and a teacher I most certainly didn't like. The fourth grade, at that time in New York City, was the year in which cursive writing and penmanship were intensified in the curriculum. My new teacher didn't like left-handers, and I was a left-hander and quite proud of it.

When my new teacher first saw me write, with that exaggerated inversion of the wrist that most lefties have, she frowned noticeably. When she next saw my handwriting, She said, "This will never do." She asked me to take the pencil in my right hand and proceeded to give me "dummy" instruction in how to hold it, right in front of the whole class. Needless to say, I was looking for a hole in the floor to swallow me up and rescue me from that humiliation. I rescued myself. I balked. Thoroughly red in the face from embarrassment, I looked up at her and said, "I can't do it this way. I'd rather do it with my left hand."

The teacher was not too happy and again directed me to do it rightie. I balked again, and soon was sitting in the principal's office. We talked. He was a nice guy. I told him about the circumstances that had brought me to his school, and he understood. He didn't change my class, but he spoke to my teacher, and while she didn't like it, she left me alone thereafter.

Two months later, in December, my brother and I entered the Pride, and kerplunk! I soon was in my third class in four months; fourth grade, P.S. 202. I didn't mind this change because, fortunately, it was a good school, with good teachers, and I was to benefit from them in many ways.

I was a good student, and for two reasons. I happened to like school because, for the most part, I was a good learner. Thanks to my mother, I liked to read and was good at it. I knew what was going on in class, and since I usually had done my homework, I was prepared enough so that if called on, I would do okay. I occasionally raised my hand, but I was rather shy, and it took several deep breaths before I could speak up before my classmates.

The second and more important reason for my school success was, of course, my mother. When she saw that I was a good student, her hopes for my attending college were established firmly. No one in my family had gone to college before, and my mom wanted it for me. Yet she never pushed me or ever hassled me about it. She simply asked how I had done in school that past week and expressed great delight at my description of my successes, achievements, and activities. The happier she was, the more I tried to do even better the next week—for her! Nor would I hold back on any major problems. I somehow was astute enough to know that she needed and enjoyed every opportunity to play mother. She was more than happy to discuss my problems with me and to help me overcome them.

Mom did all of this with my brother as well. She gave us both what would be known today as maximum quality time. She kept the focus totally on us. Whenever we asked how she was doing, she'd nod her head and smile sadly. We never heard her complain, which was amazing to both of us, and made us into noncomplainers as well. Our two-hour weekly visits with her went by very quickly. But they were essential for both of us.

My brother Bernie was only an average student; not for lack of ability, but mainly because academics just didn't interest him much. He did what he had to do to get by, but not much more. He was great with his hands and fixed things easily. He made fine models of planes and boats, and enjoyed that sort of thing. In fact, that's how he got his nickname: "Sykes." Early in his high school career at East New York Vocational High School, he took a course in boat-building and built a beautiful boat. He couldn't think of a name for it and solicited one from his friends at the Pride. For some reason, they named it the Sykes. From that point on, that was his nickname as well.

The Pride staff, in assessing each of us in the eighth grade, as was their custom, sent Bernie to a vocational high school, while I ultimately went to an academic high school to prep for college. Many years later, Bernie became aware of what he had missed. He went to night school to make up some subjects, and then, later in life, ultimately got two college degrees by attending college at night while holding down a full-time job.

But back when we lived at the Home, Bernie wasn't motivated to do well in school. Though it bothered my mother somewhat, she knew that a vocational school would teach him a valuable job skill which he could use for the rest of his life. She also knew that whenever he cared about something, he did it quite well. She knew intuitively that she didn't have to worry about him, and she was right.

This left me, however, to carry the academic banner, which I was more than happy to do. Bernie was happy enough with this arrangement. He knew how much my progress meant to mom, and he made sure to keep tabs on me so that I would continue to do well in school. He did this with affection, but also with firmness, when needed. I appreciated his being there for me, and this too was an incentive.

I liked going to school at P.S. 202. I liked my day even more when, after a few years, I was able to walk there on my own with my friends, rather than in a regimented group with the other young kids. But I almost lost this privilege when I was caught stealing fruit from a grocery store that we'd occasionally stop at on the way to school. Several of us would go into the store; two or three would distract the owner while one would pilfer an apple or pear and walk out. The owner soon became wise to us and stopped Ben Karp, our security guard, who was walking the younger kids to school, and described us to him.

Ben came over to me. "Friedland," he said, "I know that you and your friends are stealing fruit from Rosen's store, and it's got to stop!" When I protested, he put up his hand and said, "Hear me carefully. You're a leader in your group. The kids from the Pride have a good reputation, and we all have to protect it. I'm not accusing you of stealing the fruit. But you know what's going on, and you're in a position to stop it. That's what I expect you to do. If not, then your whole group is going to start walking with me to school again. Do I make myself clear?"

He certainly did, loud and clear! We didn't go into that store for a long time. The problem went away quickly.

My most memorable teacher in P.S. 202 was the one that all of us remember the most keenly, Miss Bolduc. None of us liked her;

all of us feared her. Yet she got the most from us because she was demanding and persistent. Given her odd name and her aggressive manner, it was easy to see why everyone called her "the Bulldog," though not to her face, of course. She was tenacious. When she assigned something, you'd have better done it because sooner or later, she'd "come for you"! So it was that she made me a better public speaker and performer.

I had her for eighth-grade English, and she had a standard assignment of having everyone memorize different stanzas of "Charge of the Light Brigade" by Alfred, Lord Tennyson. I was given the most dramatic stanza of the poem, "Into the Valley of Death Rode the Six Hundred," and so forth. I had never stood up before a class before to perform an oral recitation. While I was able to respond in class, it was always from the "sanctuary" of my own desk. Stand up alone before the class and recite a memorized poem in a dramatic fashion? Very daunting. My first thought was to get out of it.

"Miss Bolduc, ma'am, I do know the poem by heart. Can I come in after school to recite it to you?"

"Why?" she asked.

"Well, you know, I've never done this before, and I'm somewhat nervous about it."

Looking me right in the eye, she said, "Fine. You've just stated the reason why I want you to do it in this manner."

"What do you mean?" I asked.

She replied, "You must overcome your shyness, and there's only one way to do so, and that's by doing it. Would you like me to help you first?" "No thanks," I said hurriedly. "I'll try it on my own." I wasn't getting out of it, but I certainly didn't want any more contact with Miss Bolduc than was necessary. If that got around, I was dead!

I memorized the poem and recited it several times to my mother on my weekend visit. My turn was two days later, on a Tuesday. I rehearsed to myself repeatedly during the next day, and had it down cold. Sure enough, on Tuesday, I was called. Could I do this? The butterflies were zooming all over my stomach!

I began slowly and began to pick up confidence, especially when I saw the smile on my teacher's face. She didn't smile much, and the sight was very encouraging. Pretty soon, I was in high gear.

As I looked at the faces of my classmates, I saw their initial expressions of boredom or skepticism give way to greater interest and even smiles as I really got into it. And I did, probably in an overdramatic fashion. Nonetheless, I received an unexpected round of applause, led by Miss Bolduc. I was absolutely thrilled! When the period ended, I lingered so that I could murmur a soft "thank you" to her.

She knew full well that it was a breakthrough moment for me. She looked at me, smiled, and said, "The person you really have to thank . . . is yourself. You did it, and you can be proud of yourself." And I was.

Another thing I liked about the school was that they didn't treat us orphans much differently than the other children. This was probably because of the close communication between the school's principal, Dr. Charles Eichel, and the President of the Pride's board, Jacob H. Cohen. Both wanted us to get the best education possible. We were to be pushed as hard as anyone, especially if we could do the work. If, however, a Pride kid did have difficulties, he or she was to get as much help as needed in order to succeed. Consequently, most of us did okay at 202, which is one major reason why we all think so fondly of it.

I was in the color guard at P.S. 202. I loved it! We wore white pants and shirts with a tie. All assemblies and other full school events started off with the "march of the colors"! Striding tall and in unison, we marched in carrying the American, state, and school flags as firmly and as upright as possible. It was a big kick for me and appealed to my little boy's macho ego. Many of my Pride peers, to this day, remember the grin that was usually on my face on these special occasions.

When I graduated eighth grade, I won the Max Blumberg Medal, given to the outstanding Pride resident in the graduating class. My mother was pleased and happy. What more could I ask?

Several years earlier, Phil Craft also won the Blumberg Medal at his graduation. It was a far greater achievement than mine. For him, 202 was a different experience. Here's why.

Chapter 9

Growing Up "Mentally Retarded": My 202 Years

Phil Craft

When I grew up in the Pride, the term "retarded" was virtually unknown and rarely used. Instead, kids like me were more apt to be called dumb or stupid. I was a mistake-prone and slow learner who learned from his own errors, or else from persistent effort if sufficient time was allowed. In searching for the origins and causes of my chronic, slow learning pace, I inevitably return to my first five years of life, spent at a trauma-filled infant home in Brooklyn. It was a five-year nightmare that did me terrible harm in every possible way. I spent those influential years confused and conflicted, feeling, at the end, that I was an ugly and worthless person. Threats, taunts, and physical beatings were common occurrences for me, and I lived in continual fear of punishment or reprisal for any misdeed or mistake.

When one passes through such a frightening minefield of oppression and despair, he soon learns to watch his step and to move slowly, with painstaking care. Instinctive hesitation was my condition. I had so completely come to distrust my own impulses and judgment that I was slow to respond to most learning situations and, as a result, felt as though I had only limited ability. This behavior, in retrospect, was obviously self-protective in nature, aimed at avoiding further failure, pain, or embarrassment in the situations that challenged me daily. The repetition of such reactions developed in me the chronic slowness and rigidity of thought and action that is often an aspect of mental retardation. In short, I am "slow-witted," but certainly not "dim-witted."

This ultimately became evident when I came to the Pride shortly after my fifth birthday, in December of 1932, which put me on track to start kindergarten at P.S. 202 in February of 1933. Although long ago, I can still remember my teacher because she was so unique. She was a tall, matronly, but lovable black teacher named Miss Simkins. She smiled a lot and taught us singsong games, nursery rhymes like "London Bridge" and "Farmer in the Dell," and Mother Goose stories. She was the first nonwhite person I had ever known, and the day I met her, I instantly recalled how much I loved the taste of chocolate, which matched the dark hue of her skin.

That first positive image combined nicely with Miss Simkins's friendly demeanor, enabling me to feel comfortable and safe in her classroom, and to play with children with whom I was unacquainted. I also recall her unfailing kindness and patience whenever I faltered in learning new games and songs. I remember too her warm smile when I clung to her as she told her wonderful stories over and over again, until even I could recall many of the important details. She seemed to notice that even though I was slow, I eventually caught on and then joined in more actively, with enthusiasm, confidence, and even elation. Perhaps because of this, and also because of our positive rapport, I was placed in the 1A-3 class for the following year, rather than 1A-2. Neither Miss Simkins nor anyone else truly understood why I learned so slowly, since they knew nothing of my crippling experiences in the infant home.

For a change, I was in luck. What a perfect placement for me to start my public school career! At P.S. 202, as at other city schools in that era, kids were placed in classes based on their learning ability. The fastest learners were assigned to classes whose designations ended in the number one, where they enjoyed the aura of superiority as they progressed through the grades. The slowest students, who usually had various types of learning problems, were placed in classes designated with the number two. This probably was the city's way of attempting to disguise the ability level of these students, but it was obvious to everyone, right from the first grade. These kids, regrettably, were ridiculed, scorned, and insulted by the other children, and with the brand of inferiority firmly stamped upon them, they had to endure this right through the eighth grade.

The kids in the "three" classes were regarded as either ordinary or in transition to a one or two classification, depending upon such diverse factors as performance, effort, conduct, or even space considerations. Teachers often used grades and notations on a child's record to either reward or punish. Thus, a pupil with a negative attitude and poor conduct record who had managed to pass his final exams, and therefore should have been promoted to the next grade, could be exiled to a two class as a strictly punitive measure. Meanwhile, earnest youngsters like me, who worked hard and behaved, could remain in a three class, even though our test marks were barely borderline because our inconsistent daily performance always required additional assistance.

It is easy to see why I was thrilled with my placement in 1A-3. Given my pronounced lack of self-esteem, I was delighted to escape placement into the class where I thought I really belonged: the dreaded two class. But I lived in fear in the three class. I was afraid of being called upon lest I reveal my ineptness for all to see. So, while other, better-prepared students waved their hands when the teacher asked questions, I would anxiously summon up all I knew about the subject in order to offer some marginally correct answer if called upon. In the rare instances when I thought that I knew the answer and raised my hand uncertainly, my humiliation was painful and long-lasting if I turned out to be incorrect.

My resulting hesitation and extreme caution soon grew into a fixed and rigid pattern. Whenever the teacher introduced large amounts of new material, my mind tended to panic and even momentarily shut down under the overload. I had conditioned myself to focus on one thing at a time, and to plod my way through it in a slow but methodical manner. Whenever I departed from that style and tried to accelerate my learning of anything, I usually made errors of haste and confusion. In order to master most subjects, I had to go back constantly and review and integrate the new knowledge methodically until the facts began to relate to one other in an understandable way.

Although my IQ scores later on would indicate a normal-superior level of intelligence, I was conspicuously deficient in exercises requiring rapid thinking and decisions, abstract concepts, and even manual dexterity. In my shop classes, where only brief but detailed instructions would precede manual performance, I was incredibly slow and uncertain, always looking at the work of the better students in order to copy their methods of doing the project. Only my caution and slow work habits saved me from the ever present danger of injuring myself by using the tools or machinery incorrectly. The flawed quality of my finished work became a source of exasperation to my shop teachers, and a puzzlement to my classmates. They often said to me, "Phil, even if you're not that good in class, at least you should be able to do simple shop-work better than that." But I couldn't, no matter how hard I tried!

Thankfully, my teachers noticed that, although I was slower than others to learn, I always managed to catch up and make passing grades, through extra effort and determination. Recognizing my persistence, and also aware that I came from the Home, my teachers were all patient and supportive. It also helped, more than I knew at the time, that our principal, Dr. Eichel, was a friend of the Pride's president, Jacob H. Cohen, and instructed his teachers to be as supportive of the Pride's kids as possible.

Mrs. Simkins and Mrs. Goldblatt, my 1A-3 teacher, were both supportive of me in the highly sensitive first two years of my public school career. Had they not shown the patience and sympathy which enabled this slow kid to persevere, in spite of himself, I might easily have been headed for the two class, where I felt I really belonged. Looking back on myself as a six-year-old, I realize that I conveyed an aura of pathetic vulnerability marked by a subdued and overly compliant manner, which reflected my fragile ego and depressed self-image. Their work with me during those years, their ability to squeeze delayed but adequate mastery of the material, and finally, their placement of me in the three classes, was a great service to me. Among other things, it showed me, and others, that although I was slow, I was not stupid! How important that realization was for me! For perhaps the first time in my life, I emerged, haltingly, from my sense of worthlessness and began to enjoy school.

Another major asset was my strong love of reading. I owe full credit for this special interest to my first memorable Pride supervisor, Trig Abel. I came to love his bedtime stories, read from a wide assortment of books, which I wanted to delve into as soon as I could. Naturally, I was a slow reader, but I simply made more time available for my homework and for my "fun" reading. This consistent love of reading would help me throughout school.

Except for one significant episode, my second- and third-grade years passed by uneventfully and satisfactorily. I had one or two interest areas that afforded me pleasure and satisfaction. One of them was music. When I was seven years old, I had a sweet singing voice and a fervent love of song. Given the difficulty I had in learning anything, it was a real struggle to memorize the words of a song. Yet I made the effort gladly, since each new song I learned became a permanent and valued new possession, affording fresh pleasure whenever I sang it, to myself or to others.

One special evening, the Pride had an amateur talent contest, like the old Major Bowes Hour on radio, and I entered. I sang the song "It's a Sin to Tell a Lie," which to my naive mind sounded like a morality tale rather than a love story. To my delight, I was one of the winners, and I received a prize! Happily, it was for a series of piano lessons right at the Home, and I eagerly looked forward to them because I had always wanted to learn how to play the piano.

My piano teacher turned out to be an eager but not overly patient lady who soon became testy and frustrated. I had difficulty in learning musical notes, and even in reading the basic scale, which, of course, tested her patience sorely. However, she was visibly impressed when I was able to hum back to her with flawless accuracy each note that she had played on the piano. She said that she had never encountered this gift in one so young, and she renewed her efforts to teach me how to read music and play the piano properly. However, my fingers sabotaged me. I was so poorly coordinated that I kept hitting the wrong keys, despite her repeated corrections. Two lessons were all she could bear! She never returned for another, and I simply was told that no more lessons had been scheduled for me.

At the time, I was relieved to be rid of her and those painful lessons. They had reaffirmed to me just how ineffectual a learner I was. I had already known that I was slow mentally. Now I also knew just how bad my eye-hand coordination was. This deficiency would pop up later on when I was unable to master the skill of typing, no matter how hard I tried. "How can anyone be so dumb?" I would rage at myself. Of course, the major cause of these difficulties was, simply put, my lack of physical coordination, which penalized me considerably.

In the fourth grade I experienced my first great triumph in school, and indeed, in life. Its shape and substance came as a complete surprise.

Each June, an annual schoolwide music appreciation competition was held. The winner was the student who could best identify the main themes and lesser passages of the classical music compositions we studied in our music classes. Mrs. Jane Kerner, my music and official class teacher that year, not only had befriended me warmly, but also had inspired me with her own passionate devotion to the works of the great composers. As I began to know and learn their music, I realized, much to my pleasant surprise, that instead of being a slow learner, as I was everywhere else, I could easily memorize, and even hum accurately, virtually all the notes and movements of every composition I heard after the record was played only once or twice. The very same ability that had shown up fleetingly when I had taken those disastrous piano lessons several years before had resurfaced like a rediscovered gold mine! I was elated!

Mrs. Kerner was amazed and delighted when I brought this newly found talent to her attention, and when I demonstrated it for her. She immediately suggested that I enter the June competition. When I expressed my reservations about embarrassing myself in front of everyone, she offered to coach me after school so that I would not be too nervous or uncomfortable. By that time, she had captivated me with her genuine interest and lovely disposition. No female adult had every shown such warm personal regard for me as she did, and I loved her dearly for it.

I leaped at the chance to spend individual time with Mrs. Kerner in pursuit of our common love of music. With great patience, we spent many after-school sessions together, where she drilled me on names, titles, and the specific movements of different recordings, which she kept playing back to me until I could identify them with faultless precision. When I got back to the Pride, I would write these down in my notebook, with dogged determination, until they became locked in my memory. All the while, in other subjects and matters, I continued to have my usual learning difficulties. It was if I had two different brains, one highly efficient, and the other just sputtering along. It was puzzling!

Although I only was in the fourth grade, I would be competing with older students right up to the top grade in the school, which was grade eight. When it became known that I was in the competition, kids who knew me expressed not only surprise, but something more like shock! Their questions were generally, "What's going on here, Philip? What are you doing in this competition? Why are you out there on a thin limb, setting yourself up for a painful fall?"

This was asked or said repeatedly, and while I smiled through it all, my butterflies increased as the competition approached. Mrs. Kerner knew what was happening, and also knew how to take the heat off me. She said, "Look, Philip. No one expects much from you, so you're the underdog. Go out and do your best. If you miss, you'll get a big round of applause for being there and trying. Only you're not going to miss! And when you give the correct answers, as I'm sure you will, you're going to get a strong wave of applause, and then everyone will be rooting for you! Go get 'em! You can do it!"

With this encouragement bolstering my growing confidence, and with her buoyant smile to lean on, I began the first rounds of the competition. Sure enough, and much to my utter amazement, what she had predicted came true. When my turn came, I easily recognized the selections being played, and even supplied more information than was called for. The auditorium erupted in good-natured laughter and enthusiastic applause. Many students were eliminated in the first few rounds, but I was still there. The youngest and smallest competitor, I made it to the semi-finals!

Over the next few days I basked in my newfound celebrity status. My disbelieving classmates slapped me on the back repeatedly. "Great job, Philly! Atta-way to go, Philly! I never would-a believed it, Philly!" And so it went. Few of them thought I would go any further in the competition, and that also came through. I didn't care. I was enjoying my new status too much. Deep down, I myself didn't think that I could go further. But Mrs. Kerner did.

"Philip," she said, "you were great! And you're going to do even better. The selections will get more difficult, but they'll still be way below you. Go in there and just concentrate on the music and nothing else. You'll be fine."

I looked at her with great trust and affection. "If she has this belief in me, then I'm going to do it for her!"

I was one of the five remaining contestants. The other four, all seventh- and eighth-graders, were good musicians in their own right. In order to accelerate the pace of the competition, only abbreviated phrases of a recording were played. I knew all the answers, and one by one, three of the four other contestants were eliminated. I had made it to the finals! The auditorium was buzzing. Kids called out my name and had to be shushed. It was great! I was so excited, I forgot to be nervous!

My opponent in the finals was an eighth-grade girl who had always been in one classes. She was one of the brightest kids in the school. We both answered several questions correctly, and the suspense really built up. Then was played a piece by Debussy which she mistook for Ravel. I smiled broadly and said, in a voice that was probably a bit too loud, "Debussy"!

The contest judge turned to the audience and said, "Correct! We have a new school champion; Phillip Weinberg, from Class 4B-3!" The place went wild! I can still hear the noise and picture the scene as the judge hung the winner's medal around my neck. "You were wonderful, Phillip," Mrs. Kerner whispered as she embraced me. I looked at her with tears in my eyes. "Thank you, Mrs. Kerner. I owe it all to you!" And I did.

My fourth-grade year was significant for other reasons as well. Earlier that year, our class had been scheduled to attend a special film presentation about Abraham Lincoln and the Civil War. Mrs. Kerner knew that I wanted to see the film because of my strong interest in Lincoln. She was totally unaware, however, that I already had secretly "adopted" him as a substitute father. My own father's rejection and repeated rebuffs caused me not only to hate him but to seek, in fantasy, a warm and loving father figure. I had seen, in Lincoln's biography, the famous photo taken with his youngest son, Tad. The look of gentle affection on his worn face had captivated me, causing me to yearn hopelessly for a father just like him.

Mrs. Kerner only knew that I liked Lincoln a great deal and was looking forward to the film about him. She was shocked, therefore, when I was absent on the day of the class trip to see the film. She almost burst into tears the next day when I told her that my absence was due to my having to attend the funeral of my father, who had suddenly passed away. She hugged me tightly while her stricken face mirrored her sorrow. I had never before been embraced so warmly and lovingly. In that single moment, Mrs. Kerner became the first person in my life whom I truly loved, whole-heartedly and without reservation!

It was not long before she sought and received the Home's consent to have me visit her spacious apartment after classes, providing she brought me home before supper. Miss Predd, the Pride's social worker, was aware of my strong need for special attention, so she readily agreed to this arrangement. Benji Kerner, my teacher's young son, was just about my own age, but he attended a private school instead of 202. His own father, Mrs. Kerner's husband, had died earlier that year, so Benji welcomed my visits and the companionship they brought. I, in turn, welcomed and rejoiced in his surprising cordiality, and we soon became good friends. He was a bright, talented, good-looking boy, who, like myself, loved music. With Mrs. Kerner's ample collection of classical music records to enjoy, the hours would zoom by all too quickly before it was time to return to the Pride.

Occasionally, Mrs. Kerner had me stay for dinner, taking me back soon thereafter. I felt sheer happiness. I was on top of the world—certain that I would live happily ever after!

However, that was not to be, and my wondrous world soon came crashing down! With my unexpected win in the music appreciation contest and then my weeks of wonderful visits to Mrs. Kerner's house, I inadvertently began to goof off in my schoolwork. I felt so favored by her that I thought I would be exempt from the ordinary expectations and requirements that previously had governed my responses as a student, and to which all my classmates usually adhered. In the throes of this complacency, I missed a very important arithmetic homework assignment.

Mrs. Kerner, suddenly aware that I was taking unfair advantage of her goodwill, blew up! Her angry words, directed at me in class before my stunned classmates, tore deeply into the very soul of my being.

"You are behaving like a spoiled, ungrateful brat and should be thoroughly ashamed of yourself," she shrieked.

It would have been far kinder to strike me across the face with her hand! I was devastated. I could not flee. I wished that I had never been born. At that moment, I would have accepted instant death as my penalty!

Mrs. Kerner ended her bitter tirade when I began to cry. My deep, convulsive sobs quickly revealed the havoc she had wrought. She became contrite, but her soothing words failed to penetrate the wall of anger and self-pity that had emerged between us. I felt utterly betrayed; but I blamed myself even more for having allowed myself to love and to be loved by another person. I vowed to myself, then and there, that I never again would expose myself to such a terrible risk and have this happen to me. In that searing moment, I was too selfish and short-sighted to admit, or even to realize, that it was I who had betrayed Mrs. Kerner, my dearest friend. I knew only that the bright new world I had only recently found was now irretrievably destroyed! The new trust, which only recently had covered over the torment, anxiety, and bitterness of my earliest years, which Mrs. Kerner had so lovingly and patiently cultivated in our short relationship, had dissolved into dust.

Although I wanted to hate Mrs. Kerner and get even, I just couldn't do so. The reservoir of gratitude and affection was too deep to evaporate suddenly and disappear. My need for her positive regard had become too great to allow that to happen. Instead, the focus of my lingering rage turned to the subject of math, the cause of the explosion that had brought about my downfall. Until then, with Mrs. Kerner's help, I had been an adequate math student. But now I developed a real learning block against it which would continue into my college years.

Decades later, my therapist explained quite clearly the basis of this displacement of unconscious fury from a well-loved person to a more neutral, virtually inanimate object. However, even with this new handicap, I did succeed in remaining in level three classes throughout my public school career.

Fortunately, my love for classical music, which had always been a special bond with Mrs. Kerner, continued and grew. Although eventually our relationship was partially restored, I never again visited her home or saw her son. The deep wounds I had sustained in that confrontation never fully healed. They would haunt me for a long time, especially during my teen years, when a hidden pessimism severely inhibited my romantic advances toward girls who had stirred my interest. Each time I approached a girl I admired, a phobic anxiety would grip me, forcing me to draw back in abject fear of rejection and rebuff. I continued to believe that the best way to avoid a repeat of that traumatic experience would be to remain withdrawn as much as possible from intense friendships such as I had experienced with Mrs. Kerner, and to seek instead an emotional self-sufficiency which I could more easily support and control. I was quite content with the casual friendships that I continued to enjoy with the boys in my group because they were far safer and less demanding.

I did not enter another music competition in the three years that followed. Perhaps, as a past winner, I couldn't enter again. More likely I had become too heartsick to wish to repeat that experience with Mrs. Kerner. But by the time I reached seventh grade, important changes had taken place in my life. The fragile ties with Mrs. Kerner had disappeared from lack of contact, and I had developed a close friendship with Paul Hirsch, a buddy from the Home. I was deeply saddened, however, to learn that just before my eighth-grade graduation, Mrs. Kerner had passed away, a victim of cancer. I mourned, in my heart, for her and for Benji; and thereafter my thoughts of her always mingled gratitude with regret.

Meanwhile, as a seventh-grader, I had become more experienced, more mature, and somewhat more confident and centered as a person, thanks in no small part to my new supervisor, Lou Feigelson. His interest, concern, and regard for me brought a new hero and role-model into my life, and it was a healthy influence. When the music competition rolled around again, and my teacher invited me to compete in it, I decided to accept the challenge because I was curious to see whether I could win again.

I did, and it turned out to be easier than the first time. My intense interest in classical music had grown even stronger, and my memory had remained acute despite the fact that I wasn't listening to as much of it as before. Perhaps the level of competition also had declined. Anyway, when I won again, it was no big deal because I felt that playing football on the Home's team was even more important, and it was my standard of comparison for everything else. The emotional reward for winning the contest was less intense, and my prize, a brand-new Hohner harmonica, could not be fully enjoyed because I didn't know how to play it; and then I misplaced it soon afterwards, never to see it again.

The seventh-grade year, in general, was a good one for me. I had a great social studies teacher in the person of Mrs. Boyer, who was patient, soft-spoken, and caring about her students. Social studies already was a subject of high interest to me, but she made it even more so, expanding my horizons even further than before. She recognized my passion for Lincoln and made me the Lincoln expert in class, which motivated me to learn even more about him than before. I continued to identify with him. He was homely, spoke slowly, was honest to a fault, and had other qualities that endeared him to me. I continued to fantasize that somehow we were related. Mrs. Boyer was an encouraging figure to me that year, and I remember her warmly for it.

I had one of my best years in the eighth and final grade in 202. Mr. Feigelson had come into my life, and I had a memorable English teacher. You've already met Lou Feigelson and know how much he did for me. Now meet Miss Bolduc, one of those teachers from whom no one can hide, and who gets the most out of everyone, like it or not!

Although diminutive in size, Miss Bolduc was too formidable ever to be regarded as tiny, particularly since she addressed all of her male students as "little boy." Since she had no trouble remembering our names, which she used occasionally, it may be assumed that this habit simply made her feel taller. One morning, she had cause to summon Joseph Porto to her desk. Joe was our oldest and tallest student because he had been left back twice.

When he didn't respond right away, because he hadn't been paying attention, she repeated her directive more sharply, including the use of his last name.

"I'm not a little boy!" he protested, clearly meaning it.

"Don't be impudent, young man!" she admonished him.

"I'm not impotent, Miss Bolduc. I can get it up anytime I want!" he answered proudly.

A loud hush fell over the classroom, followed by a burst of uproarious laughter. None of us could remember anyone speaking to her like that before.

When the giggling subsided and Miss Bolduc had recovered her composure, Joe Porto was on his way to the principal's office, never to reappear in her class again.

Miss Bolduc dominated her classes completely. She let no one get away with anything in Room 515. Her way was law, inside and outside the room. Through her steel-rimmed glasses, she observed everything that went on as though peering through the telescopic sights of a sharpshooter's rifle. She'd move soundlessly about the room as we busily wrote in our notebooks or read silently from our texts. One time, she surprised a boy who had a concealed comic book inside his reader. "I beg your pardon!" she angrily shouted, making him jump two feet in sheer fright. She snatched up the comic book with the fury and quickness of an eagle seizing its prey, and only the baleful glare radiating through her glasses stifled our laughter. The boy never saw his comic book again.

Whenever she was displeased with a pupil's answer, or with any kind of misbehavior, she would loudly proclaim, "I beg your pardon!" and would repeat it until she received the correct response or a cessation of the offending behavior, which then had to be followed by an apology. Each time she asked a question, she expected her name to be included in the answer as a necessary sign of respect. An answer of "yeah" was a dangerous one, and even a "yes" response earned the student an imperious, "I beg your pardon!"

I was probably the most intimidated pupil in the English class. My fear was based on my long history of slow learning and alarm that she would cut me to ribbons when she found this out, as inevitably she must. Her homework and other assignments, therefore, took absolute priority over everything else in my life at that time. When she became aware of my unyielding effort and my perfect, albeit fearful, behavior, she began to cite me to the class as the paragon of what everyone else should be doing. This was emphasized, especially, to my classmates from the Pride. Needless to say, they didn't appreciate these references and let me know it.

In the throes of this bitter dilemma, I stewed helplessly. Finally, I decided to try bringing my homework in one day late in the hope that by doing so the "paragon" would fall off his pedestal. The ploy mollified my Pride friends, but Miss Bolduc's anger and disappointment were equally hard to bear. Gradually, I learned to placate her by turning in my next few assignments on time, but with each occasional and deliberate lapse, she became less inclined to use me as a role-model. As this became more evident to my friends, I was once again able to submit my work more promptly, and my dilemma was at last resolved.

This action on my part did more than just resolve a problem. It showed me that I was intelligent enough to solve any problem, if given sufficient time and opportunity. Needless to say, this was an important realization, and it served as a boost to my confidence and self-esteem.

Although Miss Bolduc was as much the product and symbol of her times as the dinosaurs were of their era, she was a significant and potent figure for me at P.S. 202. She might sometimes be an object of ridicule, but she could never be defied or ignored. She pushed everyone to learn at a higher level. Given my fear of her, I worked as hard as I could throughout the year, and may have learned more, as a result, than from any other teacher in the school. While there was not much to like in Miss Bolduc, she had a powerful influence on her students, which is why virtually everyone who had her still remembers the bulldog in Room 515!

When eighth-grade graduation came, I was astonished to discover that I had won the Max Blumberg Medal! This award was given to the Pride of Judea resident in each graduating class who most distinguished him or herself in some way.

"How can it be?" I asked myself. "Many of my classmates from the Pride are brighter than me, have higher averages than me. What's going on?" When I asked Mr. Feigelson to explain, he looked at me and smiled.

"Evidently, Phil, your teachers think that you are the standout student from the Pride this year. You can accept that medal because you earned it! It definitely is yours because your teachers have voted that medal to you! Congratulations! I'm very proud of you."

I felt like a million dollars! I think I wore that medal all day long until I had to go to sleep. I knew in my heart that I had been awarded it because of my consistent effort rather than my grades. But that was okay, too. What a great way to finish my public school career!

However, I was not looking forward to going to high school. P.S. 202 had become a second home to me. I knew the people and felt safe and secure there. Now would come an immense adjust-ment. I dreaded it. And unfortunately, my expectation was only too accurate.

So why did I think of myself as retarded? Simply because I was. My slowness in everything was pronounced and remained pretty much the same throughout my nine years in 202. Yet, by dint of effort and perseverance, I did succeed, but only after much trial and error. I truly was the tortoise pursuing the hares—the faster learn-ers. I suffered the hurt, frustration, and embarrassment of the slow learner, which depressed my self-esteem and clouded my mind even more. I give full credit to my pivotal teachers at 202 and my supportive supervisors at the Pride for my doing as well as I did. That is undoubtedly why I look back at P.S. 202 with such fond memories.

Chapter 10

Growing Up in the Home

Phil Craft

When I arrived at the Pride of Judea Children's Home in the winter of 1932, shortly after my fifth birthday, I was a very vulnerable human being. Given my nightmarish first five years of life, I brought to this new setting a pathetic need to be liked and a pronounced eagerness to please. Furthermore, I had a foolish gullibility, a lack of social experience and judgment, and a chronic slow-wittedness, all of which made me easy pickings for exploitation by others.

My gradual awareness of being such an easy victim aroused in me a fury, often directed at myself, and a continuing embarrassment which, each time, confirmed my belief that I was dumb and worthless. My impulse to retaliate usually was stifled by my awareness that I was too weak, too small, and too slow-witted to do so effectively. In frustration and despair, I would instead seek seclusion to lick my wounds and to review the mistakes and missteps that had made me such a helpless patsy.

Without realizing it at the time, I was beginning to use my intelligence to identify and solve my problems. Through such self-analysis, I gradually armed myself with the tools of skepticism and doubt. These, in turn, increased my sense of inner security and self-confidence by giving me more effective power and control over myself. I became less of an easy mark and even began to gain respect in my group.

Thus began a continuing, if uneven process of problem-solving which helped me to prevent or to cope with the harmful consequences of my mental and emotional hangups. With each new solution and triumph, I confirmed once again that I was not so dumb after all, and that I was capable, even though slow-witted, of intelligent thoughts and decisions, provided I had sufficient time and opportunity to activate the process. This valuable key to better adjustment learned in the Home has helped me throughout my life.

But I still had trouble in getting along with others, especially those who were physically and verbally able. Usually, after an angry argument, I'd be shattered, helpless, and virtually mute. In sheer frustration, I'd occasionally lash out in physical fury. However, even the initial advantages of rage and surprise were nullified quickly by my small size, my slow reflexes, and my awkward fighting skills.

My inevitable defeat brought painful humiliation. When I was very young, I used to cry a lot. The subsequent taunt of "crybaby" only compounded my misery, and on several occasions, the thought of taking my life suddenly seemed appealing. Who I was and where I had come from were more than enough to make me feel that I was unfit to live. Ending my suffering by ending my life seemed, at times, quite logical and even justified. However, after taking flight and remaining in solitude longer than usual, the many decent moments in the Home came to the fore and buried further suicidal thoughts.

In like manner, I resolved, when I was about ten, that I would no longer cry in public. And I didn't. When wounded, I simply fled and hid until my tears had passed, or until I felt better. I gradually learned to cry inside, without tears, burying more deeply into my psyche feelings of rage, grief, and self-pity.

Another factor which erased the hated label of "crybaby" was my recklessness in football games, combined with my spartan responses to physical pain or injury. Driven by an unconscious self-harm wish, plus a strong need to be a hero, I willingly risked and stoically accepted the physical battering I usually received in order to prove to everyone that I indeed had courage. This, along with my refusal to let anyone see me cry, helped me to create and even live up to a new persona which enhanced my self-esteem, as well as my standing in the group.

As I grew older and a little more sure of myself, I began to see that it made sense to avoid confrontations by not wearing my feelings in such an open fashion. By deliberately keeping my feelings under wraps, and even remaining emotionally detached, I could avoid and even withdraw from disputes with far less risk or jeopardy. However, on issues that really mattered, like defending my rights or protecting my belongings, I could be more effective by preparing in advance—rigidly focusing on the basic issues, and not allowing myself to be distracted from them. These strategic adaptations, fashioned by a developing intelligence based on experience, not only reduced the number of negative situations, but also enabled me to emerge triumphant in many of them.

The dynamics of group life in the Home helped me to develop the social skills that made the difference between contentment and unhappiness. When I was low, I would begin to think more about the things I savored in my daily life that could pick me up and make life enjoyable again. There was often great fun in the dorm, with friendly games of checkers, cards, parcheesi, board games, sports trivia games, and so forth. There were interesting stories read to us before bedtime by our supervisors, plus newspapers, magazines, comic books, and regular books to enjoy. We had popular songs to hum, favorite meals coming up, anticipated radio programs like Dick Tracy, The Shadow, The Inner Sanctum, Lux Theater, Dodgers games, and the Make-Believe Ballroom. We had many great outdoor games like kick the can, ring-a-levio, marbles, running bases, stoop-ball, and team games galore. Then there were the Saturday movies, summer trips, and many other things to do. Best of all, there were the good friends, either my peers or a good supervisor, who would be attentive to and supportive of me.

All of these things, and many more, made my daily life too sweet to give up, even when I felt overwhelmed with self-pity or rage or despair. The Home, in effect, was my life-saver from my own worst enemy, namely myself! If I had still been at the earlier infant home, or someplace like it, the repressive environment surely would have heightened my thoughts of suicide, with death an attractive way to end my suffering. The Home was no such place. It offered and gave too much to me, enabling me to escape from the worst of myself to the better part of my being.

When I first saw the movie version of Dickens's *Oliver Twist*, I was struck by how readily I could identify with young Oliver and his situation. I was relieved and grateful when his story had a happy ending, since such an outcome added precious hope to my own life. It was at the movies, in books, and in other media that my fertile imagination introduced me to new friends, in situations that I could control and shape, since it was of my own make-believe.

I could, for example, become one of Abraham Lincoln's little boys and finally have a kind, loving father. My fantasy enabled me to become the best friend of the hero in the Buddy book series, whom I admired and wanted to emulate. I was able to choose inspiring role-models from all walks of life who would not criticize or demean me. Since my relationships with others always seemed risky to me, I felt much safer and less lonely in this wonderful world of fantasy.

But while the cloak of fantasy was comforting to my frail ego, it could have been unhealthy. Fortunately, my life in the Home and in school had enough positives to prevent me from too deep an immersion. For that, I credit the many friends, fine supervisors, and caring teachers who provided me with real friendship and genuine concern for my well-being. They made a significant difference in my life. My own efforts to cope with my weaknesses, mentally and socially, made life a constant uphill struggle. The "helping hand" contributions of these people were of profound and immeasurable value.

With respect to my supervisors in the Home, I usually got along with almost all of them because I tended to be obliging and even overly compliant. The only one I ever truly feared was my first supervisor, Mrs. Braverman, who actually treated me with far more gentleness and patience than I probably deserved. She rarely hit me, but it was that severe, stern demeanor and that readiness to hit others in the group that thoroughly intimidated me, making me feel at risk. No doubt, she saw in me a frightened, fragile little boy who wanted to behave well but could not do so all of the time.

My shift to Miss Weingust's Midget Boys group brought great relief, allowing me finally to relax more. I only can recall one instance when I received a real beating from a supervisor. I was about eight and still in the Midgets. I recently had seen the movie *Mr. Smith Goes to Washington*, in which the hero speaks out against injustice and corruption. Always so impressionable, I tried to emulate him in real life, and the male supervisor who was my target lashed out at me with power and fury. His blows quickly subdued my protests, rekindling in me the helpless rage that I used to feel at the infants' home.

At that moment, I hated the supervisor with an intensity that I still can feel. In order to survive and achieve peace of mind, I had to

The modern Pride facility in Douglaston, NY with new function, but same mission.

The Home, The Pride of Judea Children's Home (view across Dumont Avenue).

Charlie Vladimer "horsing around" with his kids in the yard. When Charlie was there, he usually had them laughing.

Harry Koval (back row) and his smiling Senior Boys. His "positivity" was contagious! After leaving the Pride, Harry directed several senior citizen homes, and then worked for the New York City Recreation Department.

The "legendary" Mrs. Braverman and typical Midget Boys' group. Note the limited number so she could give more individual attention.

Shabbos lunch in the Home's dining room.

Patriarch - Jacob H. Cohen and Lena Blumberg, widow of Pride founder, see the children off on a summer outing.

A senior girl reading excerpts from a play on the interior steps of the yard. Author Stan Friedland is in the middle. It must have been a comedy!

Long time President of the Board, Jacob H. Cohen, and his "Bar Mitzvah boys", an annual event.

Shabbos services in the Home's synagogue.

A typical Hebrew class in the Home. Yes, indeed, they were co-ed and girls did get bat-mitzvah, though not on as "grand" a scale as the boys.

The Pride Band getting ready to march in one of several holiday parades each year. Note the fine dress of everyone.

The children in the Home cultivated "Victory Gardens" during World War II where some of the food for the Home was grown.

An arts and crafts workshop in our playroom. Developing our skills was a high priority.

A game of basketball at our summer home in Long Beach.

The Home's wartime football team. The "gnat" who played football, alias author Phil Craft, is second from the left.

Our summer "mansion" in Long Beach. It was donated to the Pride by one of its wealthy benefactors, Martin R. Sharp.

Each summer day, our post-breakfast assembly started with a salute to the flag. Charlie Vladimer is front center, and Lou Feigelson is to the front of him.

Phil Craft takes a "swing" in the Yard.

Stan and Bernie Friedland on a visit to their mother.

bury this sharp resentment, but it is still a part of me and is activated whenever I encounter bullying or injustice. During my almost fourteen years in the Pride, I received many blessings and advantages, but I did not emerge unscarred or unscathed emotionally. Fortunately, in my later personal and professional life, I was able to turn this characteristic into more productive channels.

Some eight years later, a coincidental situation occurred that was loaded with significant irony. It was well into the World War II years, and the Home, like every other place, was suffering from a manpower shortage. There weren't enough qualified male supervisors. In order to fill this serious gap, they reached into the Senior Boys group and had us take on some part-time responsibilities. I was appointed part-time afterschool assistant supervisor of the Junior Boys group, along with another Senior Boy. We both were untrained, received little orientation, guidance, or supervision, and felt quite unfit for such responsibility. I had never before had any responsibility for, or authority over, another person. Nevertheless, we tried our best to gain the group's cooperation and compliance with the Home's established rules and routines.

Sensing our insecurity and lack of resolve, the boys, seeking fun laced with some collective mischief, simply ran all over us, ignoring our requests and pleas, and rejecting our demands with blatant defiance. In sheer desperation, we used physical force. The boys now complied, but with a sullen hostility and resistance that made me feel like a Nazi concentration camp guard. Each time I had to hit a boy, I felt sick with self-loathing. The bitter memory of my own beating by a supervisor was still fresh in my mind, and here I was, doing the same to boys in my care!

Even though my weekly pay was $5, a lordly sum for a sixteen-year-old in those days, I begged Miss Epstein, the interim head supervisor, to let me quit. As a wartime employee, she too must have felt overwhelmed at times by the magnitude and difficulty of her job. Almost tearfully and with compassion, she reminded me that it was my patriotic challenge and duty to contribute in this important way in the place of men who were risking their lives in combat. I was torn by guilt and helplessness; thoughts of suicide returned, reinforced by the conviction that now it was I who was the bully, the persecutor of little kids, and one of the hated enemies I had always despised.

Who could I turn to for help? Sam Arcus had already left the Home; so Corporal Charlie Vladimer, himself a guard in a prisoner-of-war camp out West, was my last hope. My forty-page letter to him, laboriously written late at night after work over a three-week period, poured out all of my woes in a search for desperately needed guidance. Charlie did not fail me. In less than two weeks, his typed thirty-page response, filled with sympathy, understanding, and concrete suggestions, addressed each of my problems and explained, with clarity and wisdom, how each situation could be resolved. Declaring that the kids just wanted fun, not triumph, he suggested such ideas as incentives, earning new privileges, teaching them how to cooperate for group bonus rewards, going to bat for them with Miss Epstein, and so on.

I immediately put his suggestions into effect. At a special meeting with the group, I admitted to them that my colleague and I had been wrong, but if they were willing to give us a second chance, we would help them to get the extra privileges they always wanted. But they would have to show Miss Epstein cooperation and good behavior by conforming to her reasonable expectations. The boys agreed, and I readily assumed my new role, which was to help each of them in their respective efforts to achieve these objectives. This meant additional assistance for the more problematic kids, and I did this by reminding them of what the whole group stood to gain if they improved their responses. One boy, a soft-spoken but courageous kid, had taken great risks during the bad days to tell me privately how the group felt about my harsh rule, attempting, in his own way, to get me to ease up on them. Now, he was a valuable leader, urging his peers to cooperate in the quest for better privileges for everyone.

Miss Epstein, always sympathetic, was quite agreeable to the new approach and also was generous with the new privileges the boys started to earn as a group. An atmosphere of friendly cooperation and good feeling soon replaced the mutual hostility and tension. Slowly but surely, the boys permitted me to become the helpful, concerned friend that Lou Feigelson, Judge Arcus, and Charlie Vladimer had been to me.

In the months that followed, right up to the summer, I enjoyed the most heartwarming and satisfying experience in all of my years in the Home. In late June, a new male supervisor was hired, and my services no longer were needed. I volunteered for the summer-time Victory Farm Corps program, leaving a whole group of real friends behind. They were sorry to see me go, and I was touched deeply by their warm feelings. It had been a memorable and valuable experience.

Team sports played a pivotal role in the Home, in terms of social status and self-esteem, and my experiences were often not good ones. In the younger groups, punchball and softball were the popular games, and I was weak in both. My slowness afoot matched my reflexes and thought processes. But compounding these handicaps was an undiscovered visual handicap which forever denied me the depth perception required to track the path and speed of a punched or batted ball until it was upon me, leaving me helpless to catch it properly. It was not until I had left the Home that I learned that I had a condition called strabismus, with a far-sighted left eye trying to mesh with a near-sighted right eye, with both turned away from each other. (This condition also made it seem as though I could not look anyone squarely in the eye, which certainly was never in my best interest.)

Since I was rarely able to catch a ball, I usually was exiled to a lonely outfield position. There I became the intentional target for the opposing team's best hitters and the hapless recipient of scorn and derision from my teammates, especially if my errors cost us the game. Consequently, I was the last one chosen for pick-up games, and then only when I was needed to fill out the required number of positions. With each new error, the derision I received rekindled the old feeling of wishing that I'd never been born!

Thus continued a disabling pattern that had begun in the infants' home, where I had been blamed for my mother's death. Responsibility always represented potential risk or culpability, often causing me extreme anxiety, and when the guilt or shame became unbearable, it brought thoughts of suicide as an ultimate means of escape. In such circumstances, avoiding responsibility became a logical though limiting neurotic response to potential danger which, regrettably, shaped the future course of my life. Remaining unmarried and childless, and working at jobs with only limited authority, prestige, and salary, became a self-protective continuation of that pattern throughout my adult life.

As I grew older and more assertive in the Home, I began to refuse to participate in such team games. I did not need all that worry and aggravation. When I firmly stuck to this position, I began to earn some grudging respect from the very boys who had taunted me previously. I still took part, happily, in activities where winning or losing was incidental to the fun of the activity.

Of all of the Home's competitive team sports, it was in football that I finally found my own unique niche as an insignificant guard or tackle on the front line. In sharp contrast to the present, when hugeness and strength are the primary requirements for those positions, they were then the designated slots for the poorest athletes who never could be trusted with handling the ball. That was fine with me, since I didn't have to worry about the nightmarish risk of fumbling the ball or dropping a pass.

My small size and light weight, back then, did not disqualify me from either position. In fact, in my own eyes, it may even have helped me. I simply drove forward on offense, and plowed into the opposing player as hard as I could. On defense, I just stood my ground and tried to get at the opposing ball-carrier in any way possible. Often, I was too little and close to the ground to be blocked out completely; so although I sometimes was kicked or stepped upon, I still could reach out to grab the ball-carrier's foot or ankle and hang on doggedly until my teammates could complete the tackle.

It was an ideal situation for me. There were no visible responsibilities which could cause me to lose a game; only opportunities to make a tackle and prevent a gain or a touchdown. That especially was true when an offensive back penetrated the other end of our line. Then I could double back and hurl my little body at him, grabbing whatever I could catch hold of, hanging on and slowing him down until help arrived.

As my skill developed, this began to occur more and more often. My tackles per game increased, and soon I began to receive the increasing respect of my teammates and the attention of spectators. With my athletic history of having been a loser, this recognition and admiration was more than enough compensation for the pain and the frequent injuries that I sustained while making flying tackles and paralyzing head butts into the padded bodies of heavier opponents. Given my low sense of self-worth, I didn't mind sacrificing my body. It was a small price to pay for finally being appreciated as an important member of a team! It became another significant and valuable experience for me.

As a teenager, I was not exactly asocial, because I had many good friends in the Home. Nonetheless, I always felt very uncomfortable in social situations in which I was expected to behave correctly in order to impress others. Putting my best foot forward was not easy when I felt that I didn't have a best foot. I was short, skinny, homely, awkward, slow-witted, and self-conscious. The fear of failure was always upon me because I often did fail. I regularly shunned competition and responsibility because I lacked the skill and confidence to meet the expectations of others. I wasn't lazy and actually was eager to obtain afterschool work, but the ordeal of seeking and possibly being rejected for a job was too frightening to risk or to bear.

This was but another reflection of my innate sense of worthlessness, a chronic disability which often paralyzed my will and stifled my aspirations about things that preoccupied other adolescents in the Home. Nowhere was this more true than with my relationships with girls. In the Home, there were several girls, at one time or another, whose radiant personalities, striking beauty, or unique charm caused my motor to run appreciably faster, attracting my passionate attention and interest. Of course, what made them attractive to me made them attractive to the other boys, all of whom seemed far more natural, relaxed, and confident.

At that time, I had not heard of Cyrano de Bergerac; yet my situation, as I learned later, was quite similar to his. His painful awareness of his physical ugliness may have been stronger than mine, but no more of a deterrent. Like him, I dreaded the real or imagined whispered mockery and the amused glances almost as much as the rejection, pity, or ridicule I could expect in response to any romantic overtures I might very much want to make.

Although fearless in battle, Cyrano fled like a coward from any serious amorous encounter with his beloved Roxanne, and only could wax eloquent with passion and desire in the comfortable shadows of darkness. In similar situations, filled with great emotion for me, I remained mute or spoke in halting, tongue-tied monosyllables, always fearful of sounding foolish. I couldn't even write about my feelings in an articulate way, as I learned to do later.

In the few instances when I did venture to make an overt pass at a girl that I liked, my perception, real or imagined, of her displeasure or discomfort made me feel even more hideous or unwelcome than before.

It was from such moments, always after I had made a hasty retreat, that I became even more aware of the mounting presence of the rage and fury this rejection triggered within me. Once again, I felt cast out as worthless by a potential loved one. Now, in my adolescence, my fantasies contained violence, directed not only toward myself, but toward the person who had rejected me. Such thoughts frightened me, yet I was afraid to share them with Charlie or Judge Arcus. I was sure that if they learned that I was sitting on a powder keg of insane violence, they would have no choice other than to have me committed for my own safety. I began to take special notice of occasional newspaper stories about suicides or murders committed by shattered teenagers who had been scorned or jilted by the girls they had claimed as their own.

It was more than mere coincidence, therefore, that each time I ventured to reach out romantically to a girl I especially liked, I was troubled by an ominous sense of foreboding of ultimate disaster, which caused me to pull back in fear. After this happened a few times, I simply stopped trying. That particular girl, nevertheless, continued to fill a cherished, if secret, role in my fantasies. Knowing my emotional makeup, I became content to leave it at that level, which was a safer outlet and one that I could control.

I had begun to develop a pattern, in my young life, of sublimation, substitution, or simply doing without, in response to cherished things that I wanted but could not have. I would not beg outright for them, nor would I take them by stealth or force. I even dropped discreet hints, on occasion, which were ignored. I simply learned to get along without the desired object in a more self-disciplined manner. This formula, developed over a long time, has been in effect since my youth and has served me well throughout my life. To this day, I still feel quite content with relative obscurity and modest possessions because of my conditioning in the Home.

My tenure in the Inter and Senior Boys groups, when Lou Feigelson, Charlie Vladimer, and Sam Arcus were in charge, spanned World War II and marked my growth through adolescence to young adulthood. It was, for me, a period of great stress, but also of enormous growth. It was my good fortune that all three of these fine men were there in that crucial period, guiding, inspiring, and stimulating my efforts to become a healthier person. Without their invaluable input, I would have fallen though the cracks as a frightened, fragile, dysfunctional individual, ending up perhaps a suicide or an inmate in a mental institution.

The contributing role of so many of my friends to my overall adjustment and well-being in the Home cannot be overemphasized. By their own encouragement and example, I, as a slow learner, was helped to shape up in many areas, eventually tasting the sweet fruits of success as a part-time supervisor, co-editor of the Pride's newspaper, an officer of our social club, and, ultimately, a respected advisor and "elder statesman" before I left for the Army. I came into the Pride as a frightened, vulnerable little boy. I left it in much better shape.

Chapter 11

Orphans Live to Eat

Food, clothing, and shelter are the basic needs of humankind. Following this sequence, it's logical to assume that we eat to live in order to satisfy that first need. It's not that simple with the eating habits of orphans, or more specifically, the orphans of the Pride of Judea Children's Home.

The role that food played in our lives was a central one. Whenever Pride alumni get together, which is at least twice a year, the reminiscences and nostalgic stories inevitably touch upon food in one way or another. Is it symbolic? Were we deprived of our mother's milk, literally or figuratively, so that we craved food for emotional as well as physical sustenance? Interesting psychological possibilities are very much in play here, because food took on so much importance for us in the Home. We seemed to live to eat and often went to great lengths to make that happen.

Philly's Hot Dog Obsession

Phil Craft

During my earliest years at the Pride, my supervisors always insisted that we finish everything on our plates before leaving the table or asking for seconds. Most of us had little problem with this. If we liked what was on the menu, it was eaten in a hurry. If we didn't like the food, we usually were able to give it away to someone who did, and in return we would do the same for him at another meal.

I didn't like hot dogs originally. Since they were served almost twice a week, I had a mild problem with getting rid of them. However, I soon found Charlie Uretsky to take them from me, occasionally having to give up my dessert to him as part of the deal.

Whenever hot dogs were served, I usually was able to get a peanut butter and jelly sandwich by showing my supervisor my empty plate and claiming continued hunger. This arrangement continued for several years until I was sent to an overnight camp for the first time. The Pride understood the need to vary our environment whenever possible and affordable, so kids were sent to camp on a rotating basis. I was going for the first time, and, of course, was apprehensive.

Each week, the camp held a full campfire dinner so that the mess halls could be cleaned and the cooks could have a day off. Hot dogs were the primary fare for this weekly meal, and not much else. On that day, we had been very active, and I was ravenously hungry. When I saw that hot dogs were the only choice, I wasn't too happy. I asked my counselor whether there was any peanut butter and jelly; but he said no, the mess hall was closed.

Well, hunger soon prevailed over dislike, and I put as much mustard as I could on my hot dog, hoping to drown its flavor, which I had likened to cod liver oil. The first taste, surprisingly, was not bad. Not great, but not bad. Since I really was hungry, I downed the first one and admitted to myself that it wasn't too bad. I got another one and ate it unhesitatingly. I made another admission. I liked it! I ate a third. My counselor looked at me and said, "I thought you didn't like hot dogs." I answered, "I don't, except these are good." He just smiled.

So began my lifelong addiction to hot dogs. I soon loved them!

When I got back to the Pride and we had our first hot dog meal, Charlie Uretsky said, grandly, "Phil, I'll take them off you tonight for nothing." He was astonished when I replied, "Suppose I take yours, Charlie, and I'll give you my dessert for them." When he asked what had happened to me in camp, I told him, and he was very unhappy. His supply line for extra hot dogs had dried up.

I now began to barter for the hot dogs of others, using my dessert or a future delicacy as the bait. Pretty soon, I knew who to approach in order to obtain one more cherished frank, but I often failed to get enough, because most everyone enjoyed them, and those who didn't were few in number. By that time, I needed extras, and I wondered how to get them.

Before long I had it figured out. As each hot dog meal drew to an end, I would slow my eating pace while my roving eye eagerly scanned the plates on my table and the adjacent ones, in search of partially eaten wieners. Although my right eye was near-sighted, my left one had the acuity of a falcon. With the dining room nearly vacated and the plates still uncollected, I would swoop down with great precision, scooping uneaten franks or remnants thereof into my large, waiting napkin for later consumption and enjoyment. My elation and pleasure were marred by my realization that I was stooping pretty low. But I couldn't help it. I was hooked! I had become a hot dog junkie!

During World War II, Corporal Charlie Vladimer, touched by the awareness that I and another Pride kid, Paulie Hirsch, had no parents, occasionally sent a spanking-new dollar bill to the two of us in the folds of one of his uplifting letters. He'd usually write a humorous mandate, along the lines of, "Go ye forth, with Paulie of course, to Schneider's Delicatessen and have yourselves a ball!" We dutifully converted this generous gift into three wondrous trips to "paradise"!

Schneider's kosher deli was two blocks from the Pride, and it was paradise for all of us. The food consumed there ranks high up on my hit parade of the most delicious food I've ever consumed.

As my stay at the Pride lengthened, my daily existence revolved around the evening menu. The Pride had fixed nights for everything, and while I had other favorites as well, I never was unhappy on a Thursday because that was hot dog night! The occasional substitution of a different menu on a Thursday would fill me with a profound sense of betrayal and unfairness, and whatever else one feels when deprived of a beloved possession.

Today, my Pride "heritage" with respect to hot dogs continues. I occasionally make concessions now to nutritional factors, such as an occasional chicken dog. But sometimes taste wins out over health considerations. "May I have one of your well-done, all-beef hot dogs, please; and heavy on the mustard and sauerkraut, please!" My hot dog "roots" are embedded too deeply!

Our Passion for Meatloaf

Stan Friedland

Friday night was meatloaf night on the Pride menu. Everyone loved it, and trades were hard to come by. Mashed potatoes and brown gravy were the side dishes, and that is the triumvirate composing the only acceptable food for this meal.

I liked this dish so much that I played with my food. Make the mashed potatoes into a volcano-like sculpture; then pour the gravy into the opening, to be followed by small pieces of the meat loaf, so that the combination of all three can be swept into the mouth as one. Delicious! And by putting small pieces of the meat in the gravied potatoes, the meat, invariably only one portion, would last longer, perhaps into two portions of potatoes.

Our food was served family-style, on platters, with just enough slices of meatloaf to go one per person. I happened to like the end piece because it was well done, which is the way I like meat. Occasionally, the end piece was thinner or smaller than the rest, and I would lobby my counselor for a second piece. He would usually come through for me, much to my surprise and pleasure. But it was hard to conceal. When the other kids saw what I was doing, they joined in, and soon that avenue for an extra piece of meatloaf was closed. I knew I'd have to find other ways, and I did.

Food was a major focus of bartering, deal-making, bets, and prizes. We'd trade on a lot of things. Certain kids could make great hospital corners when making their beds, and they'd offer their services to kids who were terrible at it and got hassled by their supervisors. The kids used desserts or other food as their currency, which was more than enough.

In my case, I usually used some form of sports activity for my "action." To get some extra meatloaf, I'd zero in on the few kids in my group who didn't care for it that much, meaning that they ate it but not with any enthusiasm.

I remember one kid who fancied himself a good ping-pong player but was not good enough to beat me. I bet him his meatloaf against three of my desserts that he couldn't beat me with a five-point spot. He readily accepted; after all, he loved desserts and meatloaf was no big deal. I won a close first game, and he asked for a rematch, same stakes. I won the second game, and again it was close. He wanted to play again, but this time I refused. Two extra servings of meatloaf over a two-week period would be enough for the time being. We could resume again in two weeks if he wished. He didn't. The very act of handing over his meatloaf to me on both occasions was embarrassment enough, since everyone knew what had happened. Secrets were impossible to keep in the Pride, and everything that happened was usually heard through the grapevine within minutes.

Another time I bet a good basketball player my desserts against his meatloaf in a foul-shooting contest. He resisted at first, forcing me to give him a one-shot advantage. which I didn't want to do. We came out even as a result. I then talked him into a game of five-three-one and gave him a three-point spot. I was barely able to win, but winning was what counted. Another extra meatloaf! I've been hooked for life!

My Own Love of Meatloaf

Phil Craft

My encounters with meatloaf began during my early years at the Pride. It was so delicious that it quickly became one of my favorite meals of the week. Some of my sweetest memories focus on meatloaf, both during and after my Pride years.

When I left the Pride, it was inevitable that I would try to learn how to make meatloaf at home. Fortunately, my tutor was Dave Leiman, a close friend from the Pride, with whom I shared an apartment at the time. His meatloaf was the best I had ever tasted. Being a slow learner, I had to struggle and persist in order to be able to make an acceptable meatloaf. But Dave was patient, understanding, and committed to the effort, until I finally caught on. Although I never came close to matching the taste, texture, and quality of his product, my own became quite satisfying.

A few years later, as a youth worker at the Grand Street Settlement House on the Lower East Side of New York, I was assigned a pre-delinquent group of youngsters, ages nine to fourteen, who were suspected shoplifters and petty thieves. My task was to divert their interests and energies into more acceptable pursuits. They responded well to a variety of group activities, including sports, roller skating, parties, and excursions out of the neighborhood.

For the latter, I made it a practice to bring meatloaf sandwiches for boys who brought no lunch. When more and more of them began to ask for sandwiches, I realized that it was the meatloaf that grabbed them. Since this food was foreign to their Puerto Rican background, their mothers had never made it at home. They asked me to show their mothers how to do it. As I was thinking about this, one of the boys suggested that I show the whole group how to make it in the Settlement kitchen.

The cooking sessions that followed became a popular feature of the program, and thereafter, every group party and camping trip featured meatloaf. The boys became almost poetic in their praise of the meatloaf we made together. Well after the group disbanded, my periodic contacts with the members enabled me to see that they were still making meatloaf at home.

To this day, I measure restaurants, in part, by the quality of their meatloaf. It remains a delicious legacy from my days at the Pride.

The Trauma of Lamb Stew

Stan Friedland

During the war years, most of the beef produced in our country went to our military forces, causing a shortage for everyone else. Meat rationing was the order of the day. Not only was meat rationed, it became quite expensive as well. However, there was considerable sheep raising going on, for food and clothing purposes. Sheep required less grazing land and less food, and provided a double product. The older sheep, left alive for breeding purposes, produced lambs for the slaughterhouse and wool for clothing.

In light of this, the Home's ever-shrewd supply director, Mrs. Gatner, would trade in her meat rations, not for beef, but for lamb, and the less desirable cuts of lamb at that. It was inexpensive and could be made into lamb stew. Welcome then to the era of lamb stew at the Pride of Judea! Foodwise, it was a disaster!

Just as we all loved meatloaf, conversely, most of us hated lamb stew! First, its smell was awful. We had it several times a week, and whenever we did, its odor greeted us as we came into the dining room. Several peanut butter and jelly stations had to be set up so that those who couldn't eat it would have something to eat.

Don't get me wrong. It was made well and was quite edible. I used to mix it with whatever form of potato or rice was provided, and it wasn't too bad. It's just that it wasn't too good either.

Naturally, there wasn't much trading going on when we had lamb stew. Due to its limited appeal, most kids didn't ask for seconds. The few that did, usually those who would eat anything, were able to get as much as they could handle. The rest of us ate one serving, loaded up on other items as best we could, and called it a meal.

The lamb stew era lasted about three years. To this day, neither my brother Phil, nor I, nor almost any alumnus can stomach lamb stew. Lamb chops, its far more expensive relative, are quite delicious and more than palatable to all of us. But not lamb stew. Take it away!

Eat to Live, or Live to Eat?

Stan Friedland

The quest for food was a dominant activity for most of the boys at the Pride of Judea. If we got any spending money, we'd either visit the candy store across the street or else stop in at a food store on the way to school. We'd also try to get on the good side of any Senior Boy who worked in the kitchen. Because of my brother, I was lucky enough to do so.

My brother was a popular guy—a fine athlete with a friendly personality and very good looking. While this glowing description may sound prejudiced, coming from an affectionate kid brother, it's the way he'd be described by virtually everyone who knew him, and this certainly includes a groupmate of his named Abie Nagel. Abie had bad eyesight, wore thick glasses, was terrible in sports, and had no interest in school. In an effort to straighten him out, his supervisors put him in the kitchen to work with our fine but strict German cook, Fritz, and the rest is history.

Abie found a home in the kitchen and worked there not only for his remaining years as a resident of the Home, but also for pay when he left the Pride. He then became a waiter and has worked in the top Jewish deli restaurants in the Brighton Beach section of Brooklyn ever since. His work in the kitchen, and his association with Fritz, turned him around and started him on his life's career.

Abie was a good friend of my brother's, and he took good care of him, foodwise—which means that he took pretty good care of me too. But it had to be done on the sly. First, Fritz ran a tight kitchen and the food was for mealtimes only. Second, Abie did not want it known that he was favoring anyone, lest others would begin to bother him. Discretion was quite necessary, which meant operating in a clandestine fashion. Either Bernie would get me whatever goodies were available, or I would do the same for him. The fewer of us down there, the better things went. My pipeline was good, and I can recall a steady stream of small but delicious snacks that came to me in this manner.

Years later, at one of our alumni meetings, we began to reminisce about Abie, who was present at the time. The funny thing is that he provided food to many more of us than we ever suspected. We laughed at how he made us each think we were special, yet was really giving food out to quite a few kids. When we asked about this, he laughed and said, "Being an orphan myself, I knew how important food was to everyone, and I rarely had the heart to turn down a request." He sat down to a warm round of applause because he had befriended so many of us in so important a way: extra food! By filling a major need, namely our stomachs, he found a lifelong place in our hearts!

Before we depart the food scene, several miscellaneous thoughts are worth noting. The afternoon milk and cookies served a double and valuable purpose.

How do you get 250 kids, ages six to eighteen, going in all directions on school days, back to the Home safely and on time? Sounds like an enormous logistical problem. It wasn't. Serve them milk and cookies!

Every day, seven days a week, milk and cookies were served between three and four in the afternoon. That's it. Not a minute earlier, and rarely a minute later. Well, maybe a bit later if your excuses were imaginative enough. The lure of this snack was sufficient to get everyone back to the Pride pretty much on time every school day. We all attended different high schools, in different parts of Brooklyn. Some attended high school in Manhattan. Yet we were expected to have daily programs and schedules that enabled us to make it back before the end of "milk and cookies." And we did.

Our preoccupation with food does not imply any eating disorders or even that we tended to be overweight. That definitely was not the case. It's just that our appetite for food was a bit on the excessive side and may be related to the insecurity of being an orphan. Let the therapists decide.

Theft of food by the kids occasionally was a problem but never a major one. We did shoplift things from stores, as described earlier. But when detected, that stopped. Theft of food from the kitchen also occurred infrequently, mainly due to the strict security system rather than the honesty of the kids. Once, Harry Koval was approached by the director of supplies, Mrs. Gatner, who was a hard-hearted lady. "Your boys are stealing food from the kitchen," she said, "and I'd like you to punish them so it will stop." He looked at her for a moment and said, "If they're stealing food, they must be hungry. If you'll get me some extra servings for them each meal, I'll solve your problem." After further discussion and negotiations, the peanut butter and jelly supply, for those who didn't like the meal or wanted more food, was increased. Harry spoke to our group, and the stealing stopped.

When thefts occurred between the kids, usually of goodies given by family, that was cause for hot-tempered arguments and more than a few bloody noses. Many offenses were permitted, but "don't steal my food"—it was sacred!

Chapter 12

Our Religious Upbringing

Phil Craft

My Spiritual Awakening

My religious experiences at the Pride of Judea, at first glance, seem to have been quite negative. They began, painfully enough, in my Hebrew classes. All boys started attending Hebrew classes at eight years old (third grade), and continued for the next four or five years (depending on whether their father was alive) until bar mitzvah at age twelve (father deceased) or thirteen (father alive). Classes were held twice during the week for an hour and a half, and on Sunday mornings for the same length of time.

Hebrew school was hell for me! My slow learning and frequent inattention often provoked punitive and brutal responses from the teachers, causing me constant feelings of fear and dread. A slow reader of English, now I had to wrestle with the totally different symbols of Hebrew, and for a long time they made no sense to me.

The Hebrew teachers were given to the use of corporal punishment, the disciplinary method so prevalent in yeshiva education at that time. Raps on the knuckles with a heavy ruler, smacks on the head for misbehavior or inattentiveness, and similar uses of force were the norm as the teachers tried to make fear a major motivator. I hated them and I hated Hebrew!

This distaste spun off into our Friday night and Saturday morning shul services. Try as I might, I didn't know what was going on, and as a result, found the services long and boring. My misery was compounded because I felt again the inadequacy of my retarded learning ability.

I couldn't even enjoy the Jewish holidays. Not only didn't I understand them enough to appreciate them, but they constrained me from more enjoyable play activities. We had to remain in our "good" clothes through all of Rosh Hashanah and Yom Kippur, and just laze around and do nothing. As a restless boy who enjoyed his play activities, I resented the holiday restraints, and in this I was not alone. Our Saturday punchball games were often stopped when members of the Pride's board of directors and their friends, all of whom were Orthodox Jews, came by to visit. How could we desecrate Shabbos if we were being brought up Orthodox?

As all this indicates, my initial encounters with Orthodox Judaism were not very favorable. It represented much that I feared and resented. Worst of all, though, was the negative portrayal of God presented by my first Hebrew teachers. They depicted Him as a remote deity, all-knowing and ready to pounce on anyone guilty of transgressing the accepted practice. They made Him into an angry, jealous, punitive entity, marginally protective and not really on your side.

Thus, they invested God with the worst human qualities, and made Him accessible only via prescribed and correct Hebrew prayers and rituals, which effectively shut me out! In desperation, I turned to Him in my usually naive and innocent way. I began to pray using my own words and thoughts, and if nothing else, found this more comforting.

Much to my satisfaction, I began to think that God was responding to my prayers. The things I had "discussed" with Him sometimes were straightened out, and I was very heartened by this. If I had this more direct line to God, then certainly I didn't need the unpleasant ranting and raving of my Hebrew teachers. They were no longer of any relevance or value. I began to look elsewhere for a doctrine that I could believe and embrace. I wanted religion to be a major part of my life, but one that would have real meaning for me.

In this quest for a new faith that I could really believe in, I began to explore other religions and viewpoints. As I began to ask questions of my gentile friends, I began to read about Jesus, the Hebrew teacher from Nazareth. The more I read about his preachments and philosophy, the more he made sense to me. I was particularly impressed with his Sermon on the Mount, and his view of

God as a caring, loving father—something I was deprived of in my own life.

Although I was never able to accept the formal Christian doctrine that Jesus was the son of God and had come from an immaculate conception, his views and preachments on human behavior appealed to me. I exhausted the libraries and had extensive conversations with gentile classmates of all denominations about their religious doctrines and the thin differences between their various Christian denominations. When I found something that appealed to me, I was happy to take it in as if it were mine and to ignore the rest. It was as if I were knitting a quilt of religious swatches that appealed to me and then cloaking myself in it.

I also was influenced by the inspiring figures I encountered in books and in movies. This was a very impressionable era for me. Memorable influences included the Harriet Beecher Stowe classic, Uncle Tom's Cabin, the Father O'Malley character portrayed by Bing Crosby in Going My Way, and the priest played by Gregory Peck in Keys of the Kingdom, whom I found inspiring both in the movie and the book.

But I kept coming back to the lofty example of character set by Jesus himself. Instead of feeling brainwashed about him because of my Jewish upbringing and environment, I eagerly enjoyed each new discovery and increased understanding of this complex subject. In my excitement, I even tried to share some of what I had learned with my closer friends at the Pride. Their good-natured surprise and amusement at my new religious convictions and missionary zeal did not faze me.

I discussed what I had learned, and the emotional fervor unleashed by my discoveries, with my supervisors, who were understanding and perceptive, and did not get uptight about my "heresy" or try to suppress it. Not only did they understand my search for a religious path that could sustain me, they also respected my seriousness in tasting different religions. They were strong enough not to be concerned about the possible consequences to them or to me should it be discovered that I was straying from the Orthodox faith. The protective atmosphere thus provided by adults I respected and even revered helped me to continue my important quest.

I attribute to the Pride, therefore, the important impetus in helping me to make the transition from religious confusion and alienation to a greater degree of substance and clarity. It was because of the Home that my widened spiritual awakening was allowed to begin and take root. The elements of a strong, enduring faith, which first emerged there, continue to sustain me and to enrich my life in the most important ways. Today, I am neither observant nor actively affiliated with any established religious group . However, I have an abiding belief in God and continually bear strong witness to His active presence in my daily life. This has provided me with a deep faith that has helped to sustain my courage and hope in troubled times. It has enabled me to endure a tough life and to grow in wisdom and self-esteem with each challenging experience.

Rabbi Haklai

Of all the Hebrew teachers and religious personages whom I remember from the Pride, only Rabbi Haklai really impressed me in a positive way. He was there when I was in the Intermediate Boys group, just before World War II. His stay was all too brief, but he left me with an indelible image of his passionate devotion to God, undiluted and untainted by any blatant need for physical domination over the children, as was typical of the religious personnel who worked with us. Indeed, his personal fervor was so intense that to me he seemed like an ancient biblical prophet crying out in the wilderness, beseeching us to forsake our casual indifference to religion and prayer, and to reach out with more commitment and love to the deity he loved and worshipped.

When I first encountered Rabbi Haklai, his religious demeanor was so intense that I thought he was an eccentric zealot. When from his podium, he first called out, "Harken unto God, you rebellious children of Israel," I was amused, then shocked, then sheepish as I began to take him more seriously. As the magnetic nature of his delivery made me actually listen to his words, I began to realize the worth of his messages.

Although Rabbi Haklai had a loud, booming voice in shul, he always spoke to me in soft, gentle tones, conveying a feeling of real interest and concern, instead of the premonition of impending punishment I was so familiar with from my other Hebrew teachers and rabbis. He seemed to have a deep sincerity and purity of soul that set him apart from the rest.

Quite frankly, I was often bored during our long, tedious Shabbas services, and occasionally I would fall asleep. One of our rabbis used to smash my face into the prayer book when this happened. But in Rabbi Haklai's time, I'd awaken with some sixth sense to find him staring at me with a look of hurt and disappointment that made me feel truly sorry for this lapse. As a result, I firmly tried to stay awake and pay attention, and did so more with him than with anyone else.

The rabbi was a big, burly man, an emigré from prewar Palestine, who brought to us first-hand accounts of Jewish culture, history, and tradition. As such, he had a unique eminence and status with all of us, which explains his strong impact. There was another factor as well. He was married and had a beautiful and unspoiled little daughter who usually attended our services. Whenever he looked over at her, which was often, there was a radiant warmth and joy in his smile. To me, who long and often had craved such parental affection, this display on his part stirred both admiration and envy, making him an object of respect and trust, despite his religious preaching and scolding.

I remembered Rabbi Haklai long after he left. I used his love for and devotion to God to explore and develop my own pathways to Him. Then, and only then, did I really begin to understand the rabbi's devotion and single-mindedness, not only toward God, but also toward his own mission as a representative of his God. To this day, he is my benchmark figure of what a man of God should be. His combination of holiness and compassion enabled me to have a receptivity for and need of religion in my life rather than the fear and resentment caused by the brutal approaches of his peers. I truly am beholden to him for this invaluable, lifelong legacy.

Is There a Just and Kind God?

by Stan Friedland

Unfortunately, I fell into the resentment and indifference category toward religion, which was well underway for me before I checked in at the Pride. My experiences with religious training there only increased my alienation, but they would have had to have been outstanding in order to have turned me around. Unfortunately, they weren't.

One of my first memories—vivid and unforgettable, burned deep into my psyche—was of my mother kicking and screaming as she mourned the untimely death of my father. He died of a heart attack at age thirty-seven; my mother was thirty-four; I was three and one-half. Soon afterwards, my mother developed multiple sclerosis and had to be confined to a wheelchair in a hospital for chronic diseases. As I grew older, I remember thinking repeatedly, "What kind of God would visit these tragedies on this most deserving of people?" It jaded me then, and no subsequent experience or person ever dislodged the anguish I experienced every time I saw my mother and thought about the rank unfairness of her life. If anything, my seven-year stint in the Pride, during a very impressionable period of my life, only enhanced this antipathy and served to further my alienation from religion and God.

As is typical of Orthodox Judaism, the children at the Home began attending Hebrew classes to prepare for bar mitzvah at age eight and continued until the event itself. With no father alive, I would be bar mitzvah at age twelve, as compared to age thirteen for those with both parents alive. Since I came into the Pride at nine, I was thrust into Hebrew classes that met on two afternoons a week and once on Sunday mornings.

I didn't like them, and for a variety of reasons. As an avid sports fan, I loved my games, not as a spectator but as a participant, actively and at full tilt. Coming back after a full day of school only to have Hebrew class was a drag! It was an imposition that blocked me from a far more enjoyable activity, and I resented it. I tolerated Hebrew class because my mother would ask about it as part of my educational package. Of course, she wanted both Bernie and me to be bar mitzvah and to receive a good Jewish education.

The second reason is that the teachers were poor. Either they were from the "rap the knuckles or skull club," or they were just downright bad teachers and the kids ran roughshod over them. I definitely was not a goody two-shoes, but I'd rather have had order and some decent teaching going on than the noise of a poorly disciplined classroom which descends regularly into pure chaos.

Unfortunately, the latter prevailed, and most Hebrew classes were a waste of time. I couldn't wait for my bar mitzvah, if only to finish with Hebrew classes.

Ironically, I wound up taking three years of high school Hebrew and earned an 81 on my three-year Regents exam. I didn't want to take Hebrew but was sort of forced into it. The Home was midway between two high schools, and if I wanted to go to Thomas Jefferson High School, which I did, then I had to take Hebrew because they were just starting it. So I did, and it turned out to be a blessing in disguise. I had two of my best high school teachers for the three years of Hebrew, and I learned a great deal. They made me fond of the language but couldn't quite dispel my initial distaste for the ceremonial trappings of Judaism.

I didn't like our shul sessions either. Friday night ("erev Shabbos") and Saturday services were a big bore. Because we were all usually so restless, these sessions were subject to frequent shouting and other disciplinary actions as the Hebrew staff and rabbi tried to make us pay attention. As a result, they were not pleasant experiences, turning me off still further.

Our annual bar mitzvahs were held in one of Brooklyn's finest hotels, the St. George. We had the synagogue part at the Pride on a particular Shabbos, and the next day, we had a luncheon at the St. George. I was bar mitzvah with about eight or nine others, and we actually enjoyed ourselves on both days. In fact, after the Sunday luncheon, we went swimming in the St. George pool and had a great time.

Of course, I knew even then that the bar mitzvah was an important part of the Pride's fund-raising campaign. We would all duly pose with the Pride's president, Jacob H. Cohen, and the picture would be prominent in the Pride's fund-raising requests for the next half to full year. Journal tickets would be sold, as well as tickets for the luncheon at the St. George Hotel on the Sunday following the bar mitzvah. It was the Pride's biggest money-maker for the year and usually did very well.

But all that time in Hebrew school left a bad taste in my mouth. I vowed, even then, that when I had kids, I would not subject them to anything of the sort, so that they would love their religion rather than have an ongoing dislike of it. As each of my three boys turned eleven, we had him tutored at home by a good Hebrew teacher. Not only did he prepare them in the Torah passages to be read on the forthcoming occasion, but he taught them Jewish history, culture, and other relevant topics. As a result, my boys do not dislike religion and even get some pleasure from it on occasion. My oldest son, in fact, enjoys Judaism and observes it quite regularly, especially on holidays. Too bad I can't say the same.

Even though I'm critical of the religious education taught by the Pride, I don't blame it for my inability to find peace and comfort with the concept of God. I was driven by my need for a kind and just God, but I could not find Him. On account of my mother's horrid fate, exacerbated by even worse events on a never-ending continuum, it is simply too difficult for me to conceptualize an omnipotent, omniscient deity.

However, I do have a strong sense of being Jewish, and that has always been true. Today, I regard myself as a strong secular humanist Jew. I'm interested in Jewish culture, history, the State of Israel, and the values of the Jewish family. In this important regard, spending seven formative years in a Jewish orphanage was valuable in helping me to develop an identity that is an important part of my total being.

Chapter 13

Birds and Bees Fly at the Pride

Stan Friedland

When you have 250 boys and girls, many well into their teens, living in close proximity to one other, you have a fertile environment for an interesting heterosexual education. That was the daily situation at the Pride, and that is what most of us experienced.

In my own case, I considered the daily proximity to girls a strong asset in my social and sexual development. They were there to relate to, and in order to relate to them successfully, one had to experience the social contact repetitively in order to develop some satisfactory skills. This was very helpful to my preadolescent awkwardness, a painful stage from which no one is exempt. I was in the Home from age nine to age sixteen, and my daily contacts with the resident girls helped my sexual development.

This does not mean that model behavior between the sexes was necessarily the norm. It wasn't. It does mean that having had a large number of girls to relate to daily, many at your age level, and many of them quite attractive as well, was a richer social setting for all of us. We related to one other more frequently, more naturally, and more comfortably. The aura of just talking to a pretty girl lost its stiffness and intimidation the more you did so. Their presence and availability also minimized our need to seek outside relationships. We could ogle the pretty girls at school, at whatever age we were, but we usually had our girlfriends at the Pride and didn't have the normal pressures of getting one on the outside. It worked quite well for me and for many others.

But even for those without girlfriends, just having the girls there increased our sense of fun and adventure! The girls had their rooms on the third and highest floor so that the boys couldn't look down and spy on them. This didn't mean that we didn't spy on them. We did, and we never stopped trying to do so, even when we were thwarted. The key to our doing so was the roof, the ultimate high ground.

After our supervisor checked us into bed, a few of us would sneak out the balcony door, wedge a piece of wood into the opening, and on bare feet ascend to the roof. Off we'd run, soundlessly, to our best vantage points, to gaze into the windows of the older girls who were getting ready for bed. One night, as one of the prettiest girls was coming back from her shower draped in her towel, several of us waited in rapt anticipation for the towel to drop. Suddenly, a familiar voice boomed out, "What are you guys doing up here?" It was Charlie Vladimer. He had caught us in the act! The five of us were herded back to our room and grounded from playtime for a week. We agreed, however, that it was well worth it . . . almost!

When the girls had been warned to keep their window-shades drawn all the time, and were doing so, we simply paid one of the more cooperative of them a dollar (which was a lot in those days) to raise one particular shade (closest to our target and vantage point), and she did so. Another girl proceeded to close the shade. Our girl pulled it back up again. When it was pulled down for the third time, it stayed that way and we were out a dollar, with not much to show for it. We were always trying!

The roof was always a place for this type of scenario. It was dark, had many alcoves for hiding, and appealed to the more adventurous of us. Several of the really daredevil kids used to scale the ledge to get an even better view of the girls. One misstep and they would end up three floors down. I tried it once, but it was too scary.

I had a number of girlfriends during my seven years at the Pride, each corresponding to my specific age needs at the time. My first was a pretty girl with a great smile, and we used to enjoy "ranking" on each other in a teasing, good-natured manner. It was not politic then to be seen holding hands, and so we'd take walks out to the summerhouse (the large-sized gazebo that extended out into the playing field) and talk, hold hands, and do some awkward smooching.

When she left, I developed a sort of platonic friendship with a girl who taught me how to dance. The Home regularly held Saturday night socials, and early on I couldn't dance too well. This girl was cheerful, upbeat, and a great dancer. She took me in hand and taught me how to dance, and I became a rather good dancer as a result. It was the era of the Big Band—Benny Goodman, Glen Miller, Tommy Dorsey, Harry James. Saturday-night radio shows featured the entire range of music, and we didn't need to buy too many records, although we had a good collection, thanks to our supervisors. Many pleasurable Saturday nights were spent in this harmless, fun-filled manner. It paid to have learned how to dance because it always was so enjoyable, and it made it much easier to approach girls.

Then came several girls who didn't return my affection or advances. They were hot and cold and kept several of us on a string. We'd all do our show-off things to impress them, which, more often than not, backfired. It rarely deterred us from trying again, whether we fell on our faces or not. With our active hormones urging us on, it was important to always be in the game.

My next best "love affair" at the Pride was with a beautiful girl who returned my affections in an equally warm manner. Soon we were regulars on the roof. In those days, heavy kissing and petting were as far as one went with a "nice girl." When the girl's reputation was questionable, it was more acceptable to go "all the way." But my girl was too nice, and our passionate sessions on the roof satisfied our needs, despite the restrictions. It consumed the better part of my last year there and served to make my sudden departure that much more painful. I came back on weekends to play ball. But with no means other than public transportation, I was confined to that one Saturday afternoon per week, in which I invariably played ball all of the time. We soon drifted apart and our relationship ended.

But it didn't for many others. There have been twenty or more marriages between onetime residents of the Pride of Judea, and several more between supervisors. My brother Bernie was in a longtime relationship with a girl at the Home. However, when he went into the Navy for a year, she eloped with an outside guy, only to have a hellish life thereafter.

Mr. Abel, the supervisor Phil calls Trig, met his future wife at the Pride. She was a very striking woman, and they made a great-looking couple. To our regret, of course, their pairing and plans also led to their departure.

Sam Arcus became a supervisor at the Pride in his early twenties. By his account, he quickly noticed a very attractive Senior Girl, who, soon after her departure from the Pride, became his wife. This year, they celebrated their fiftieth wedding anniversary!

Harry Koval met his future wife, the beautiful Sarah, when she too was a supervisor. They too are closing in on fifty years of a good marriage.

The social needs of boys and girls while growing up are quite pronounced, and often cause maladjustment, anxiety, and unhappiness. For many of us, the Home was a good environment where our needs could be satisfied more easily. The recollections of our alumni when we asked them about this were overwhelmingly positive. Many mentioned relationships that were like "brothers and sister," reflective of the comfortable environment and the friendly relations between the sexes.

When I left the Pride, I felt myself fully at ease in relating to the opposite sex in all situations. Having had good experiences with them, I was rarely embarrassed or intimidated in my future contacts, even when trying to impress the special ones. The same appears to have held for most of the other Pride alumni. My brother had the same confidence, as did virtually all of his friends and Pride peers. We had our full share of the "birds and the bees" at the Pride, and for most—though not all—of us, the experience was beneficial!

Chapter 14

"What? Are You Sick Again?"

Phil Craft

My First Encounter

For every youngster at the Pride of Judea, the infirmary was, in function and symbol, the point of entry, the Ellis Island, to a new life of unknown challenge and anxiety. Every entering youngster would be kept there for several days for a physical exam and for general observation and evaluation.

When I arrived at the Pride in 1932, I thought at first that the infirmary was the designated site of my own well-deserved ordeal. Beset with acute panic and despair, I cried bitterly and incessantly despite the valiant efforts of the Pride's longtime physician, Dr. Sarah Demick, to comfort and reassure me. Having already been subjected to five long years of blame, mistreatment, and rejection, I had become too angry and suspicious to readily trust the motives and intentions of any stranger. After three days of self-inflicted suffering, sheer exhaustion, and a growing submission to the fate before me finally achieved what simple reason and a kind person could not; I finally wound down and shut up.

My first contact with Dr. Sarah Demick was a good one. Russian born and educated, she had been at the Home for some time before I arrived. It was to be her major career site for a long while afterwards as well, spanning some twenty-five to thirty years in all. For most of the other children, during her long career, she was a figure taken for granted, but for me, with horrendous treatment from adults as my norm, she was a welcome change, and at a pivotal time. She was the first sympathetic and supportive adult I had ever encountered. Here I was, a wailing, hysterical new entity, and

109

she made repeated and patient attempts to calm me, to reassure me, and to make me feel welcome.

Knowing that an effective pathway to a frightened little boy was through his sweet tooth, she plied me with ample portions of tasty food, and delicious desserts of ice cream and cake. She was gentle, concerned, and supportive, and I will always appreciate that first contact with her.

Helping immeasurably was the presence in the infirmary of two other boys, both six years old, who were there simply because they were sick. Allied with Dr. Demick's efforts to console me was the unexpected friendliness of Charlie Uretsky and Stanley Jacobs, who tried hard to make me feel welcome and told me how much I would enjoy my new home.

As I look back, I realize that Dr. Demick must have enlisted their active involvement in becoming my welcoming committee, but it certainly was well received and needed at the time. She also had me remain in the infirmary for an extra day until they were well enough to leave and to accompany me upstairs, where they could look after me as a new member of their group, the Midget Boys.

Charlie and Stanley helped to ease my early adjustment into the Home and remained steadfast friends in the years that followed. Thus, the infirmary, for me, became a positive and vital bridge to my new life at the Pride.

My Tonsillectomy

Since I was in good physical health for the next two years and did not need to visit the infirmary during that time, nothing happened to change my appreciative attitude toward my benefactor, Dr. Demick. However, all that changed with my next medical crisis, my tonsillectomy.

When I was seven, another boy and I were told that we were going on a special outing to the wonderful Steeplechase Amusement Park in Coney Island. We were astonished to find ourselves, at the end of the trip, at the Beth Moses Hospital, where Dr. Demick was waiting for us. This rude shock, mingled with my own intense fear of the unknown, and a sharp feeling of betrayal, caused me to explode into rage and violent rebellion. I absolutely went nuts!

Only the powerful, determined efforts of the hospital attendants, the tight restraints of the heavy straps that bound me to the table, and the application of choking ether could subdue me effectively in preparation for the removal of my tonsils. I had been lied to and betrayed! I felt abandoned once again, and by someone I thought I could trust!

When I finally awoke, my throat hurt and it seemed as though hours had passed. Then I was given something that made me sleep again. It was dark outside when I awoke again. My cries brought a running nurse to the room, and she told me that Dr. Demick had left hours before but was sure to return for us in the morning. My fears, always so close to the surface, prevented me from believing that Dr. Demick would come back, and I cried myself to sleep in this strange and lonely room, in total despair. I truly doubted that I ever would see her or any of my friends in the Home again, and I wondered what would become of me and the other child from the Home.

My elation at seeing Dr. Demick, early the next morning, transformed her face into something beautiful to behold and quickly blotted out all of my suffering and pain. Her confirmation that we indeed were going home filled me with a surge of hope and joy, causing my depression and resentment to evaporate instantly! I felt like a condemned man who had just been given a reprieve.

The Home's infirmary, where we were taken to recuperate for the next few days, became for me, again, a happy place of deliverance and celebration. I did not even mind being denied solid foods, since along with lots of ice-cream and jello, we also were allowed extended visits from our friends. It was a joyous few days.

Here I was, at the tender age of seven, and my two experiences with Dr. Demick and the infirmary had been significant ones. Both had started painfully. Yet both had ended in happiness and virtual ecstasy. Nevertheless, I was happy, on both occasions, to return to my group upstairs.

My Painful Earache and a Lifelong Discovery

When I was about thirteen, I experienced a painful earache of increasing intensity which soon reached, then breached, my threshold of tolerance. Too big now for tears, I went quickly to the infirmary. In my helplessness, I prayed fervently that Dr. Demick would know how to stop this agonizing pain before I went mad.

Knowing and confident, she quickly prepared a hot water bag, applied it to my ear, and smiled reassuringly as my relief soon became evident. Although I thought that I'd be allowed to return to my group, this was vetoed quickly when a routine reading of my temperature registered at 102.7. My disappointment was mitigated by my gratitude, not only to have the pain gone, but also to know how to treat it for myself in the future. But there was an added bonus. This incident was my introduction to Dr. Demick's fabulous orange juice, the most delicious concoction I had ever tasted, which I drank greedily before going to sleep, and which I could enjoy again in the morning.

The next day, I was delighted to see Dr. Demick approach my infirmary table with an orange juice pitcher in hand. Sure enough, it was full of the magic elixir that had made me forget my pain the night before. As I drank three glasses in rapid succession with insane delight, her dark eyes mirrored a feeling of satisfaction mingled with a slight trace of wonder that I might have flipped my lid overnight. After a brief examination, I was discharged back to my group. Once again, I was delighted! I now knew how to treat any future earaches, rendering them harmless, and I also knew who made the best orange juice I had ever tasted!

"What? Are You Sick Again?"

Stan Friedland

I was a pretty healthy kid and did not have much real need of the infirmary during my seven-year stay at the Home. That doesn't mean, however, that I wanted nothing to do with the place. In fact, I wandered into it every now and again, because we viewed it as a vacation retreat in times of stress or need. For me, those times occurred in the dead of winter, when the weather would get so bad that the cozy sanctuary of the infirmary became an ideal resting place for a day or two. That's when I most needed an acting performance of Academy Award caliber. Dr. Demick had pretty good radar for phonies, so it had to be good. Let's see: I have no temperature, sore throat, running nose, etc., etc. How about an upset stomach, nausea, and diarrhea? That's the ticket; let's go.

Since I wasn't a frequent visitor, I made it through the infirmary gates on most of my tries. I really didn't want to be out of school much, since I valued my schoolwork and grades. Thus, I relished those occasions when I could rest in the comfort of the infirmary, have my meals brought to me (though, when I did the stomach routine, I often had to suffer the consequences of a restricted diet), be able to catch up on my pleasure reading, and generally lead a lazy existence. In the middle of the winter, this was most desirable.

Once I successfully got into the infirmary, I could watch the efforts of my friends as they made their play to be admitted. One of them, a real character, tended to overdo it in frequency, and I was there one day when he tried to get in.

Dr. Demick greeted him with her classic, "What? Are you sick again"? Not to be daunted, Eddie said, "My earache is killing me, Dr. Demick. I couldn't even sleep last night."

Dr. Demick examined him: ears, nose, throat. She smiled. "Eddie, you're fine. Go to school." He protested. "I'm not kidding. My ear is killing me!"

Dr. Demick had no nurse during the day. She handed Eddie an empty hot water bottle and said. "Here. Fill it up with the hottest water and hold it to your ear as long as you want. But do it on the way to school, because that's where you're going! Next. What? Are you sick again too?"

And so it went. Especially in the worst weather of the winter season. Those of us who successfully got in usually razzed those who tried and failed. That was the game part of it. When legitimate illness occurred, the medical care was quite satisfactory. Dr. Demick was from the old school and stayed with the basics. Since we were a healthy lot, in general, we usually needed some bed rest, some aspirin, and a lot of fluids, including the ever-present chicken soup. This timeless formula usually worked quite well. When something out of the ordinary happened, such as a bone break, Dr. Demick took the patient to the hospital for more specialized diagnosis and treatment. This is where some of her weak points surfaced.

As Phil indicated in his account of his tonsillectomy, Dr. Demick did not always tell the children what was about to happen to them. Maybe she wanted to shield them from anxiety, but in any case she often told them something else, or nothing at all. While she was a competent physician, for the most part, she was not a warm or overtly compassionate person. Therefore, medical situations requiring hospital treatment were usually not good experiences. Fortunately, I was never in this category. But my brother was.

He broke his shoulder playing football and was brought to the infirmary. After a brief examination, Dr. Demick informed him that he required hospital treatment to treat the injury. She put him in a car, alone with the driver, and had him taken to the hospital, where he was sent upstairs, alone. A doctor set his shoulder in a sling cast, but he was kept overnight for observation, in a room with two octogenarians. After a sleepless and uncomfortable night, the driver reappeared to bring him back to the Home. Dr. Demick showed little concern during this time. She had seen to it that Bernie had appropriate care, but did not provide the attention and concern that would have eased the experience for him.

Another problem area was Dr. Demick's relative insensitivity to the needs of the girls when they experienced menstrual problems. Although her physical examinations were conducted in private, she had a loud voice and her comments could be heard easily by everyone waiting in the outer office. She might be heard telling the girls, "When you menstruate, this is normal. This is what's going to happen each time. Get used to it." The recollections of many female alumni indicate that they were often embarrassed and humiliated when they went to her with these problems and difficulties. Nor did she do any group hygiene with them to prepare them for these physiological changes. She left that important task to the regular supervisors.

Dr. Demick, Russian born and educated, came to the Pride in the late twenties and stayed through the early fifties. The length of her tenure there was much more of an asset than a liability. She knew all about institutional life for kids, knew their needs, etc., and generally developed user-friendly practices and procedures to meet those needs. Her system worked fairly well over the years, as reflected by the positive views of most alumni when they were asked to rate the medical treatment they received at the Pride. With some exceptions, most had fairly satisfactory recollections of her and the medical care provided.

Basically, Dr. Demick was a known quantity, a familiar person, and we liked the stability she represented because it was very reassuring. We knew what to expect from her, warts and all, and that was fine. She was an old-fashioned doctor and stayed with remedies of long standing. For example, everyone in the infirmary had to take castor oil each day, dispensed by her own hand, and of course using the same spoon for the entire population. If you faked your way into the infirmary, that was the price you had to pay, and we accepted it as such because the perks were worth it.

In general, Dr. Demick's medical care and life in the infirmary are held in positive regard, which is no small achievement, considering the challenging setting and the active clientele.

Miss Gorelick

The junior member of the medical team at the Home was the longtime night nurse, Miss Gorelick. Another Russian emigré in the nononsense mold of Dr. Demick, she provided night coverage of the infirmary and also made rounds of the dorms to ensure that all was right with the Home's children.

Our view of her was mainly through these nocturnal visits as she made her nightly rounds. Wearing heavy shoes with leather heels, she could be heard approaching from a long way off. Not infrequently, we were engaged in various mischievous activities and would try to fool her into thinking that all was well and we were "following the rules."

Miss Gorelick was a registered nurse and was up to the task of providing fundamental medical care as needed. In an emergency, Dr. Demick, who lived nearby, could be called, and the twenty-four-hour coverage net was complete. Miss Gorelick also was at the Home for a long time, and while she was a stern and imposing figure, her long tenure was reassuring enough to compensate for any deficiencies.

The two Russian women made for a strong medical team, and we knew that we were protected in case of illness.

Their presence represented another vital part in the mosaic that produced the institution's solid care of its children.

Chapter 15

The Summers Were a Treat

Phil Craft

The Orphans' Day Outing

The annual Orphans' Day Outing at Coney Island was the most eagerly anticipated event of the summer. It was sponsored by the Police Anchor Club of New York City, and New York's finest certainly did get involved.

On that special day of the year, children from every orphans' institution in New York City were bused to Coney Island for a full day of "feast and fun" on this world-famous beach. Under the protective eyes of an impressive array of uniformed police officers mounted on motorcycles, nothing was too good for the happy boys and girls riding in scores of chartered school buses on the way to their favorite outing. I can't recall any boy, in any of my groups, ever missing this outing, unless he was seriously sick or incapacitated.

Dressed in newly laundered play-clothes, and with neatly combed hair and clean faces on display, we would want to show the kids from other orphanages, as well as the outside world at large, just how well cared for we were, hopefully drawing smiles of approval from all who saw us.

Eagerly descending from our buses, in orderly columns under the watchful view of our supervisors, we carefully scanned the many huge banners and printed signs for the special logo of the Pride of Judea which marked the designated meeting place for the more than 200 kids from our Home. This would be our base for the day, where we would start all of our many wonderful activities.

Since it was almost midday when everyone was assembled and settled, the first order of business was, of course, lunch. An abundance of delicious frankfurters, in huge pots of freshly boiled water, were brought to us, waiting to be placed into fresh buns. Small bottles of soda, encased in ice, were opened quickly and given out as we passed in line. You could have as many of both as you liked. Then small cups of Breyer's or Horton's ice cream would be removed from refrigerated trucks slowly cruising the beach, and these made for a delicious dessert.

Then, after a rest interval, it was off to the ocean for a refreshing swim, but only after a strong lecture on safety and the need to stay with your buddy. After being buddied up, we would be walked into the water and supervised as closely as possible. After the swim, a wide expanse of spread blankets and towels surrounding the big Pride sign would be ready for the returning bathers, and a few minutes of needed rest. Then we had our afternoon options. You could go to Steeplechase Park for several hours of fun rides, or you could stay on the beach for more sun and fun, playing many games.

I often tried to do both. Steeplechase Park had an assortment of great rides, and this would be our only time all year to experience them. After several exciting hours there, it was back to the beach for more good food and our share of sun, surf, and games. Throughout the afternoon, more hot dogs would be gobbled down and more soda and ice cream would be consumed, without pause or worry about cost or quantity.

On this wonderful day, orphans became pampered royalty whom grownups strived to please. And then it ended. It always ended all too soon as the late afternoon shadows arrived much too quickly. We boarded our buses, tired but happy, for the long ride home, rushing for window seats so that we could watch, with fascination and delight, as the motorcycle cops weaved in and out of formation, occasionally sounding their sirens, either spontaneously or in response to one of our frequent pleas to do so. Group songs and chants, rising above our endless chatter, echoed from each bus and became the loudest when we passed another bus and joined the unspoken competition of seeing who could drown the other out in good-natured song.

As we made the turn off Linden Boulevard for the last few blocks to the Home, loud, enthusiastic cheers would ring out for our driver first, and then for any other favored individual. Our police escort was long gone by then. We were alone, but content with our warm, fond memories of this special occasion when each of us had been king or queen for the day.

Other Outings and Bus Trips

Phil Craft

During the summers in the thirties, there were other bus trips to ocean beaches and these always were fun. As a little kid, the waves seemed huge to me, and it was exciting to jump them, thereby mastering them and surviving.

Every trip also brought with it the great pleasure of a bag lunch. For me, these were a special delight in that they offered a tasty departure from the prepared meals back at the Home. The bag lunch usually consisted of two sandwiches and a fruit, accompanied by a half-pint of milk.

My classes at P.S. 202 took many trips. We went to the Brooklyn Museum, the Botanical Gardens, the Bronx Zoo, the American Museum of Natural History, and the Hayden Planetarium. Given my restricted background, all of these trips opened up my world a lot more and were a valuable part of my education.

But my favorite trips were those taken by the Pride. With my friends all around me, with the anticipation of a delicious bag lunch, and with enjoyable destinations ahead, the Pride trips were my favorites. And who can forget the exuberance of Charlie Vladimer as our bus turned down Elton Street on the last block of the journey, as he led us in a rousing cheer for the bus driver!

Seagate

Phil Craft

The directors of the Pride of Judea recognized early on the value of getting the kids out of the hot city during the summer and placing them in a setting where they could enjoy themselves every single day. They proceeded to make some key acquisitions and moves that resulted in outstanding summers for all of us.

In the pre-World War II days of the late thirties, the Pride rented a large house on the beach in Seagate, Brooklyn, which was adjacent to Coney Island. Every summer day, the children would board buses for the 45-minute ride to the house, and another enjoyable day at the beach.

I enjoyed our trips to Seagate a great deal. Even today, I still recall rolling along Linden Boulevard, passing the familiar, fortress-like building that was our school, P.S. 202, and then moving on to the attractive seaside area of Brooklyn where we soon would get off at the Coney Island exit. The sounds of traditional camp ballads mingled with popular Hit Parade songs echoed loudly from our moving buses as each new tune was introduced spontaneously, almost before the previous one had ended. The spirit of anticipation and fun was etched vividly on our smiling faces as we sped happily to our seafront destination for another bright, warm, sunny day at the ocean.

Food, as usual, was a topic of anticipation and conversation. Following later, the Home's big, black delivery truck would be carrying our individual bag lunches and half-pint containers of milk, and also "bug-juice" for snacks before we went home. During the ride to the beach, there'd be lively speculation, and even some swapping, like stock market futures, of lunch sandwiches whose contents were still unknown. Bologna was the premium kind, followed by American cheese and hardboiled eggs, with peanut butter and jelly bringing up the rear. The thought of food was never far from our minds.

Each of us carried a bathing suit rolled up in a clean towel, ready for some quick changing as soon as we arrived. The girls used rooms on the main floor, while the boys changed upstairs. Of course this meant our best peeping efforts, but their shades and doors were always shut tight. Anyway, we really had come for the beach and ocean, and so it was arrival, change, and onto the beach.

For someone like me, living since birth only in the large, brick buildings of institutions, the quaint two-story wooden house held a strange and special fascination during that first summer. I felt a strong desire to explore all of its rooms as if it contained a life of its own that I never had experienced. But this sensation always gave way to my desire to get out on the sunny beach with the rest of my friends and dive into the attractive surf.

There was lots to do on the beach, in addition to going into the water. Running bases was a favorite. We played touch football. We played catch with just about every type of ball. We played tag and many other games requiring running. We constantly built sand castles and whatever else our imaginations could conjure up. We buried any friend who succumbed to sleep at the beach, and the trick was to do it without awakening the victim until he was as deeply buried as possible.

When we went into the water, we were guarded very carefully, reflective of the tragic drowning of Pride kids only six or seven years before in the Rockaways. Our days at the beach were just loaded with good fun, and repetitive as they were, we couldn't get enough of them.

The bus rides home also had a warm, fuzzy feeling. They'd be punctuated by even more raucous singing as we whiled away the almost hour-long ride back to the Pride. As we neared Elton Street and the Pride building, one of our counselors would shout, "Three cheers for our driver," and the rousing "Hip, hip, Hoorah" was not only for him, but for the day as well. We were home again, just in time for a delicious supper.

During the war, when we moved into our new summer residence in Long Beach, I initially felt pangs of loss and regret that the happy times at Seagate were now only fond memories. While we all came to enjoy Long Beach very much, our time at Seagate was special and I remember it with sweet nostalgia.

At Long Beach, During the War Years

Phil Craft

In 1943, a wealthy philanthropist and major benefactor, Mr. Martin Scharf, donated two lovely homes in Long Beach to the Pride of Judea. These homes, a scant block from the boardwalk and ocean, provided many enjoyable summers for the Home's children.

Located in an attractive section of this small Long Island town, there was nothing between the Pride's homes and the beach, giving the enclave a feeling of luxurious isolation and privacy. The town also sported a new air-conditioned movie theater and a large municipal pool, both of which were used extensively by the Pride's kids. Games of chance and skill dotted the boardwalk, usually at a nickel per try. Bikes could be rented hourly for a modest fee.

When the Pride first acquired these homes, only the lesser one, called the "Annex," was available for use. The "main building," formerly a mansion, with wonderful marble pillars and impressive ornateness, required extensive renovation in order to accommodate all of the Pride's girls and its entire staff. The boys were to be housed in the Annex, which was closest to the beach, and more than comfortable enough for us not to be jealous of the more impressive main building.

During that first summer of 1943, only the Intermediate and Senior Boys moved into residence at the Annex house. Everyone else continued to be bused out daily, along with a full load of needed supplies from our home base in Brooklyn. As a member of the Senior Boys, My groupmates and I felt like pioneers, and we warmed to our new daily life.

Under the able direction of Sam Arcus, our competent and innovative supervisor, we had a most enjoyable summer. The Judge promoted an atmosphere balanced with excitement, relaxation, and relative serenity, at minimal cost and difficulty. We played ball, went swimming, roamed the boardwalk and other places of interest, cooling off in comfort at the beach, in the pool, and even at the movies. We spent a carefree, idyllic summer, sharing many adolescent adventures and experiences. While I was to enjoy several more outstanding summers at our "home" in Long Beach, that first one was the most memorable because it was just that, a totally new experience of beachfront residence that affected all of us quite deeply.

As if that wasn't enough, another powerful first happened to me one summer. I fell in love!

For the first time, at the tender age of fifteen, I fell hopelessly in love—with Josephine Valente, the new lifeguard at the municipal pool. Jo, as everyone called her, had gained that position of prestige and responsibility, not only through obvious merit, but also as a direct consequence of the wartime manpower shortage. Nonetheless, no one witnessing her confident, forceful manner and her effective performance ever questioned her competence or authority. Although she would tolerate no nonsense regarding safety, she also was much respected and appreciated for her patient and dedicated efforts to teach children and other beginners to swim better and with greater confidence and enjoyment.

Since I usually was uncomfortable with authority figures, I initially bristled at Jo's tough, strident manner and openly rebelled, defying some minor rule just to stubbornly assert my autonomy.

She quickly put me in my place by restricting me from going into the water for the entire day. Regarding her now with new respect, I also grew increasingly aware that, in total contrast to my earlier, matronly tormentors, Jo actually glistened, especially when wet, with a radiant loveliness that stirred my admiration, mingled with feelings of adoration and desire.

Daily weather changes suddenly assumed new meaning, since they determined whether or not the outdoor pool would be open. I started to view each dark cloud with ominous foreboding, and for similar reasons, I no longer welcomed weekends because the pool would be crowded or Jo would be off and therefore away from me. Now, each new sunrise signaled the pleasant possibility of being near Jo again. This included our regular group swim sessions with her, plus running errands and doing special chores for her and others on the pool staff.

I also needed, and received from Jo, special instruction in floating and treading water. My aquatic skills were quite weak, as reflected by my having to be rescued the previous summer by one of my Pride friends. Following that near disaster, my attempts to learn how to swim had been frustrated by fear and inability to relax, despite the efforts of several well-intentioned instructors.

However, Jo's own involvement injected a new factor into the situation because my devotion to her was so deep that I was ready to place my life, and thereby my complete trust, in her capable hands. Her very touch sent tremors of delight through me, which I vainly tried to suppress or conceal by attempting to relax in her gentle, comforting grasp. With a wisdom and understanding quite rare in one so young, she tactfully pretended to ignore the obvious signs of my rapture and excitement, and patiently persisted until I indeed learned how to float and tread water.

Early on, however, it became quite clear to me that this relationship could never ripen beyond simple friendship. The differences in age, family background, financial position, and religion were all so great as to make it futile from the outset. My feelings, despite their intensity and sincerity, were, after all, only those of an inexperienced and immature young boy. Nonetheless, Jo's understanding, sensitivity and tact, and her genuine regard for my feelings, enshrines her in my heart forever.

The summer of '43 indeed was memorable and was one of my favorite summers ever.

Heavenly Long Beach!

by Stan Friedland

I loved our summers at Long Beach . . . but I almost lost my life there!

Imagine being a have-not kid familiar only with the concrete streets of the city. Now, suddenly, you are living in a gorgeous home one block from a beautiful ocean beach and attractive boardwalk. The pauper had become the prince! That's the way I felt during our summers in Long Beach.

Though I only visited there on day excursions in '43, my group moved into residence in the Annex in 1944. The daily schedule suited me fine; many activities and considerable free time. Basketball on the attractive basketball court; handball on a great handball court; at least two long sessions on the beach daily, with the option of going to the pool. For rainy days, the game room was well-equipped, plus arts and crafts and other skill-development possibilities. The food, however, was just okay because these were the war years, and meat rationing was compensated for by an excess of meals featuring lamb stew, which I hated.

Big deal! It could not deter the enthusiasm and excitement of the days. Occasional bike sessions on the boardwalk; gaming sessions at the boardwalk arcades, money permitting; frequent trips to the attractive Laurel and Lido movie theaters. Life in Long Beach was great! Then I almost drowned!

Our daily schedule was an attractive one. Wake-up, dress, wash, and then flag-raising around the flagpole before breakfast. Morning activities, lunch, a full afternoon, and then, about an hour of quiet time before dinner. Since I loved the beach and the water, I occasionally absconded before dinner for a solo swim. I liked the solitude of having the beach all to myself. I didn't have to share it with anyone.

On this occasion, it was sunny and windy, and the surf was kicking up. I was all of thirteen in the summer of 1944 and quite confident of my swimming ability. Without any hesitation, I dove into the waves and began my normal swim outward. I could feel the pull of the current, which made me pause from swimming too far out. I then began my second habitual pattern, which was to float on my back and be lulled by the motion of the waves. After a few minutes of this, I took stock of my position and was surprised at how far out I had been taken in such a short time. I began swimming toward shore. When I looked up, it was almost as if I hadn't moved. The undertow was strong and the current was moving out from the shore.

"No need to panic," I thought and began resolutely to make for shore. Only I wasn't making much progress. It hit me very quickly that I was in trouble, and I doubled my efforts to move forward. Ten minutes, then twenty, and I was tired.

I was making progress, but now I was in the vicinity of the rock jetty that came out at right angles from the beach, and it was not user-friendly. But my energy was waning and I seemed to have no choice. Closer and closer I came to the rocks as the current seemed to sweep me right at them. "Perhaps I can simply grab on for awhile and rest," I thought, when boom, a wave launched me right onto one and I felt the sharp pain in my side where I had landed. I did grab on, and was able to get enough rest to kick off and struggle toward shore.

An eternity later, probably ten minutes, I lay gasping in shallow water, too weak to immediately stand, but safe enough to count my blessings. The beach was still deserted, and for once I really wanted to see someone . . . anyone. When I crawled onto shore, I felt the pain in my side, and when I looked down, my whole side was covered with red welts and skin-burning abrasions. It was not a pretty sight.

Walking quickly back to the Annex, I snuck quietly into the shower room and reveled in the longest hot shower I had ever taken. When I finally appeared in the dining room, a good half-hour late, my lame explanation was that I had fallen asleep on a back bed and no one had awakened me. Since I was not given to tardiness, this excuse was accepted and I was able to get my dinner.

I told no one about the mishap, not even my brother. When it came to safety, he was very firm that I not do anything foolish to endanger myself. If he found out what had happened, he would have been angry at my stupidity, and so I decided to leave well enough alone. Though my side hurt for the better part of a week, I was grateful to have survived in one piece.

I did not swim in the ocean alone again. Nor did I want to. Somehow, the thrill was gone.

But this didn't diminish my love for our summers in Long Beach. They were terrific and memorable! The have-not kids had a luxurious summer home in the best of locations—and we certainly made the most of it!

Camp Vacamas

Stan Friedland

For the summer of 1947, when I would reach my sixteenth birthday, five of my Pride friends of similar age and I were given the opportunity to work as dishwashers in a social service agency camp, Camp Vacamas, in Kingston, New York. The pay would be $250 for the eight weeks, with a $50 bonus if we stayed the full time. That was big money to all of us, and we readily accepted.

This opportunity was part of the Pride's excellent policy of preparing its children for life on the outside in every conceivable way. Its administrators were receptive and encouraging about after-school part-time jobs, providing we came home for dinner and for the afterdinner homework hour that was a staple of each day. Because of the obvious experiential benefits, they encouraged the older kids to work during the summer in self-contained settings, which was why we were at Vacamas in the summer of 1947.

For me, it was a big step. I never had been out on my own before. My brother had enlisted in the Navy the preceding year, and I had seen him but once when he came home on liberty. Now I would be leaving the nest for the first time, and it was an exciting adventure. It was not unintentional that I would have five companions from the Pride with me. We were to be each other's support team, and that would prove to be of great value to each of us.

I set three objectives for myself that summer. First, was to stay the course and reap the full $300, which was the most money I had ever earned. The other two were to learn how to drink and like beer, and to smoke and enjoy doing it. In my adolescent mind's eye, macho men smoked and drank beer. That's what the ads said, and that's what I wanted to be, a macho man. I was far from the watchful eyes of my brother and mother, both of whom would disapprove vigorously. "What the heck. Let me try it and we'll see what happens."

The only trouble was, I hated the taste of both, with a passion! Both were foul tasting and foul smelling. What was a guy to do? I drank every brand of beer I could find, and smoked every brand of butts in existence. No luck! Their taste was yuck! A Coke was far tastier and satisfying. I tried hard for eight weeks, but at the end of the summer I was a confirmed nonsmoker and nondrinker of beer. Just my tough luck!

But everything else went quite well. The work was quite easy, especially since there were eight of us, five from the Home and three guys from the inner city of Philadelphia. They were pretty nice, and we all got along quite well. We bused the camp tables and washed the dishes and silverware. Once we got the hang of it, we'd be finished about an hour after each meal, making it about a six- to seven-hour day. Then we had the run of the camp's facilities, as long as we didn't interfere with any of the kids' activities. Since all eight of us were very sports-minded, we constantly had things to do in a friendly undertone of rivalry.

While it was fun to be on my own, I missed my family and my friends. I became a prolific letter writer, since I knew how much my mom enjoyed letters from her children. She, in turn, would send me a regular chain of postcards that summer, each one written in an upbeat manner, reflective of her courageous desire to be a positive influence in our lives, something at which she was most successful.

The last several weeks of the summer dragged on because, by then, we were tired of the routine and of one other. Close exposure to the same people, day in and day out, can be wearing. Yet, despite this, we got on quite well, and it was apparent that our Pride commonality made for a bonding force among us.

When the season ended, we stayed for several more days to close down the camp. We reveled in the peaceful isolation of the place and enjoyed the Indian summer weather of the late summer. When the director gave us our checks, complete with bonus, I was a happy person. It had been a valuable and enjoyable summer, and I was going home with more money than I'd ever had. It was a good feeling!

Little did I know that in less than a month, I would be asked to leave the Pride, because the new executive director felt that age sixteen should be the new maximum for reasons of economy and ease in handling the children. The joys of a fine summer evaporated very quickly, and I was thrown into a very difficult and frustrating year.

Chapter 16

The Unhappy Ones

Stan Friedland

The Pride of Judea Children's Home had its share of unhappy children. They came into the Home unhappy, they remained unhappy, and they left unhappy. There are a good number who want nothing to do with the current alumni organization, lest it remind them of their unhappy years in the Home.

Virtually every child came into the Home unhappy. In itself, placement in an orphanage meant that something was amiss, and that the child could not be cared for in a normal family way. Death, divorce, desertion, poverty, or illness reared their ugly heads as the usual culprits. The children were the victims of these family destroyers and usually came into the Pride feeling abandoned and very much alone.

It was the challenge of this institution to turn them around. Life had dealt these children lemons, and the Pride had to convert that into the proverbial lemonade. That it was able to do so for so many of us is testimony to its high quality. Yet there were those who remember their years in the Home in less than a favorable light. In what follows, one of them eloquently explains why.

The Children's Home

"Brick walls a prison make, and iron bars a cage."

My home, for most of my youthful life, was a large, dismal red brick building on Dumont Avenue between Elton and Linwood Streets in the East New York section of Brooklyn. Behind the building, surrounded by an iron-bar fence, were a gazebo and a large playing field.

The October night had not yet fallen. I was standing in a corner of the football field—I say the football field because it was the football season now, and the field changed its play with the seasons. I was holding tightly to the iron bars and looking through the fence at the neatly arranged two-family homes on the tree-lined street directly across from me. Two kids were playing kick the can. My eyes and cheeks were moist. I wasn't crying because the kids were playing kick the can; it was because they were outside and free. I was not.

This was my sixth year behind bars. I'm ten now, and I'll never get used to this place. Never. Some kids love it here; I hate it. No, it's not a reform school, or a place they send kids to if they commit a crime.

Actually, we get good food and acceptable clothes, although my clothes seem to hang very loose, and sometimes my pants fall down.

Kids come here if they're orphans—you know, if they lost both parents or have only one parent. I'm in the latter category, my mom having died when I was very young.

The Home isn't so bad; we have nice activities, baseball, football, basketball, and such, and we do go outside to school. My brother and sister are here with me too. They may have adjusted to this place a little better than I did. I'm not sure because I really don't remember much about them in this place, but I detest it here. I'm lonely and unhappy all the time. You ask why. Well, that would be another story. Let me continue this one, about my escape.

Tonight is the night I'm going to run away. There's no doubt about it! I've had more than enough. Yesterday, I got smacked around again, by that big bully M.B. I don't want to tell my brother because it would result in another fight. No, I've had it. I'm going tonight.

I've got it all planned. I'll sleep in my street clothes and won't take a shower. I've got $3.10 saved, for my ready cash. I've already packed some extra clothes in a bag, and was able to sneak a piece of chicken, a boiled potato, and some bread from tonight's dinner. Yes, I'm really ready to go.

I sleep in a dormitory with a bunch of other kids. When they're all sleeping, I'm going to go. I just can't walk out the front door. There's a big, fat policeman in a dirty gray uniform standing in the front hallway. His name is Carp, Randolph J. Carp, and he stinks worse than any fish. He'd sure as anything grab me easy and kick my butt. No, the front door is out for sure.

I'm going to hide in the chicken coop. There are no live chickens in the coop, just garbage cans and plucked chicken feathers. Every morning, at about five o'clock, the garbage truck comes to take out the garbage. You guessed it; I'm hopping on the truck and out I go. I haven't decided where I'll go yet; just out will be a good start.

Suddenly a hand grabs my shoulders and holds me against the fence; the voice of M.B. blasts in my ears. "Hey, runt, crying again? Get your hands off the fence and your tail up to bed or I'll . . ."

I turn and let go a vicious kick at his knee. He releases me and I take off, with him in hot pursuit, like a cat after a mouse.

"I'll break your head, runt, when I catch you," he shouts, as he chases after me, holding his leg.

"He's always picking on smaller kids," I think to myself as I run toward the building as fast as I can. With other kids now in sight, I breathe a sigh of relief. I knew he never would hit me in view of others. Scooting up the steps to my dorm, I wash and jump into bed with my clothes on.

Time passes slowly, and soon the kids' chattering has stopped. The last bed-check has been made. I lie quietly for what seems like an eternity, just looking up at the clock on the wall. Finally, it's three-thirty, time to go.

I pick up my extra clothes and food, and silently make my way down the stairs and out the back door to the chicken coop. The early fall air is cold and clear. Shivering, I open the door and hear a loud squeak. My heart stops, but looking about and seeing nothing, I creep inside, close the door, and hide in the corner behind a large garbage can.

I waited for what seemed like hours, my eyes getting heavier and heavier. "I'll just take a little nap for a few seconds; the noise of the garbage truck will wake me if I fall asleep," I told myself.

I opened my eyes and blinked as the afternoon sunlight streamed through the open door of the chicken coop. I had slept my escape away.

Stretching from my cramped position, I stood up and walked out into the bright afternoon light, and bumped right into my supervisor. The kids called him Uncle Jack. But he was nobody's uncle; he just liked little boys.

"What the hell are you doing in the chicken coop?" he shouted. "Wasn't your breakfast enough? I saw you take an extra orange juice." He smacked my butt as I ran toward my favorite place—the far end of the football field. I held the bars again and stared out at the kids playing across the street.

"I'll try again. Nobody ever misses me," I cried to an empty field.

But, of course, I never ran away. At sixteen, I was released and finally set free of the iron-bar fence.

I'm not sure what effect being in the Pride had on my life. I do know that it was an emotional hell for me. Time has changed my life, and most of my ill-fated memories have faded into oblivion. But every now and then, something said or written will resurrect my unpleasant experiences in the Home, and I react with unexpected passion.

Unhappy Moments

All the members of the Pride of Judea's alumni organization were canvassed about their recollections of their lives in the Home. One question was: "What did you least like about the Pride and why?" The following are some of the answers.

From a girl who was there for seven years: "Rigid rules and lack of warmth and sensitivity by some supervisors. I often missed having the love and attention of at least one close parent, to whom I could confide."

Many other responses touched on the same theme. "I didn't have adults to share my emotions or feelings with when I needed to." "There was a lack of real love." "There were just too many kids for the supervisors to spend any real time with us, individually. I envied my outside friends who had their parents to return home to every night."

Many responses touched on the unpreparedness that many felt upon leaving the Pride. This was especially true for those who left at age sixteen, rather than the earlier ones who left upon high school graduation. However, most of the respondents also felt that their initial sense of helplessness was only temporary and was caused by the "culture shock" of the total change in routine and environment encountered in the outside world.

The other main category of response to this question referred to the bullying that took place between the kids, both physically and verbally. One significant comment was, "If you weren't a good athlete, or even active in sports, you tended to get picked on a lot more by everyone. " Regrettably, this was the case. Athletic ability directly affected the pecking order of the social scene, and the least talented and active kids, boys and girls, got hurt the most in their peer relationships.

Discipline at the Pride:
The Good, the Bad, and the Ugly

All youngsters, at every age level, require firm, effective discipline. Providing it is the greatest parental challenge, and has been since the beginning of time. If it's a formidable task for parents in the privacy of their own homes, think how difficult and challenging it was on an institutional level with a population of orphans.

However, on the whole, the Pride disciplined its charges quite well. Any youngster, in a situation requiring discipline, is going to be unhappy. To get a more objective look at the quality of the discipline, the current alumni were asked to "describe the type of discipline you received at the Pride when you stepped out of line, and was it effective, and why?" The following is a compilation of their responses.

"I was confined to my dorm room during play periods for a week or more. I regarded that as a minor inconvenience at the time. But now, looking back on it, I do believe that it was effective because I wanted to be with everyone else."

From a woman: "In my five years, I never was struck by anyone, and always appreciated that. When I got into trouble, I was sent to my room or to the office and was not allowed to participate in fun events. This usually worked. Losing a privilege made one feel even more left out and I didn't like that. So I usually corrected my misbehavior."

A male response: "When I was in the Midgets, I occasionally was spanked by Mrs. Braverman. As I grew older, I had privileges revoked. Neither was effective because I always seemed to be in trouble!"

Another male: "When I was seven, I remember Mrs. Braverman hitting me with her leather strap because I received a C in conduct at P.S. 202. I was so upset that I ran away by climbing over the fence and walking about a mile to my grandmother's house. My mother lived there at the time, but she was away at work. But my uncle was there, and when he saw how upset I was, he took me by car to Coney Island, where he treated me to some rides and food. Then, promising to tell my mom what happened, he took me back to the Pride. My mom was there the next morning and gave Mrs. Braverman a nice piece of her mind. She never hit me again."

Another: "Not being able to play ball or go to the movies. You bet it was effective!"

Another: "I had a supervisor who made us hold a pillow with arms stretched out fully. It was very tiring, but we tried to do it to show him how strong we were. When we finally got too tired and had to let our arms drop, he ridiculed us, or else smacked us lightly on the head. I also had privileges taken away, such as movies and sports. Both kinds were effective for me. In fact, I appreciated them even then. I felt then, as I do now, that we needed that discipline to develop into better people. I think that it worked, too."

Another: "I was in the Pride for twelve years, and the discipline that worked the best for me occurred on but two occasions. Both times, a supervisor that I liked very much gave me an unexpected slap in the face for something I had done. It was so unlike him that it jarred me into thinking about what I had done and I vowed to correct my behavior."

As one might conclude from the above recollections, discipline at the Pride was varied, moderate in severity, and generally effective. It paralleled the methods employed in a conventional home setting and seems to have been appreciated by our alumni in retrospect.

My own experiences were in full agreement with the preceding observations. I cannot recall ever having been struck by an adult during my seven years in the Home. And I was not a saint, by any means. I was confined to my room and deprived of privileges on numerous occasions. Nor did I play the unfair game, where the "you're being unfair" routine is laid on the adult by the child.

When we were punished, we usually had it coming. In fact, half the time, we had done more than was known by the supervisor. So we usually took our punishment in stride and went on from there.

The generally good tone of the disciplinary methods used reflects favorably upon the supervisory staff of the Pride throughout its years. In all of their recollections, the alumni can remember only one really sadistic supervisor who left an indelibly negative imprint. In general there was a positive, supportive climate that helped us so much.

Chapter 17

Memorable Characters

Phil Craft

Several people stand out in my mind, not only because they played some role in my life, but because they were colorful and significant enough to be known by everyone and to have an effect on the entire institution. They are, simply, memorable characters of the Pride.

Big Ben Karp

For almost as long as I can remember, Ben Karp's gray-uniformed hulk was a familiar and reassuring figure in the Home. Unlike Mr. Bumble, the bossy, greedy workhouse superintendent pictured in "Oliver", the musical film version of Dickens's *Oliver Twist*, whom he strikingly resembled, his was a benign, good-hearted presence in the halls and on the grounds of the Pride. It sometimes seemed odd to me that someone so massive and formidable-looking would be working in a place inhabited by so many small, skinny kids. This incongruity, which no one else seemed to notice, occasionally made me laugh.

Mr. Karp, as I respectfully addressed him, was charged with enforcing rules and generally preserving order. This he did with an impartial sense of duty and, sometimes, a trace of reluctance, since he valued the goodwill, if not actually the affection, of the children.

Nowadays he'd be called a security guard; yet to most of us, he was more than that. From time to time, he displayed genuine interest in our activities, even to the point of becoming an occasional participant. Sometimes, when he came to bat as a designated hitter in one of our frequent softball games, he was able to drive the ball well beyond the summerhouse, sending the outfielders scurrying in pursuit. With each prodigious blast, I instantly and naturally linked him with the immortal Babe Ruth, thinking of their remarkable similarity in girth and explosive power at the plate.

Sadly, however, Mr. Karp's leg speed and physical conditioning were quite limited, obliging him to settle for a hard-breathing double. The image of him lumbering breathlessly into second base is a vivid memory of mine. The members of his team would give him a rousing cheer, which brought a good-natured smile to his face.

If he was able to linger in order to get up a second time, he would enjoy the backward movement of the outfielders as they moved ever so deep in respect of his awesome power. That too brought a smile to his face, as did our remarks when we ran into him during the next few days. Such interaction made him a more real person to us.

Mr. Karp walked the younger kids to elementary school each day, which now, in retrospect, reminds me of a huge shepherd tending his sheep. This image is actually quite accurate, because he hovered protectively around us at every intersection and possible area of danger. He did this quite well, with nary an accident or crisis that I can remember.

When school was let out, his large figure was our reassuring assembly point for the walk home. When we got back to the Pride for our afternoon treat of milk and cookies, he occasionally joined us, with probably as much enjoyment of the refreshments as experienced by any of the children.

Now, many decades later, I more readily appreciate that during that time of radical change, when the world went from peace to war, Ben Karp was a constant, predictable, and protective force in our lives at the Pride. While the world beyond the walls was growing more volatile, stressful, and even dangerous, he loomed each day as a visible guardian against harm or threat from the outside. Although I once took for granted the sense of security his presence conveyed, I came to realize, many years later, that Ben Karp had been far more than just a huge landmark in our midst.

Miss Mazer, My Homework Room Teacher

Since well before my first day in Class 1A-3 at P.S. 202, Miss Fanny Mazer already was mistress and custodian of the homework room at the Pride of Judea. Situated in a spacious corner classroom on the main floor, and facing Dumont Avenue, this room became my mandated place for homework and study throughout my entire elementary school career. All of the residents had to spend an hour in this room every day in order to do their homework thoroughly. This rule was an excellent one and was another important reason why virtually all of the Pride kids got through school, with many becoming excellent students in the process.

Although Miss Mazer was small in physical stature, she was an imposing and straitlaced individual who would not tolerate disruption or disrespect in her domain. She was the rigid arbiter of any disputes that might arise, and such was her authority that her decisions were beyond challenge or appeal.

Always a stickler for neatness, decorum, and proper grammar, Miss Mazer labored mightily over the years to correct my countless flaws in syntax, manners, and deportment. For many years, I was sufficiently awed by her bespectacled and disciplined presence that I struggled mightily to improve in my many areas of weakness. To my lasting benefit, she harbored an irresistible urge to fine-tune my correct use of words. When I once asked her, "Miss Mazer, can I sharpen my pencil?" she replied that I should ask instead, "May I sharpen my pencil?" citing the distinction between ability and consent.

Among her greatest passions was her unending crusade against careless waste. Because I learned slowly and only after great effort, I had unintentionally become a real challenge to her in this area. She simply could not bear that my repeated errors in arithmetic and grammar were committed, indelibly, on "good paper," thereby requiring correction and repetition on new paper. She grew so frustrated that she began to issue me old scraps of paper that she dutifully collected for this purpose. Summoning me to her desk, she would thrust this odd assortment of paper into my hands and direct me to do my homework and corrections on them before then transferring the completed and corrected versions into my notebooks.

Sharing, even then, a similar devotion to frugality, I was happy to comply. Who could have known then that years later, when my creative writing efforts began in earnest, I invariably would experience a serious writing block whenever I attempted to write on "good paper"! I dealt with this phobia by collecting and writing on used paper, such as handbills, junk-mail, and even the blank inside surfaces of used envelopes. The mother of my "adopted" Turkish family (to be explained in a later chapter) also provided vast quantities of discarded paper from her job as an office-cleaning woman. With this option, my creative spirit soared, and I knew that I would never run out of paper.

Miss Mazer, therefore, played a significant role in my early life. A weak, slow-learning student, I always needed help to master my schoolwork. Not only did she provide it for me on a daily basis, but she also took a personal interest in my progress, which I needed desperately.

For these reasons, she is forever enshrined warmly in my memory, and is recalled fondly each time I reach for a discarded piece of paper from my huge pile. This story, in fact, was written on discarded, recycled paper, which is the best symbolic commemoration of the important role she played in my life and in the lives of many others.

Jerry, My Photography Teacher

Most children arrived at the Pride with few resources in terms of wealth, family connections, or people who would later be able to open doors of opportunity for them. I, in particular, was impoverished in this respect. Every bit of attention and advantage I received came directly from some caring person who came to the Home and then became helpful to me in some way, sometimes for only a brief period. Such an individual was Jerry, the volunteer photography teacher, who came to the Pride when I was twelve.

Jerry brought cameras, rolls of film, darkroom equipment, and chemicals. In addition to his excellent photography skills, he brought some key qualities that made him an ideal teacher. He had great patience, sensitivity, and persistence, plus the ability to convey facts and ideas simply and clearly, and with an empathy which encouraged us, not only to learn, but to succeed.

Because I learned quite slowly, Jerry devoted more time and attention to me than to anyone else. He rooted for my successes with such genuineness that I regarded him not only as my teacher, but as a good friend. Gradually, he taught me all of the basic steps in developing film and making prints. He let me use his Baby

Brownie camera, and supplied me with enough film so that I was able to practice everything, from shooting pictures correctly to the subsequent steps of the development process. Such repetition served to increase my skill and confidence, and provided additional proof that, although slow, I could master new things and enjoy them. Jerry opened a new window on the world for me, because photography, since then, has been a valuable part of my life.

Since I had few adult friends to really trust, Jerry became very important to me during his brief stay. He asked me to keep the Brownie, urging me to continue taking and developing pictures in the darkroom, which he would leave well stocked. He left before I could venture to inquire why he was going, and I never did find out the reason. However, his camera became my single most valuable possession, and with it came a growing collection of photos of my friends in the Home and at school, and even some of myself.

The camera was a magical tool that gave me a previously unknown power to record an image in time, from start to finish. Photography was another valuable source of self-confidence.

The growth and changes in the years that followed were duly recorded on film with that special camera, which I even took to the Army with me. The collection of photos, now grown in number, was left in the special care of Charlie, since they were of great value to me.

As the years passed and my circumstances changed, photography continued to occupy much of my free time, even while my cameras, picture-taking techniques, and darkroom skills developed and improved in my own home photo-lab. Although I grew more involved with the scenic aspects, people continued to be my favorite subjects, and photography itself brought me closer to them. My pictures marked the growth and changes in the children, grandchildren, and older members of my adopted Puerto Rican and Turkish families, who have come to mean so much to me in my adult life. These pictures, in fact, form the nucleus of their own respective family collections. Furthermore, the adults in one poor Puerto Rican village sport black-and-white photos portraying their own childhood visages and family events, all taken during a bleak period in their lives when my semi-annual visits provided their sole chance to be photographed and to receive free copies. These were duly and proudly displayed all over the village and seemed to validate their very existence.

I obtained such satisfaction from this "public service" that I soon turned my camera in a similar manner onto my own neighborhood's Little League program, with much the same happy results. I then concentrated on family weddings, christenings, parties, graduations, and other special events. What a joy it was to capture such happy times for people and to see their pleasure when I gave them the completed photos as a present.

Wherever Jerry may be now, his contribution to the quality of my life is immeasurable. I am uniquely blessed to have known him and to have had him introduce photography into my life. He is one of the people who inspired me to follow in his footsteps, with the premise that indeed "it is more blessed to give than to receive!"

Jacob H.: Patriarch of the Pride

One morning recently, while seated on a crowded city bus, I overheard a loud conversation in which a passenger was reviewing the various pronunciations of the name of our sixteenth president. When he mentioned "Ibraham Lincoln," he suddenly struck a familiar chord which instantly evoked the faded memory of Jacob H. Cohen, the ancient but indelible patriarch of the Pride. It recalled for me, the memory of more than sixty years ago, when he declared with definite certainty and obvious pride that indeed "Ibram Lincoln was a Chew" before an attentive audience of highly impressionable children at the end of a Shabbos service in the shul. I still can remember how proud that made me feel, since at age seven, my hunger for new Jewish role-models exceeded my thirst for historical accuracy.

Jacob H. Cohen was the president of the Pride of Judea's board of directors from 1939 till the early sixties. He had been brought onto the board by his close friend Max Blumberg, the founding father of the Pride. When Max Blumberg died in 1939, there was no doubt as to who would become the Pride's second president: Jacob H., who had long been the number-two man. If Max Blumberg was the founder and sculptor of the Pride, then Jacob H. was the patriarch who preserved and sustained his creation.

But at that early time of my life, Jacob H., as everyone called him, was a rather comic figure. Totally bald, with a heavy but quaint East European Jewish accent and a distinctive facial twitch, he evoked in a little boy like me the same mirth that made Charlie Chaplin and S. Z. "Cuddles" Sakall, a character actor, special film favorites of mine in later years. I viewed him as an odd, benevolent figure who seemed to hearken unto little children, posing pleasantly with them for a constant stream of promotional photographs, and often the only adult in many of them. For example, there was no official bar mitzvah group that didn't have its picture taken with the indispensable Jacob H.

Filtering things through a child's eyes, I always was surprised by the respect and deference Jacob H. received from the adults in my life. To them, of course, he was a formidable figure of authority, harboring a superior status of which I was not even vaguely aware. Years later I learned that in addition to his stature as head of the Home, he was the owner of several nearby lumberyards, and a man of considerable wealth and power in the community.

Jacob H. was a philanthropist, a term I naively defined at the time as a rich person who obtains great pleasure and conspicuous acclaim from making large donations to charity while simultaneously underpaying and exploiting his employees, with, of course, less publicity. This impression was formulated in 1950, when the Pride's staff members unionized and went out on strike for higher wages, better working conditions, and more money to be spent on the kids in their charge. As soon as he learned of their union affiliation, Jacob H. Cohen fired them all on the spot! The group included veteran supervisors like Mrs. Braverman and beloved ones like Harry Koval.

In the years since then, I have often wondered how one should measure an individual whose impact, direct or otherwise, on lives like mine looms larger and larger with the passage of time? I now realize, more than ever, that when my own needs were most urgent, I received sustenance, schooling, and protection within the secure shelter of the Pride, while others, equally needy, but less fortunate, were compelled to struggle for survival outside, where many floundered and fell by the wayside.

In a more mature retrospect, while we may have laughed at the comic figure presented by Jacob H., his appearance in those photographs served as part of frequent and skilled fund-raising campaigns that kept the Pride afloat, enabling it to care effectively for me and my fellow orphans. Jacob H. Cohen played an important leadership role. He invested an extraordinary amount of his time and a good deal of his life in preserving the high quality of the Pride which enabled it to be such a good Home for all of us.

Charlie Vladimer had a very good relationship with Jacob H. because Jacob H. knew how effective and popular he was with the kids. When, in the mid-forties, an executive director of the Pride had a forceful disagreement with Jacob H. and was fired, Charlie was asked to be the interim director. Soon afterward Jacob H. offered him the directorship on a permanent basis, but Charlie was keen on going to college, and stayed on only as a floating supervisor.

However, Charlie got to know Jacob H. quite well and came to like him. Whenever we discussed him, Charlie would remind me that Jacob H. had his share of faults—he liked things done his way; he had no patience for unions, either in his lumberyards or in the Pride; he installed people in pivotal positions and backed them if they were obedient rather than competent—but despite this authoritarian streak, he really did love the kids in the Pride and the institution itself.

Jacob H. played the lead role in acquiring the Long Beach homes that became such a great source of summer enjoyment for so many of us. He single-handedly led the fund-raising campaigns each year and made sure that all the Home's budgetary needs were met. He even made sure that fine teachers of music, drama, and dance were available to us, either at the Pride or by visitation of the kids to them. He cared a great deal, and he backed up his interest with a forceful, hands-on style of management.

Though Jacob H. is now just a remote figure from my distant past, I prefer to remember the positive, more contributory aspects of his unique personality. I now am able to appreciate more fully all the good things he did for me and the hundreds of other kids who lived in the Pride. In this regard, he indeed was an important figure in our lives. Since few of us are likely to have said it to him back then, it's more than time to say, "Thank you, Jacob H."

Chapter 18

The Girls Remember the Home

No book about an orphanage like the Pride of Judea Children's Home would be complete unless it contained representation from both genders. Since both co-authors are men and offer the perspective of the male gender, we reached out to some articulate female alumnae who lived in the Home at different times. Their views and perceptions present the important female perspective.

Adele Rosenthal Arcus

I was placed in the Home in 1932 when I was almost six years old. My mother had died right before that, and my father's illness, chronic asthma, required him to live in the more temperate climate of Southern California.

The Pride of Judea was chosen because we were from that neighborhood. My older sister would be able to visit me every Sunday and walk me to our aunts, uncles, and cousins, all of whom lived nearby. Nonetheless, the initial move, from real home to institutional home, was traumatic. At that tender young age, I was all alone in a strange place with unknown people.

My first three days and nights were in the infirmary, under the care of Dr. Demick. She checked me out, as she did all new kids. The process wasn't only physical; she wanted to see the nature of my overall adjustment.

Then I was placed in the Midget Girls group under the supervision of Miss Fiedler. She was a middle-aged lady, very sensitive and very kind. I took to her immediately as a much-needed mother figure. The girls in the group were quite nice too, and since I always made friends easily, it wasn't long before I had made a surprisingly good adjustment to my new home.

During my first several years at the Pride, the dorms were rather large, with many girls in a room. About three years later, partitions were placed strategically so that there were only about six girls to each diminished room. We enjoyed this change because it gave us more privacy and intimacy. Fortunately, the girls in my group were very nice and we got along remarkably well. We progressed through school together and enjoyed good friendships.

Through the years, my supervisors were generally quite nice too. I can't recall any of them ever being unpleasant or harsh. We seem to have liked them all, although since there was a high rate of staff turnover, we were prevented from really getting close to any of them.

One of my favorites was Miss Epstein, whom I had as a Senior Girl. She made me a monitor, which was the first special position I ever had. I was assigned to the Junior Girls, where I had to make sure that they had clean clothes each day, and then I had to help them get ready for school. I also helped serve their food in the dining room and assisted in getting them ready for bed. It was a great experience. Being the younger sister myself, I felt as though they were my little sisters, and I enjoyed taking care of them.

In general, life in the Pride was quite pleasant. I always had my friends around me for positive companionship. There always were things to do which kept us quite busy. We'd play volleyball and other sports. We had dramatics, and I fondly recall my roles in some plays. We had a drama club that met weekly with an outside teacher who was very stimulating. The members would select a new play with the guidance of our teacher. He would recommend several, let us know the specific attractions and challenges of each, and then let us make the final selection. We'd get the scripts, go into rehearsal, and ultimately put the play on for the entire Home, and even invited guests.

This was an important activity for us. Everyone learned how to speak loudly and clearly, which did wonders for our self-confidence. We'd be very nervous beforehand, but afterwards we'd feel great! The Home always had this activity, and it was a valuable experience for virtually everyone who participated.

I also took some piano lessons, but my teachers never stayed too long. They kept changing all the time. I believe this was because they were involved in a Depression-era public works program.

Hopefully it was not because of my piano playing. Unfortunately, my instruction was interrupted so often that I never learned how to play the piano. Some of my peers did, however, much to their great satisfaction.

I enjoyed the Friday night and Saturday morning services in our synagogue. I remember being asked to light the Shabbos candles one Friday night before dinner. That made a big impression on me. I enjoyed the spirituality of it, as well as the kinship of a large family. Being part of a family meant so much to me at the time. I also enjoyed going to Hebrew classes and fully appreciated the Jewish education and experience that I received.

The daily schedule was a full one, and since I felt that each activity had value, I really enjoyed my days. For example, we all had to go to a homework room for one hour daily. That made sense to me, and I made good use of it. There was a good balance between work and play, and the fullness of the day worked well for me. Later, when we went to high school, I liked the degree of freedom that it gave us. We came and went on our own, and if we behaved and were responsible, it was like an unrestricted life. My Pride friends and I particularly enjoyed this feeling because it made us feel equal to the girls on the outside. It minimized our resentment and sensitivity about our status.

The food in the home was generally good and plentiful. Everything was kosher, and we learned about the dietary laws and why things were done that way. We had very nice Seders at Passover, when the food was especially good and well served. I have fond memories of those Seders and of how much I enjoyed them.

The Pride also understood our social needs and had supervised boy-girl activities for the older groups. I remember our weekly dances with the Boys groups, and also less-frequent ones where another orphanage might be invited. For example, we met with the boys from the Hebrew National Orphans' Home in Yonkers on several occasions, and these events generally went well. Not only did they satisfy our normal social needs, but they were the springboard for teaching us the social niceties, such as dancing and how to interact with the opposite sex.

I left the Pride when I graduated high school in June, 1944. All of the older kids left when they reached this point, and it was a good policy. It enabled us to reach closure in our public school careers before moving into the adult phase of our lives. At that time in my life, my father had returned to New York but was still quite ill and required medical care. Initially, I was going to live at the Girls' Club, a place like the Y, where many Pride graduates went if they had no other family place. My wonderful sister, who always looked out for me, persuaded the aunt with whom she lived to make room for me. I finally got to rejoin my family. I already had secured a job at a local hospital, with the help of one of my high school teachers, and so, I was all set.

As I look back at my twelve years in the Home, I firmly believe that I was far better off for having been there than I would have been had I remained with my father. The Pride met all of my needs remarkably well, and my stay there was really a very positive experience. If I had remained with my father in our very small apartment, with not much income to support us, my sister, only a teenager herself at the time, would have had to care for me. It would not have worked too well. and life in all respects would have been quite unhappy. In careful retrospect, I was far better off for having been in the Home. It was a good place for me.

No question, then, but that I am indebted to the Pride. Not only did I have a comfortable existence there, but I formed many great friendships which have continued to this day. I also met my future husband there. Sam Arcus and I started dating when I was in my last year at the Home. Sam, in his early twenties then, was in his first full-time job as Senior Boys supervisor. We even left the Pride at the same time, which, of course, was a great comfort to each of us.

An important part of our courtship was our friendship with Fritz and Edith Lowenthal. They had escaped Nazi Germany, and their first jobs in this country were at the Pride. Fritz was the head cook, and Edith supervised the staff dining room. They became dear friends to us, and I learned a great deal from them. They were at our wedding in 1946, and we were very happy that they lived long enough to know our two children.

Based on what I know of orphanages, the Pride of Judea Children's Home was tops in overall quality. It provided children who badly needed it with a sanctuary that met most of their needs. As compared to foster homes, which often were temporary, or placement with relatives that might provide marginal comfort, the Pride provided a secure, pleasant, strongly developmental Home that met all of our needs quite well. If such a place could be replicated today, which is an interesting possibility, it would be a strong option in the care of orphan, indigent, or even abused children.

The Next Generation: The Forties

Anonymous

I was in the Pride between 1944 and 1951, and while it was not always a happy place for me, it did provide me with a strong foundation that has served me well in life. I think that I've maintained a realistic view of my time there, and these are some of my recollections.

I loved many things about the Pride. High among them was going to Long Beach every summer. It was like going to a great summer camp because I enjoyed everything about it. We put on shows to which we invited the public. It was like a fund-raiser for the Home, but it also showed off our talents. We had fun, but performing also does wonders for your self-confidence, and it helped me a great deal.

Our summer home was like a mansion, and the Pride threw several card parties on its spacious lawn that also were heavy fund-raisers. The Pride had many auxiliary chapters, and their members were a major source of its income. The fun part of these events for us was that we would get paid for helping out. We served as a sort of waitresses, getting soft drinks, light refreshments, or anything else desired by our assigned tables.

The Pride would take us to ballgames, and since I was a good athlete, I followed the sports scene and enjoyed these games. They also took us to the circus and other events. When I had my own children and took them to similar places, I realized how great the Pride was in enriching our lives. There weren't too many places that I took my kids to that I hadn't been to myself.

Then there were the holiday celebrations, where we would receive special clothing to celebrate the respective holiday. The dining room would be filled with boys in shirts and ties, and girls in nice dresses. That made the occasion special for us and elevated the importance of the religious holiday. We also had some great Purim festivals where we acted out the Purim story in play form.

I simply was ecstatic to be *bat mitzvah*, at no less a place than the luxurious St. George Hotel in downtown Brooklyn. We were wined and dined and presented with more presents than I, for one, ever had received. I was only eleven and a half at the time, probably the youngest ever to have a *bat mitzvah* at the Home. They had very few girls that year, and they knew I'd be leaving before the next such event. They also knew how much I enjoyed Hebrew school and what a good student I was. How thankful I am to them for this memorable event which I remember clearly to this day.

There were many things that I didn't like about the Pride. Some of the rules seemed rigid and unfair. When applied by some poor supervisors, they grated on me. Throughout my stay, I often missed having the intimate love of at least one parent-figure to whom I could confide. I also found the discipline to be rather strict.

Two particular incidents at an early age have left an indelible impression on me to this day. The first involved my entire group having to bear the punishment of marching around the summer-house, out in the field, over and over because some children in the group had been reported by our public school as being unruly in going to and from school. Since I was not at fault, I became quite frustrated by the ongoing length of our walk, and I muttered something under my breath, which was overheard by one supervisor. He confronted me and asked what I had said. When I told him, "What do you think we are, horses?", his hand flew up and slapped my face—and hard.

I was astonished, and humiliated! I had never been hit before. I immediately ran up to my dorm, but I was so enraged that I tried to take a large mirror off the wall so that I could hurl it to the floor. Since I was only about eight years old at the time, I'm glad that I didn't have the strength to succeed.

The second incident occurred in Long Beach that same summer. All the kids seemed to have money in their accounts but me. I really felt deprived about it and asked the person behind the table if I could have candy even though my account was down to zero. She said that she'd give me some candy if I got the head supervisor's approval. However, when I looked for him and couldn't find him, I returned to the table and flat-out lied, telling her that I had seen the supervisor and had his full permission.

Little did I know that the person at the desk would check my story out, and how upset the head supervisor would be. Just as I was getting ready for bed, he came into the room, and in front of everyone, he gave me quite a tongue-lashing. I was deeply embarrassed and humiliated.

This incident left a lifelong impression on me, and taught me an important lesson very early on: that before you lie again, think about the consequences, because most of the time, you will be caught and feel worse afterwards! Now, years later, I firmly believe that the supervisor overreacted, and that it would have been better and more attuned to my feelings if he had taken me aside privately, instead of in front of everyone else. It was obvious, however, that he wanted to make a point so that others would not do the same thing.

Well, in one way it worked! My strong conscience overwhelms me at times, and I find it difficult to tell even a small white lie.

The boy-girl relationships at the Pride generally were good. My interest and ability in sports enabled me to have friendly relationships rather than romantic ones. I enjoyed our monthly social dances as well. However, I didn't like the way the boys teased the girls about their developing bodies and about sexual matters. For some reason, this seemed to inhibit me in this important area, which took me a long time to overcome.

I also didn't like the total lack of sex education, which left me quite unprepared for my first menstrual experience. I started hemorrhaging in school and wound up in the Pride infirmary. Instead of being told what was happening to me, I was given vitamins, as if I had an iron deficiency. Given this type of treatment, I don't recall ever having a meaningful discussion on this important matter with anyone.

The food at the Pride was good, for the most part. I had a job helping Abie Nagel in the kitchen, and I enjoyed working there. Abie had a heart of gold and would always give me some extra snacks and food. He was well liked by everyone, and justly so, too.

As far as school went, I believe that I developed a very strong work ethic in my school work because of the Pride. As a result, I always tried to do my best, and this approach worked out quite well for me.

I received an excellent religious education at the Pride. Mr. Jacob Greenberg, a Hebrew teacher who also led Shabbos services, encouraged and inspired me to be the best even after I left the Home. In fact, he arranged for me to receive Barton's chocolates every Jewish holiday, such as Hanukah and Passover, for two years after I left the Home. He kept us entranced by his wisdom and knowledge. He had a fun side as well. He would put on magic shows, and I enjoyed assisting him whenever he called on me. Although he was a large, heavy-set man, whom some kids ridiculed, he left a lasting impression on me.

Another person who made a positive and lasting impression was Harry Koval, even though he was the Boys supervisor. He was so fit and such a good athlete.

My major difficulty was in not understanding or accepting that girls were treated as second-class citizens when it came to sports. I was just glad when no one said that I couldn't play with the boys. I remember being able to outrun some of the boys and wondering why I couldn't be on the track team!

All things considered, the Pride played an important role in my life. I recently was honored by the American Jewish Congress as a Person of the Year. Preparing my acceptance remarks forced me to think about the Pride and its effect on my life. Here is what I said about it:

> Due to various family problems, much of my early childhood was spent in the Pride of Judea Children's Home, an Orthodox orphanage in Brooklyn, New York, where my character was shaped and molded. During my years at the Pride, I developed a strong conscience of what was right and wrong, an enduring set of religious values steeped in the Bible, a desire to help others, and a thirst for learning. All kinds of sports, music, dancing, and crafts were available, and I developed my interests and skills in them. As a result of these many developed interests, I lead a more abundant and enriched life today, blessed with the energy and good health to pursue them.
>
> Although not born with a silver spoon in my mouth, and coming from what many may consider to have been a disadvantaged background, I have felt truly blessed that somehow, through environment or inheritance, there was ingrained in me the tremendous drive and ability to overcome whatever adversities came my way. In other words, despite some difficult times in my childhood, I still was able

to view the glass as half-full, rather than half-empty. Fortunately, along the way, I was surrounded by many individuals of all ages who served either as substitute parents or as good friends. They all helped to reinforce a positive attitude in me and gave me the confidence to always set my sights higher, no matter what my goals were.

The Namesake of Our Alumni Chapter

Our alumni organization, affiliated with the Pride of Judea Mental Health Center, located in Douglaston, Queens, is called the Rose Nadler Schefer Alumni Chapter of the Pride of Judea Children's Home. Our name is in memory of a lovely person who spent fifteen years of her childhood in the Home, and who thought that it was invaluable in shaping her life. A moving tribute to her, written by her daughter, herself a prominent writer and magazine editor, reflects, not only Rose's beauty as a person, but the prominent role that the Pride played in her life.

Tribute to the Memory of Rose Nadler Schefer

Dorothy Schefer

Those who knew Rose Nadler Schefer often heard her say that she came from a small family. Aside from her three sisters and brother, only three childhood friends, with whom she grew up, knew that she was raised in the Pride of Judea Children's Home during its early years as an orphanage for children whose parents had died or could no longer care for their children themselves.

Rose Nadler and her sister Toby entered the Pride in 1924, the year their father, Meyer, died and their mother, Frieda, became too ill to care for her five children. During the rare moments that she spoke about it, which was always to her children, Rose had only the happiest memories of her years in the Pride. She said she never felt deprived. Or unloved. Or that her early life had been unfair.

As she would all her life, Rose not only made the best of things, she turned them to her and others' advantage. She became a woman of strength and determination and purpose. She befriended others, helped them, and encouraged them. She attributes these deeply rooted altruistic values to Dorothy Schwartz Rosenberg, her longtime supervisor during her years at the Pride. To Rose, Dorothy was teacher, mentor, and surrogate mother. When Dorothy died of cancer in 1947, Rose named her first daughter, born a few months later, for her.

Dorothy Rosenberg nurtured, guided, and loved Rose. She encouraged Rose's interest in assuming more responsibility as she grew older, stimulating her to take on the role of big sister to some of the younger children there, and eventually putting her in charge of the young ones.

In 1938, the year before Rose graduated from high school and left the Pride, she discussed her future with Dorothy Rosenberg. More than anything, Rose wanted to become a nurse. Dorothy Rosenberg offered to arrange this and to be there for Rose whenever the need arose. She nominated Rose for a scholarship offered by one of the Pride's benefactors, in memory of his son. Its first recipient was Rose Nadler.

Rose met her great love on a blind date when she was just fifteen and a half. Eli Schefer was a freshman studying engineering at the City College of New York. They married in 1942, after Rose graduated, with honors, from nursing school. Theirs was a love affair that lasted forty-seven years. They were inseparable and totally devoted to each other.

Three children were born to Rose and Eli: Michael, in 1945; Dorothy, in 1947; and Phyllis, in 1948. Rose stayed home to raise her children. When they went off to school, she became president of the PTA. When they were of camp age, she became a camp nurse and took them to camp. Because of her early years in the Pride, she was passionate about family life. Rose fully understood, perhaps more than most, the significance and value of deep and loving attachments.

With their children grown and off to college, Rose resumed her nursing career full-time as a private-duty nurse. She had the very special gift of being able to touch the lives of strangers, who soon became her friends.

Matilda Schefer, Eli's mother, had been active in one of the Pride of Judea's auxiliary chapters. When she died in 1981, Rose, wishing to honor the memory of her mother-in-law and dear friend, renewed her relationship with the Pride of Judea, now a mental health center. In the next four years, as was typical of her, Rose gave fully of herself to this cause. She joined two different auxiliaries and gave her time, energy, and support to their varied fund-raising activities.

Rose always said that her Pride contributions were rewarded in the most unexpected but meaningful ways. It was at a Pride spring luncheon that Rose recognized two of her closest friends from the Home whom she hadn't seen in forty-five years. It was a special and joyous moment for the three, and their friendship quickly was renewed.

Going into the winter of 1983–84, Rose, buoyed by her happy renewal with her old Pride friends, planned on activating the Home's alumni chapter so that many more could share in the excitement of meeting their old Pride brethren again. But it was a dream never to be realized. Rose lost a four-month battle with cancer and passed away in May, 1984. And, as she had lived her life, so she faced her death with the same bravery and courage. She would have been moved to discover how large her extended family had become. Hundreds of her relatives and friends came to the synagogue to wish her farewell.

Ironically, it was not long before another group of Pride alumni, independent of Rose's friends, convened a massive reunion of hundreds of alumni which was a joyous and emotional occasion. An active and energetic alumni chapter was formed, with several hundred members. Its officers were asked to name the chapter in memory of Rose Nadler Schefer. They readily consented and were happy to do so.

Chapter 19

Our Pride Brothers: Then and Now

The children who came into the Home always came in feeling vulnerable and unhappy. They had been uprooted from a setting that was, at least, familiar and set down in a strange environment. Even if they had siblings with them, they generally felt alone because they were separated into their respective age groups. With adult supervisors coming and going at a frequent rate, a major source of social support for each child was his or her peers and friends.

It is no surprise then that as we look back at the Pride of Judea, we think fondly of good friends who by virtue of the close proximity of our lives were more like brothers and sisters. Indeed, as our alumni frequently reminisce about their lives in the Pride, there are many easy references to good friends as brothers and sisters. This chapter will present brief profiles of some Pride brothers who either were good friends or had notable achievements.

Whitey

Phil Craft

As a young boy growing up in the Pride, most of my heroes, like Abraham Lincoln, Knute Rockne, and Lou Gehrig, lived on the pages of the books and newspapers that I read. A special one, Pee-wee Reese, also was scrapbook material for me, in terms of his daily achievements.

But one real live one, Lou "Whitey" Kaplan, was group-mate, teammate, quarterback, and captain of our own varsity football team. I can't recall now how or when he became our captain. But whether this title was official or honorary, there never was any doubt that Whitey was not just our team leader, he was the inspirational force who truly energized our collective efforts. In any crisis or tight spot, he was the guy we looked to, and he rarely let us down.

Long before we got helmets, the sight of his blond hair blowing wild in a stiff wind was like a banner or battle-flag to rally around, to lift our spirits and spur each of us to play as hard as we could. We usually fielded a smaller team, in size and in numbers, than our opponents, and we always faced an uphill struggle in our games. Time after time, when we were down, battling near our own goal line, Whitey would come up with a spectacular play to turn the tide our way and to infuse fresh confidence and zip into our tired hearts and bodies.

We all played both defense and offense, and he was a standout at both. Sometimes our opponents, recognizing the impact of his great play and leadership, would call out derisively, "Hey Blondie, we're going to get you!" They were only wasting their breath, as their taunts fell on deaf ears. He just seemed to play even better.

Nobody was more dedicated, or worked harder than Whitey to help us win. Many of us, inspired by his example, tried to match his courage and endurance by playing on, despite painful blows and bleeding wounds. Overmatched and underequipped, we usually took a pounding but came back for more. It was Whitey's belief in himself and in us that enabled our team to often come back against more formidable adversaries, and then prevail.

With Whitey leading us, we were defeated occasionally, but we rarely were beaten. We became known for our never-say-die spirit, and would go down fighting, if we went down at all.

Whitey's daring play selection often kept our opponents off balance, enabling us to gain vital yardage. He was a talented ball-carrier, a good passer, a superb blocker, and a determined tackler. But most of all, he kept us playing together, helping one other out and rooting for one other. He literally was our Jack Armstrong, all-American boy!

When Whitey left the Pride in 1944, much of the joy and spirit of our team seemed to depart with him. A mournful lethargy seemed to descend upon us which made our own football efforts less crisp, less precise, and less consistent. They lacked the special spark that heretofore we had taken for granted.

Then one afternoon Whitey returned for a visit, and for old times' sake ran us through our old plays during a practice session.

The effect was electrifying! Suddenly, our plays were executed with new purpose and precision; with crunching blocks that were made, not missed; with passes that were caught, and with a ball that was carried through a gauntlet of would-be tacklers, and not fumbled. For me, it was like a mystical experience which, fifty years later, still hovers with great clarity. On that special day, I knew, without confusion or doubt, why Whitey was one of my genuine heroes.

In his after-Pride life, Whitey Kaplan maintained his level of excellence. Always a strong student, he graduated from the City College of New York with a B.S. degree. He then pursued a master's degree in bacteriology at the University of Kansas, obtaining it in 1950. Next, he went to work at the prestigious Sloan-Kettering Institute as a cancer researcher, rising to the level of senior researcher during his thirteen years there. During this time, he attended Cornell University, which was affiliated with Sloan-Kettering, earning his Ph.D. degree in microbiology in 1957.

In 1965, Dr. Kaplan went to work for Merck Labs, where, for the next twenty-eight years, he did important pharmaceutical research, helping to develop many drugs "found in nature" for human and animal use. By the time of his retirement from Merck in 1993, he had risen to the important position of director of microbial physiology and fermentation development, and had gained an international reputation in his field. He had been elected a fellow of the Society of Industrial Microbiology, and chairperson of the Fermentation Technology Division of the American Society for Microbiology.

Just as importantly, Lou has had a long and happy marriage. He and wife, Fran, are the parents of three fine children, who, in turn, have made them happy grandparents. Today, Lou Kaplan, retired but busy with many pursuits, is on the executive board of the Pride's alumni organization, and is a mainstay of our regular yearly events.

Whitey Kaplan lived in the Pride for over eight years, between the formative ages of eight and sixteen. What impact did the Home have on him and what role did it play in his life? Here are the answers, in his own words:

> Without a doubt, if I had not been in the Pride during my early years, I am certain, at least from an educational point of view, I would not have attained the educational goals that I eventually reached, and the

subsequent career success that I was to achieve. Why do I say that? None of my siblings ever went beyond grade school; they had to go to work during the depression era of the thirties. If I had remained at home, after my mother's death, I too would have been thrust into the job market. Unfortunately, education was not a priority in my family. However, at the Pride, I must have shown some ability in school because I was encouraged to pursue my education as far up the ladder as possible.

The two persons who influenced me greatly in this area were Sam Arcus and Mrs. Asya Kadis. The former was my intelligent, sensitive, and caring supervisor at the Pride, and the latter was my psychotherapist, who assisted me immensely in overcoming my speech impediment to a great extent, and also helped me to surmount many other personal problems. All of this wouldn't have happened if I hadn't been in the Home during those years.

It is clear to me as well that my stay in the Pride also prepared me for the challenges of marriage and family. By that, I mean that I knew that I'd have a wife and children and that I'd be darn sure that they wouldn't lack for anything. I was more determined than ever to be successful and to instill in my children the importance of being "menschen," of caring for others less fortunate, of pursuing their own educational goals, and of doing the best in whatever endeavors they undertook. I am happy to say that all of these expectations have come to fruition.

The sports programs at the Pride helped me considerably by sharpening my competitive edge. I was fortunate enough to have athletic abilities in team sports, and the ability to excel and be a team leader probably had a lot to do with my future growth and success. It also taught me that cooperation and good team play are the surest ways to get things done effectively. Had I not been in the Pride, I doubt that my future would have been the same, or nearly as good as it was!

Sykes

Phil Craft

Sykes's real name was Bernie Friedland, but the only one who ever called him that in his latter years in the Home was his kid brother, Peewee Friedland. Tall, rangy, straightforward, and a very good athlete, Sykes was a popular person whose friendship was eagerly sought and sincerely valued. His social poise and rugged good looks, combined with his innate good nature and concern for others, made his widespread popularity among his peers, both male and female, readily understandable. If the term "regular guy" had not already been invented, it specially would have been created to describe him.

I first met Sykes in the Junior Boys group when we both were nearly twelve years old. He easily bonded with everyone despite his recent horrendous experience in an abusive foster home. His upbeat attitude and solicitous concern for his kid brother immediately struck a deep and responsive chord in me, since I craved but never had received such brotherly affection. Indeed, it was mainly their vivid accounts of their ordeal in the foster home that caused me to change my initial hesitancy about being adopted into outright opposition to adoption, effectively ending that one possible opportunity, and reshaping the course of my life to my ultimate benefit. A life without Charlie Vladimer and Sam Arcus, and so many others who made incalculable contributions to my own development and happiness, is too frightening to even contemplate.

One important relationship that Sykes and I shared together was our close, positive rapport with Lou Feigelson, our treasured supervisor, who had reached out to each of us in sympathy and friendship, well beyond the boundaries of his official duties. On some Saturday afternoons, when our peers would be going to the movies, Mr. F. drove the two of us, in his own car, all over the city, ending up each time at his mother's house in Queens, where we were received with warmth and friendliness. We enjoyed these outings very much and were delighted to follow him when he was reassigned to the older Intermediate Boys group, so that we could sustain what had become an important relationship for both of us.

During this period of our lives, football became very important to us because we now were old enough to join the Home's regular teams, complete with uniforms, game schedules, regular practice sessions, and coaches. Sykes caught on quickly as an end and occasional running back because of his tall reach, sure hands, the ability to get open for passes, and his good blocking and tackling skills. He quickly became one of our premier players. Although, we often were hard-pressed to win our share of games.

When we were about fourteen, we graduated together from P.S. 202 and were assigned to the same high school, the East New York Vocational High School Annex, which was nearby. With his greater maturity, self-confidence, and considerable talent in the manual arts, he managed the transition more easily than I. In fact, it was because of his talent that he earned his nickname, Sykes. In a boat-building class, Bernie built a beautiful model of a three-masted schooner. When he brought it to the Pride, he still had not named it. For some reason that no one can recall, his close friends named it The Sykes, and soon everyone was calling him by that name.

I was delighted to have Sykes as my schoolmate! Even as his presence and influence had provided a measure of security and comfort for his kid brother in the Home, they now provided shelter and protection for me in this new and unfamiliar setting. I already knew I was fortunate to have had his friendship in the Home, but I valued it even more in high school! His good companionship and assistance helped me greatly at that time of my life.

After two semesters, our exploratory program of courses ended and we parted school ways. I was off to the School of Printing, in Manhattan. Sykes would be going to the main building, where he made the varsity basketball team that won the city vocational high school championship that year, with the final game played at Madison Square Garden.

Life at the Pride during the years of World War II was marked by instability, frequent change, and great stress. Older friends continually were leaving to join the service; male supervisors were in short supply and the staff changed often. The Senior Boys were recruited to fill in as supervisors, and often as not, did not do too good a job. In all of this uncertainty and turmoil, one consistent item stood out: Sykes's little radio.

Every evening, this small but valuable possession provided a precious measure of comfort, enjoyment, and predictability to our daily lives, earning its special place of importance on the chair beside his bed. It was our dependable entertainment center, presenting prime-time programs that became regular favorites of ours. Jack Benny, Eddie Cantor, Bob Hope, and Fred Allen visited us weekly through the medium of that radio. Though Sykes owned it, we all reaped its ample rewards, and the radio enjoyed special immunity and protection from our frequent horseplay in the dorms. Not even the Norden bombsight drew more caution and care. That chair and that radio were off-limits, and they never took a hit.

Since the radio was his, Sykes could have turned on any station he chose. But, reflective of his social-mindedness, he always reached out for consensus in selecting the program. Only when a disagreement arose that threatened to become a heated dispute did he become the final arbiter of program selection. Invariably, that settled the matter, because his roommates knew him to be fair-minded. The only requirement he had was for the last person up to turn off the radio before going to sleep. That special chore most often fell to me. My inordinate slowness with my homework, my work on the Pride newspaper, and my long letters to Corporal Charlie Vladimer often kept me up later than everyone else. I was more than happy to do this task and to preserve that valuable little beacon.

With the lights off, the little radio didn't just connect us to the outside world; its gentle glow lighted the path between each bed and the bathroom. It had become an institution within our institution.

When Sykes graduated from high school, he did not leave the Pride right away because he had been drafted into the Navy and would be going in a matter of months. He found employment and paid room-and-board expenses to the Pride for the interim period. Once more, our paths paralleled, because in March of 1946, we both went to the same induction center, where we parted, he to the Navy and me to the Army. I would not see him again until we both had returned to civilian life and learned that our jobs were near each other. We then met for lunch periodically—joyous occasions for me because I continued to regard him so highly.

When Sykes came out of the Navy, he returned to his previous position, but then decided to put his strong craftsman skills to fuller use. He apprenticed as a sheet-metalist at the Brooklyn Navy Yard, scoring among the highest of those taking the three-state qualifying test. He quickly rose to the rank of journeyman and then, after he married and started a family, took a better position in private industry as a sign-making sheet-metalist.

Here, his popularity, competence, and strong social skills brought him to the attention of his union leaders, and he was appointed by the executive board to replace a retiring union official who was in charge of pensions and health benefits. Working many years in this post, he not only earned a bachelor's degree in labor management, he also took his union's pension plan from a precarious, deficit status and helped make it into a healthy and attractive plan that other unions sought to emulate. His retirement dinner was crowded with people getting up to express their thanks and gratitude to Bernie Friedland for his singularly fine work on their behalf.

On the personal side, Bernie and Lil, his lovely wife of forty-seven years, have three grown and married children who have given them five wonderful grandchildren. He is an active member of the Pride's alumni chapter.

Through all the years that I've known and cherished my friendship with Sykes, there always was one thing that puzzled me. When he and his brother Peewee came to the Pride, they arrived as survivors from an abusive foster home experience. Others surely would have been damaged, suspicious, and embittered. Yet in all of my experiences with them, they seemed confident, competent, good-natured, and concerned for others. As years and even decades passed, this became even more evident and pronounced in their successful, happy lives, brightened by that same care and sensitivity for others which each had shown in the Home.

Where, I wondered, had the Friedland brothers drawn the strength, resolve, self-assurance, and empathy for others, even at such an early age, that I, and others like me, always had to struggle to gain? As Stan and I prepared the chapters for this book, the answer finally became perfectly clear. Each had been drawing these resources from a remarkable lady who, although imprisoned by the chains and pains of multiple sclerosis, had lived with a fertile intelligence and an unconquerable spirit, accompanied by boundless love for her children and a good heart for people. Their own goodness and their many achievements are an eloquent and continuing tribute to that wonderful lady, their mother. I wish that I had been privileged to know her.

What impact did the Home have on Sykes Friedland, and what role did it play in his life? Here are his answers.

> I always looked at the Pride as being a very positive time in my life. I had just come from a very bad situation, and the Pride really provided a much better environment in all respects. We had and did many things that other kids with parents, living around us, could not do. The Home certainly gave me a strong sense of self-reliance, namely,

that you had to do things for yourself because they wouldn't be done for you! That principle has guided my entire life, and it's been quite beneficial. The Pride played an important role in my life, and I'm happy to say that it was a good one!

Sloopy

Phil Craft

During my time as a Senior Boy, one of my closest friends was Morrie Sloop. In a geographical sense, there was no one closer, since my bed was located at the dorm entrance, and his was right next to mine. We always were the first ones to receive the wake-up call of our supervisor, Judge Arcus, when he came in each morning. As a light sleeper who always heard the wake-up bell, I invariably escaped the dubious honor of being dumped, mattress and all, onto the floor. This was the fate of those less fortunate bodies that remained supine and inert under the covers as the Judge made his early morning rounds.

"Sloopy," as Morrie was universally and affectionately known, was one of the Judge's favorite targets. In fact, the Judge had a unique fondness for him, drawn, like most of us, to his unfailing good nature, high spirits, and singular lack of pretense. Sloopy had what some might call an innocent, childlike faith in the fundamental goodness of people, a belief which reflected his own sincerity and his genuine concern for his friends. In a Hollywood film, he would be cast as the loyal, caring, supportive buddy.

Sloopy shared with me an intense interest in and enduring love for anything connected to football, whether in the Pride or on the outside. It was a constant topic of good-natured banter and serious conversation between us. We'd constantly talk about our own Pride team, on which we both played, or of an upcoming Notre Dame game, or any other timely football news.

The two of us were passionate, loyal members of that large, though unorganized fraternity called the Notre Dame Subway Alumni, which meant that we loved the Notre Dame football team with a blind passion. We pored eagerly over newspapers, sports magazines, and even borrowed or bought books, for anything, important or trivial, about the Fighting Irish. Names like Knute Rockne, George Gipp, and the Four Horsemen were enshrined reverentially in our own list of football greats, while more contemporary heroes, like Coach Frank Leahy, Johnny Lujack, and Angelo Bertelli, became living objects of devoted admiration and emulation.

Morrie and I enjoyed many wonderful afternoons roaming the deserted playing field at the Pride, passing and catching a football. During the football season, this activity was almost a ritual with us, and we both looked forward to it daily.

When he wasn't used as a reserve fullback on the Pride's football team, Morrie played right guard, next to my position, which was right tackle. We alternately blocked on offense or tackled on defense as a coordinated unit. It was like a game within a game. Our backs ran many plays through our positions, confident that our synchronized blocking would open the necessary holes for big gains. On defense, we often shared tackles, since we both were small and depended on each other. To cope with the inevitable pre-game jitters, we spontaneously developed a secret ritual; we slowly and alternately would pop each other's fingers with a gentle pull, listening intently for that magic sound each time. Then we would wait expectantly for the opening kick-off, more confident that we could handle anything that came our way.

Those moments of closeness were valued and treasured by the two of us. We developed a strong camaraderie which, since then, has bridged the obstacles of distance and time, thriving today as a warm and lasting friendship. Even as I write these words, Sloopy's smiling face looms near, looking as it did in the early 1940s, and also as I remember him when I last saw him, several years ago.

Morrie left the Home before he graduated from Boys' High School in Brooklyn. After graduation he took a job with his uncle, in a metal-spinning plant. Not liking it, he took a sales job and immediately discovered his life's work. He was ultimately in sales in the cosmetics industry for the next twenty-eight years, working for leading companies such as Max Factor, Cody, and Chanel. He won frequent awards, such as Top Salesman In the Company and Top Ten in the Country.

On the personal side, Morrie married a lovely woman, raised two fine children, is now a proud grandparent, and lives happily in semi-retirement in Florida. Prior to that, he and his wife, Ina, played an active role in the growth of our alumni organization.

Serving briefly as its president, he made many valuable contributions. As for the role of the Pride in his life, Morrie had this to say:

> I very much appreciate what the Pride did for me. First, it enabled me
> to remain together with my older brother and sister. Next, it taught
> me to be competitive, to hold my own, which especially came in
> handy in my sales career. Also helping my career was my ability to
> handle and even enjoy a fast-paced life, which I learned how to do in
> the Home.

Our War Hero

Stan Friedland

Marvin Koppelman was the most heavily decorated Jewish soldier
of the Korean War. What he did in the military was typical of what
he used to do in the Home. Marvin was my friend and roommate,
and I smile when I think of him.

He was outgoing, personable, and not too comfortable with
authority. Though intelligent, he didn't care too much for the routine of school and was not a serious student. But he was an excellent athlete, and our games with him were spirited and enjoyable.
Even in the midst of a hotly contested game, his good nature would
keep all of us, even the overly intense, on an even keel, so that we
all had a good time. Everyone liked Marv.

After high school, he left the Pride, and, after working for a
while, joined the service. We all lost contact with him . . . until we
picked up a newspaper one morning, and there was his face staring
back at us!

The Korean War was in a critical stage and Marvin had just
earned his second Silver Star for gallantry in action. For the first
one, he single-handedly had knocked out two enemy roadblocks
with a bazooka during the Taejon withdrawal. The second medal
had much more of a story to it than appeared in the papers.

When his unit was about to be overrun during an enemy
attack, Corporal Koppelman again took a bazooka to a nearby hill
and held off the advancing enemy until his unit could pull out.
While doing so, he was knocked unconscious by an exploding
mortar shell. When he came to, he was being removed by ambulance to a safe area. Once there, he asked about his men, and when

he learned that some were wounded and still on the battlefield, he asked the driver to return and pick them up. When the driver refused, Marvin pushed him aside, jumped in the ambulance, and returned to pick up his wounded buddies, driving them to safety through considerable fire.

Marvin's superiors were thinking seriously of disciplining him, but his men leaked the story to the press and he was awarded a well-deserved second Silver Star.

After the war, Marvin worked in the business world, married, and had three daughters. When his first wife died of cancer, he remarried and helped to raise two families. He subsequently passed away while only in his fifties.

Professor, If You Please

Stan Friedland

The entry on Professor Roy Lachman in Who's Who in Southwestern Universities says, in part: "He has written extensively in journals, books and publications, and is recognized as a leading authority in the field of artificial intelligence. He has been a professor at many universities, and currently is a full professor of Psychology at the University of Houston."

Roy Lachman is an alumnus of the Pride of Judea Children's Home. Roy was in the Pride for six years, between 1938 and 1944. He is remembered as a fun-loving, good-natured individual with an active sense of humor. But the most interesting account of the impact of the Pride on Roy's life comes from Roy himself.

I've had a lot of good fortune in my life, because the road has not always been smooth, especially in the early years. One major piece of good luck was having Sam Arcus for a supervisor in the Home.

Sam and the other supervisors worked horrendous hours. Despite that handicap, Sam attended CCNY several nights during the week. He continually communicated to us enormous enthusiasm for knowledge and learning. He'd come back from school and often convey his wonderment at the material he just had covered in class, with great delight. He shared many of his college experiences with us, everything from dissecting a fetal pig in biology to his class debates in political science.

Needless to say, this made a profound impression upon me and on my cohorts, as well. I remember a boy, one year older than me, saying that he was going to emulate Arcus and also work his way through CCNY. Sad to say, this did not come to pass, as he was killed when his plane was shot down in World War II combat.

Nor was that the end of Sam's contribution to my life. I left the Home shortly after my sixteenth birthday, and I certainly was not ready for the outside world. Coming initially from a dysfunctional family background, and with no family support to count on, I faced my future with considerable uncertainty. Sensing this, Sam Arcus continued to offer invaluable guidance. He showed me how to look for a furnished room in the New York Times classified ads, what questions to ask, how to find a job, and various other things indispensable for one's survival. Throughout that period, Sam and his new bride, Adele, were enormously supportive, providing me with wise guidance (even when it went unheeded), and always showing me great kindness.

I then began a number of years in the service, first in the Merchant Marine and then in the Army. After my discharge, some eight years later, I took full advantage of the G.I. Bill and resumed my education in earnest. I did indeed "follow Sam" by attending and graduating from CCNY with honors, and ultimately earning a Ph.D. from New York University in experimental psychology. I have been teaching and researching at the university level ever since.

The good luck in my life includes my marriage to a lovely woman and the presence of a wonderful daughter. Indeed, my background enables me to appreciate them that much more.

The Pride certainly played an important role in my life. These were our formative, years and consequently the Pride has to be the cornerstone of our personalities, styles, and whatever else we are. However, the Pride was not particularly effective in preparing us for the outside world. On departure, most of us lacked the practical skills that are needed to make one's way successfully. Fortunately for me, I had an "angel" in my corner.

Comic Relief

Stan Friedland

Allen Schwartz is a person I like to remember from my years in the Pride. Though several years my junior, he had that great ability to make people laugh. Since I tended to be on the intense, serious side, his good humor and affability were most appealing.

He also had another quality that I enjoyed. He needed protection . . . though not really. He was very skinny, and I used to call him, "Kid Candle, one blow and you're out!" Regarding him like a kid brother, I took him under my wing and made sure that no one picked on him. However, he had pretty much the same positive effect on others, so that he really didn't need much of my protection, even though I enjoyed providing it.

Allen had several other things going for him that endeared him to others. He was a good athlete in all areas. A starting guard on the Pride basketball team, he often was the high scorer. He was a sneaky good hitter in softball and punchball, and did things you wouldn't expect from such a runt. He was also a talented entertainer, and he loved to sing and perform before an audience.

Quite often, when meals weren't ready on time, our resourceful supervisors, Harry Koval and Charlie Vladimer, would have Allen and others put on a brief performance in the dining room, and they were good enough to distract the children from their growing hunger. To the Pride's great credit, it recognized the value of the dramatic arts in the total development of a child. Allen, and others of like aptitude, received lessons, both in and out of the Home, in singing, drama, and even tap dancing.

Another thing that endeared Allen to me was his love and concern for his younger sister and brother. Their mother had deserted the family early on, and despite his good intentions, their father, who had to earn a living, placed them in separate foster homes. Eventually they were reunited at the Pride, where Allen enjoyed his kinship with them between 1945 and 1950, when he left. His father remained a loving and attentive parent, visiting regularly and remembered by everyone as being a fine guy.

After leaving the Pride, Allen went to work with his father, who had his own window-washing business. Following him to Detroit, Allen kept the business going when his father passed away. Today, in the Detroit area, Allen is a mini-celebrity, and is known as the "Singing Window-Washer and Comic Too." Not only does he do comedy and singing performances at functions and for his customers, but he also contributes comedy material to newspapers and radio stations.

He was for me, my Pride peers, and people who know him today a valuable source of pleasure and laughter. He was a good kid brother in the Home.

Manny

Stan Friedland

I really didn't know Emanuel Fineberg in the Home because he is six or so years younger than I, but we may have had some overlap. He remembers me for having kicked him off the basketball court one time so that my cronies and I could have the court. But Manny is my Pride brother because of his strong work in helping to reunite the alumni and in forging a strong alumni chapter.

Manny was in the Pride between 1947 and 1953. The Home would only be in existence for six more years as an orphanage, and he gives us a view of it in its final era.

Manny did not like a number of things about the Pride. He was unhappy with the practice of using the older boys as enforcers even though they lacked sufficient training and supervision. He didn't always feel accepted as part of the group and found some supervisors indifferent or insensitive. He also felt that the Pride was weak in preparing kids for life on the outside, observing that his own career preparation took place long after he had departed.

But there were many plus factors too. Manny received an excellent religious education, often assisting with the Shabbos services. He became a skilled clarinetist, thanks to extensive music lessons at the Pride, which enabled him to earn admission to the High School of Music and Arts, then one of the most prestigious high schools in New York City. At that time, Julius Nierow was the executive director of the Pride, and his son Peter was a talented pianist. Peter convinced Manny to audition for Music and Arts, and he did so well that he was accepted. He spent four strong years there, which he always has valued. His friend Peter, who attended Music and Art with him, went on to a fine career as a pianist, performing under the name Peter Nero.

Manny attended CCNY and became a varsity fencer, winning championships in that activity. He credits the Pride for helping him to develop his athletic skills. He earned a Ph.D. in psychology from Fordham University, and worked as a school psychologist for many years in the New York City schools. Manny still is a practicing clinical psychologist, and credits the Pride for "making me interested in helping children to save them from the vagaries of their lives."

Manny is married and a grandfather. His son is a professional woodwind musician. He has been, and continues to be, a strong leadership force in the Rose Nadler Schefer Alumni Chapter of the Pride of Judea.

Chapter 20

High School and Beyond

Stan Friedland

My Story

The Home had a system for evaluating the scholastic ability of its children and then sending them off to the high school that best matched their talents and interests. The idea, of course, was to make the match that would best help each child prepare for a future of economic self-sufficiency. If a child's elementary school academic record was either satisfactory, average, or lower, the high school placement generally would be in a technical or vocational high school, so that a trade could be learned, reflective of the child's aptitudes and interests. If the elementary school record was strong or superior, then an academic high school, with the intent of going to college afterwards, would be the pathway chosen. While the Pride's advisers had the dominant role, the families, and to some extent the children themselves, were involved in the decision.

For me, there was no doubt. My mother had her heart set on my going to college, and that was fine with me. Not only had I done well in elementary school in academic areas, but I had no interest or talent in any trade or technical area. I was enrolled in Thomas Jefferson High School in an academic curriculum.

"Jeff," as we called it, was a good school then, though large, as were most city high schools. While I had been a big fish in a little pond at P.S. 202, it was the reverse for me at Jeff. However, I enjoyed the challenges and was up to the tasks of doing well. In my sophomore year, I was placed in the honors classes in English and social studies, and in Regents-track classes in the other three academic areas. Again, that was fine with me. It meant, in my estimation, the best teachers, and it made my mother quite happy. Indeed, the teachers were good. They brought their subjects to life and minimized the boredom that comes along when the novelty of school wears off and routine begins to prolong the movement of the clock.

I was acutely aware of two things which differentiated me from my classmates in high school. Whereas in P.S. 202 there had been Pride kids all over the place, I was now relatively alone, with no kids from the Home in any of my classes, and not too many in the entire school. I became more sensitive to the fact that I lived in an orphans' home, and while I wasn't ashamed of my status, I certainly did not wear it on my sleeve. Consequently, I rarely reached out to make closer friendships with any of my classmates, even though they were quite nice. I was sociable enough, but only in the context of school activities.

Secondly, I brought up the rear in my honors classes. While I had a respectable 87-plus average in high school, it lagged far behind the mid-nineties of my honors classmates. I didn't mind this too much. Since I was happy to be quiet in class, I was content to let the real brainy kids monopolize the various discussions that took place. Fortunately, I did well in the big tests, especially the Regents exams, which counted for 20 percent of the final grade.

I vividly remember my eleventh-grade American history teacher as he read out the American history Regents test scores from the week before. When he came to my name in the alphabetical sequence, he sort of paused and looked out at me and smiled. "Ninety-four, the second-highest mark in the class!" I thought he was kidding and looked up at him skeptically as if I might be the butt of some joke. "Oh yes!" he exclaimed. "You did a great job!" And I beamed. It would be my highest Regents grade ever. My mother would be delighted as well.

An unexpected incident occurred during the early part of my junior year which shaped my college career. My mother thought that it would be wise for me to learn how to type in preparation for college, and so I selected a typing course for my eleventh-year program. Before the school year began, the Pride played in a Long Beach softball league, and I was playing my usual position at first base. Our shortstop, Bernie Pearl, had an arm like a rocket, but often didn't know where first base was. Sure enough, in a late inning play, with the score tied, he threw the ball way off to my left side. As a leftie, I could only attempt to block it with my bare left hand, which is what I did. Crack! Not one, but two fingers went up in smoke!

The upshot: no typing for me that year. Instead, my advisor suggested bookkeeping, for the credit value, and without much thought, I consented. Well, it turned out that I not only liked the course but got a 98 in it. My mother knew what to make of this. "It's quite clear," she said. "You've got a good head for figures, and accounting is the profession for you. Accountants earn a good salary, and there are many opportunities in the field. It's ideal." When my mother talks, I listen. Okay, it will be accounting for me as my college major.

My yearbook caption is worth noting. It read:

Here's a guy swell and gay,
Going to City College to study CPA.
Ambition: Businessman

I'd have had a heart attack if that was my caption today! How the times have changed!

During my sophomore and junior years in high school, several things happened in the Home that were significant to me. First, my brother enlisted in the Navy in 1946, which meant that we would be separated for the first time in our lives. While I didn't really need Bernie to look after me, his presence was always greatly reassuring. We were close; we had an active relationship, and it was nice to be able to see him every day. It was a first for me when he left, and while I missed him, I was old enough by then to not need him for my general well-being. That was a plus for pushing my self-reliance and independence one notch higher.

The second occurrence was my taking a surprisingly valuable drama course at the Pride. A drama teacher had been brought in to give several sessions in drama to the Senior Boys and Senior Girls, but separately.

Some sage person knew that we'd be too distracted if the classes were coed, and so they were held apart. The teacher was good and made us emote, not from any script, but from any situation that he, or we, would choose. The value for me was that I discovered that I had a tongue, and a good one! Quiet and shy throughout high school, I only spoke when I had to and raised my hand only occasionally.

The three drama sessions really turned me on to the value of self-expression. No, I was not stage-struck. For those of us who responded to the teacher, the stimulus opened us up like proverbial clams. I was much better after that in being able to speak up in class, or before a group, without feeling deathly nervous. It was an important experience.

One of the major bright spots in my unhappy senior year in high school was the open door that the Pride had left for me on weekends. I and the other sixteen-year-olds had departed after the new executive director changed a long-standing policy and made sixteen the ceiling age for Pride residents. However, the director took Saturday afternoons off, leaving the place under the very able care of Harry Koval.

Harry, who had been my favorite supervisor, had not known that we sixteen-year-olds were to be gone until after it had happened. Word filtered back to me in my foster home in Sheepshead Bay that Harry wanted to see me on any Saturday afternoon. When I returned to the Home on the very next Saturday, Harry apologized profusely, stating that he had known nothing about it, and then inviting all of us to come any Saturday afternoon to play ball and use the facilities.

It was a grand gesture from a grand guy, and we were happy to oblige. Arriving after lunch, we'd play full-court basketball until our tongues hung out. Then we'd retire to the kitchen, where our good friend Abie Nagel, who was working there, gave us as much ice cold milk and cookies as we wanted. My brother, Bernie, would be there most of the time, which made it even better. He had been discharged from the Navy earlier that year and now was living with my Aunt Yettie. I would go with him to her place afterwards for an enjoyable dinner before returning to my foster home.

What the Saturday visits represented was that the Pride really hadn't let me down! Harry Koval, to me, was more representative of the Home than a new, unknown person who just happened to have been appointed executive director! Harry's explanation of his own ignorance of the matter and his opening of the Pride to us for those enjoyable Saturday afternoons did much to restore my faith in the overall goodness of the Home. It had been a good home for me for seven important years, and this was a much better way to take my leave of it than my sudden departure just months before.

The year 1948 was an important one for me. I graduated high school, began college, and rejoined my brother by moving into my aunt's house. My mother's older sister, Yettie, was married to Sam Freiberg, and they lived in a large apartment in the nearby Crown Heights section of Brooklyn. Living with them were my mother's younger sister, Tillie, and her younger brother, Nate. None of them eked out more than a meager living, which is why they lived together. While collectively they always had been interested in, and responsive to, my brother and me, they had never been able to afford to take us out of the Home and care for us.

It was good timing for Bernie that when he was discharged from the Navy in 1947, Uncle Nate was finally getting married, which opened up his room for Bernie at our good Aunt Yettie's place. He had to pay room and board, of course, which he did by going to work for Bernard Scharf, the benefactor who had donated the two Long Beach homes to the Pride. There was no room for me at Yettie's until 1948, when Tillie also got married, quite late in life. I then moved into her empty room, with my room and board being paid for partially by the Jewish Board of Social Services, and partially by working part-time.

I was delighted! I didn't like my foster home, although it was through little fault of the couple and more to do with my abrupt departure from the Pride and my strong distaste for any foster home placement. But most importantly, I was going to be reunited with my brother again and also with Aunt Yettie, who, childless, had always treated us like her own children.

It was a big deal to me. I had been only five years old when my mother had been forced to place us in our first orphanage. I had really never experienced a normal home environment with my own family, at least nothing that I could remember clearly.

Furthermore, aside from my devoted love for my mother, I loved and enjoyed Aunt Yettie. She was a great cook and homemaker and always had treated us as well as her meager resources would permit. Her husband, Uncle Sam, drove a bus or a cab throughout his career, with a barely adequate income to show for it. An old-fashioned guy, he never would hear of Aunt Yettie's working, and so, even with no children, she remained a homemaker. Unfortunately, Sam was a smoker and somewhat tense, both of which contributed to his erratic health.

Although I was tickled pink to be moving into a place that I could really think of as "my home," there was a substantial dark cloud in my life that would take its inevitable toll. My mother had developed a diabetic condition, which, when added to the ravages of multiple sclerosis, was weakening her rapidly. Once again, she would put on a brave face so as not to worry us. Never a complaint from this courageous woman as she headed into the final year of her life.

In order to pay my expenses, I enrolled in the afternoon-evening session of CCNY's Baruch School of Business, which was on Twenty-third Street in Manhattan. I got a part-time job in the garment industry for as many hours as I wanted per week, and my college career in accounting had begun.

I lasted one year at CCNY. I found everything related to accounting to be supremely boring and uninteresting. Although I persevered in my classes and passed everything, my grades were only average. The final stimulus, however, was the death of my mother.

When I finished the second semester, I thought that I would come back in the fall and see if my new courses generated more enthusiasm and interest. I took a job as a busboy-waiter at a Catskill Mountains hotel because I could earn good money. I wasn't too happy with my mom's condition, though. She was deteriorating visibly, and when I told her that perhaps I shouldn't go away to work, she wouldn't hear of it. Bernie would be around. With that as some form of assurance, away I went.

My mother passed away on July 12, 1949, at the age of forty-nine. She had been confined to a wheelchair in an institution for her last thirteen years. Yet she had been a pillar of strength to me and had provided support and inspiration just as if she had been with me daily. And she had been. Her death hit me quite hard. I can remember as if it were yesterday how my knees shook when the rabbi asked me to shovel earth onto my mother's lowered casket, which is part of the Jewish burial service. The sound of the earth falling on her coffin went through me like a shot from a gun, and I thought that I would fall over. My philosophy about death evolved from that painful experience. I was determined not to let her go. She would live within me and I would be guided by what she represented and stood for.

I didn't go back to CCNY. Whereas my mother might have been disappointed by my dropping accounting as a college major and career goal, now it didn't matter. My definite dislike and disinterest spurred me to look for another career pathway. I discussed the situation with a friend who was about ten years my senior and whom I respected very much. He asked me what I liked to do the most. Without hesitation, I said, "Sports; I like to play ball." He said, "Have you thought of physical education? You can become a gym teacher and coach, and make sports your career."

The idea set off bells in my mind. I did some research on the topic and found I liked it even better. Rather than go to the uptown campus of CCNY, I decided to transfer to Brooklyn College. It was a significant and productive move. Not only did I enjoy every minute of the new curriculum and school, but it also heralded my entry into the wonderful field of education, which would become my life's career. To add rich topping to the cake, I met my future wife, the second great lady in my life!

I came into Brooklyn College as a sophomore and took mainly the required liberal arts subjects that were prerequisite to the major core. What a great school it was! Only four large buildings, an airy, attractive campus, and some very good teachers. I was enjoying myself.

My junior year revolved mainly around classes in my major field of physical education, and I was looking forward to this program. One fall course was in first aid, and the teacher used an old-fashioned Delaney book to seat his students alphabetically. I found myself seated next to an attractive girl by the name of Frances Friedman. We laughed about the similarity of names and then went about our normal business, with little social interest on my part because I was dating another girl at the time.

One day we had to tape each other's ankles in a practice session, and then we had to remove the tape. My legs are a touch on the hairy side, and Miss Friedman had taped too high. When she ripped the tape off, as we were taught to do, I saw all of the constellations. I let out a shriek so loud that it brought the entire room to a halt.

Fran was mortified. She was embarrassed for herself and red-faced because everyone knew that she was the cause of my pain. However, before long we were both laughing about it, and from that point on, we began to enjoy each other a lot more. I asked her out in January of the following year, and the rest, as they say, is history.

We married in June, 1952, right after my college graduation. It certainly had been an enjoyable college experience for both of us. Many years later, sitting at the graduation ceremonies of Harvard University, where my eldest son had earned a law degree, I turned to my wife and said, "I'm delighted that Steve has gotten such a high-quality education. But when I remember how much we enjoyed and got out of BC, I don't think I'd trade places with him." And I wouldn't; it was that good.

I've had a truly wonderful career in education. It's had some interesting twists and turns, probably caused by my upbringing as an orphan. For example, I decided to make a quick exit from physical education in order to become a guidance counselor, where I felt that I could be of more help to young people. While starting my teaching career in a tough Harlem junior high school, I also pursued my master's degree in guidance at Columbia University. A full day of teaching, followed by a 4:30 p.m. class, usually found me asleep twenty minutes into the class. No matter.

Two years later, degree in hand, I was hired by the Bethpage, Long Island, schools to start their first junior high school guidance program. I wrote a group guidance curriculum for that age group, taught the classes, and also did individual counseling with the students assigned to me. I coached the basketball team and had the best of both worlds.

Four years later, I took a similar position with the Great Neck, Long Island, schools, and soon transferred to their South Senior High School, where I enjoyed ten interesting and vital years of counseling high school boys. My work as a school counselor was always marked by my interest in my students as people rather than as students. In other words, their overall adjustment was more important than how well they did in school. I always involved the parents so that the family could work harmoniously rather than at odds with one other. My seventeen years as a school guidance counselor were fruitful and fulfilling.

Another unexpected twist of fate turned my career in another important direction. During my stretch as a counselor in Great Neck, I was elected president of the Great Neck Teachers' Association, which had about 600 members at that time. Two years in this capacity made me realize that the school leaders who make the big decisions did not always have the welfare of the kids as a top priority. It stirred in me a strong interest to become a school administrator, where I would be able to do much more for students. Taking sabbatical leave, I enrolled in the doctoral program in educational administration at Columbia, with the idea of becoming a high school principal.

My first administrative job was in none other than Long Beach High School. The prodigal son returning to one of his hometowns! But soon, doctorate in hand, I secured a position as high school principal in Bayport–Blue Point, a small town in the southern part of Suffolk County, Long Island. I remained there for twelve very enjoyable and productive years.

It was a demanding position but the best one for creating a total school environment that had the welfare of students as its top priority. My background and roots could not have served me any better for the multitude of human problems and predicaments one encounters as a principal. My high school won some singular honors during my years there. We were a finalist for Long Island Community Service High School of the year in the early eighties, for our many community service programs. We won awards at the state and national levels. In the late seventies, I was chosen High School Principal of the Year after my entire faculty signed the required application, something the judges had never seen before. The closing statement on the application, probably pleased me the most. It read, "Never have we had a principal who is so concerned about the total welfare of each student. Meeting their needs is his top-most priority!"

I retired in 1986, after thirty-four years of service. Only, I didn't really retire. I opened up an educational consulting firm and continue to be very active in education. I conduct training workshops for teachers and administrators that will help them to modernize their approaches to students. I write articles for educational journals and have had regular radio and television shows dealing with education. It's been a full and varied agenda, and truly a labor of love!

On the personal side, I have four delightful children, all of whom I'm very proud because they're fine human beings. I'm married to the same lovely woman, and our next anniversary will be our forty-sixth!

I often reflect on the effect being an orphan has had on my life. I believe that it has given me far more positives than negatives. Firstly, I'm an appreciative person. What others may take for granted, I appreciate to the fullest. My family, and its welfare, takes center stage. My wife and I have been there for our kids. This is not to say that I've been a great or even a superior parent. I haven't. It does mean that I have been a conscientious and devoted parent because I know what it's like not to have a home and family, so that I fully appreciate my own, from its inception.

Lastly, on the shame-pride spectrum of having been an orphan, I probably register an eight toward the pride end, but it's an internal, quiet eight. There's no need to conceal it or reveal it. It's just there, part of my pedigree. If and when it comes up, or needs to be discussed and revealed, it is, easily and forthrightly. I'm pleased to have been president of the alumni chapter of the Pride of Judea Children's Home for the past eight years. It has enabled me to keep in touch with my childhood friends, and to maintain a give-back posture to its namesake: the Pride of Judea Mental Health Center.

My Story

Phil Craft

Due to my learning difficulties at P.S. 202, I never contemplated going to an academic high school as did my brighter, more confident friends. In any case, what with my total lack of family resources, the Home decided that a trade school would prepare me best for an occupation in which I could support myself after I left the protective cloak of the Pride. Together with Bernie Friedland, off I went to my new high school, the annex of the East New York Vocational High School, and the placement was quite agreeable to me.

It was not much more than two miles distant from the Home; so in nice weather, we could save the nickel carfare by walking home from school, or by making the journey on roller skates. But the brief exploratory courses in machine shop, electrical wiring, aviation mechanics, boatbuilding, etc., were quite beyond my ability.

Only in printing with movable type was I even remotely capable. My fingers were clumsy and slow in setting type, and my mind moved only slightly faster; so even there I always struggled to catch up. Only my growing aptitude in reading, spelling, vocabulary, and writing offered any possibility that someday I could become a proofreader of printed texts, albeit a slow one. At the end of this two-semester introductory program, I was assigned to the New York School of Printing, located on Thirty-fourth Street in Manhattan.

The stark complexity and potential confusion of traveling alone each day to a new school in Manhattan, which would commence in September, caused me acute distress and even nightmares that summer. I would be required to ride on three different subway lines, involving two pivotal transfers at stations with unfamiliar names. If for any reason I missed either connection, I would be helplessly adrift and alone in a strange universe. I had not yet learned to use a telephone, and I didn't even know the Home's number. Even if I could summon the nerve to approach anyone for help, I wouldn't know how to define my problem in words. My long-buried fears of being abandoned and forsaken now loomed again. I was terrified!

With the approach of the new school year, a visible pall of gloom and despair descended upon me. Thankfully, my wonderful supervisor, Judge Arcus, recognized my depressed mood, and listened with patience and understanding as I poured out all of my worries and fears. His calm confidence reassured me, helping me to recall other crises we had faced together when his clear vision and practical wisdom had enabled me to reduce the complexity of some seemingly insoluble problem to more manageable proportions. With persistence and great patience, he drilled me on my steadily growing knowledge of the train stations of my route to school and all the steps I had to take in my round-trip journey each day. He also reviewed the corrective steps I could take in case something went wrong.

When the first day of school came, Judge Arcus quietly walked me to the train station, and with a last pep talk and pat on the shoulder, saw me off on my fearsome journey. With his remembered words guiding me through the trip, as if he were with me, I handled every transfer point with faultless precision. With repetition, his instructions became so clear and certain that I could even imagine myself now teaching them to someone else!

And, in a manner of speaking, I did. Many years later, as a professional social worker, I had a similar opportunity, and the distinct pleasure and satisfaction, of providing the same helpful guidance to a profoundly challenged adolescent client enrolled in a special education program. Although that equally trusting youngster had never known Sam Arcus, the good Judge's inspiring symbolic presence was as real to me then as it once had been during my own period of trial and stress.

During my first days at the new school, I drifted and floundered like a helpless fish trapped in a turbulent current. Fortunately, another caring adult came to my rescue. Mrs. Schneirson, my perceptive homeroom teacher, promptly recruited and guided the supportive efforts of a cadre of older students, many of them seniors, who enthusiastically "adopted" me, taught me the ropes, and smoothed out my adjustment path by enlisting the aid of their own friends throughout the school. When, at last, many of them graduated or went into the service, at semester's end, I had already begun to take hold with greater independence and self-confidence. What a wonderful "reclamation" job they had done at this pivotal time in my life, and how much I owed to everyone involved.

Even with all this help, I had to stay up late virtually every night, laboriously wading through difficult and lengthy reading assignments, completing homework, or studying for tests, just to keep pace with the school performance and learning progress of everyone else. The playing field called school was still tilted against me, and I had to persevere with far more effort than my peers in order to make it through successfully. Fortunately, by this time, my school records had alerted my teachers to my learning pattern. They knew that I was a slow learner, but could and would succeed given the added time I needed.

At the start of each new term, some of them took me aside to assure me of their willingness to be patient and suspend any negative judgment as long as I continued to make steady progress according to my usual pattern. Spurred by their special interest, I worked even more diligently to keep faith with these understanding and supportive teachers.

This was made more difficult, however, when, because of the manpower shortages caused by World War II, I was asked to become a part-time afterschool supervisor of the Junior Boys back at the Home. By then I also was involved heavily with the Home's newspaper, the Pride Survey, which included a regular column, articles, and correspondence with alumni in the armed forces, including long letters, some thirty to forty pages long, to Corporal Charlie Vladimer.

Under the burden of these special commitments, plus the heavy demands of my schoolwork, I had the dubious distinction of being the last boy in the Home to go to sleep each night. Then, with the special help of Frank, the night watchman, I was the first to be awakened in order to start my long journey each day to my high school, which was the farthest away of anyone's. (The habit of early rising proved particularly fortunate several years later, when, as a garrison soldier stationed in South Korea, I awoke prematurely early one morning to find our hut utterly ablaze. I quickly aroused my bunkmates, and we were able to extinguish the flames. My early rising tendency probably saved our lives.)

In January, 1946, I did graduate with my classmates, gaining a vocational diploma without any distinction for excellence. Nevertheless, the loud, vigorous applause my peers gave me for hanging in there and earning a diploma despite formidable obstacles meant more to me than if I had been chosen class valedictorian. I was out of school, finally.

Military service for fourteen months followed graduation; and then, soon afterwards, an entry-level, low-paying job in a small, family-owned print shop. During this time, I lived happily in Army Hall, a CCNY student residence which, before the war, had been the Hebrew Orphan Asylum. Although it was one room, I had the pleasure of sharing it from time to time with good friends from the Pride, plus Charlie Vladimer, who was well on his way toward a degree from CCNY.

Around this time I began to assist Charlie, each Sunday morning, in his volunteer role as cubmaster at the Hebrew Educational Society, in Brooklyn. Helping out with many worthwhile activities and successful events, I not only gained much knowledge about working with groups of youngsters, but soon became so obsessed with the challenges and special satisfactions of this work that my printing job began to lose its priority and importance as my future career.

I wanted to follow Charlie, Sam Arcus, and Lou Feigelson into the field of professional social work, even though my learning handicap made this seem like a hopeless dream. But Charlie not only was optimistic about my chances, he was downright enthusiastic!

"You've already overcome many obstacles in the past," he said, reminding me, in particular, about my initial difficulty in working with the Junior Boys group and then turning that venture into a rousing success. "If this is what you really want to do, Willie," he said, "it's worth your best efforts, because nothing else will bring you a happier life."

Charlie's support and encouragement made me absolutely jubilant. We began to project long-range goals and immediate plans. "The key," he said, "is to go steadily forward, but at your own pace."

Like Sam Arcus before him, Charlie helped me to reduce this ambitious, far-reaching campaign into smaller and more manageable segments, making it much easier for me to focus my efforts. A flexible timetable emerged, specifically geared to my own pace.

Viewing this vision through Charlie's clearer, more experienced eyes transformed what once had been a quixotic impossibility into a glorious, exciting adventure. With the financial support of the G.I. Bill, not even the necessity of returning to high school for the Regents credits required for college entrance dismayed me or diminished my enthusiasm to begin the long journey.

With Charlie actively helping and encouraging me, I either would succeed or make one hell of an effort in the process! He made his own strong ego part of mine, constantly infusing me with his unconquerable optimism and empathy, while at the same time helping me to remain focused on each of the tasks that had to be done. He always was near, either to congratulate my small successes or to brainstorm new ways of overcoming stubborn problems.

Charlie's strong, persistent advocacy of psychotherapy as an integral part of this undertaking proved to be, literally, of life-saving value. This powerful source of added support became a vital factor in enabling me to cope with my most severe mental stresses and emotional conflicts over a period of nine long years of change, challenge, and psychological growth. It especially was important when defeat, disappointment, and despair occasionally threatened, not only my emotional balance, but also my very motivation to live. As I became more intensely involved in therapy, I grew strong enough to stand more solidly on my own, a development which made me less dependent on Charlie's support; but also one that he enthusiastically welcomed and encouraged.

As in my earlier schools, I again received substantial help from many quarters. At the Stevenson School in Manhattan, a private institution staffed by, and also catering to, returning servicemen, I took Regents and college-prep courses, taught in a more relaxed, less formal atmosphere. I also learned, for the first time, how to study with less wasted effort, and prepare more effectively for exams. I completed four years of academic work in but a year and a half, which pleased me to no end. I was ready for college.

At New York's City College, I succeeded by concentrating on preparing for exams rather than on completing homework assignments, as had been my habitual pattern in public school. I was coming of age as a student.

It only took me four and a half years to earn my B.A. degree, a time frame considerably shorter than I had expected. Summers, I worked as a camp counselor, and after classes, I worked in the cafeteria, which covered my modest rent and food costs. My G.I. benefits helped to pay for my therapy. It was an uphill climb, but with a little help from my friends, I made it! I felt as though I had climbed a difficult mountain and now stood on the summit. And I had!

Upon my graduation from CCNY in June, 1950, my bank balance was near zero. My veterans' benefits had been used up, and, in addition to self-support, I wanted to raise some money for graduate school. With my new college degree and my group-work experience in summer camps, I applied to and was hired by the New York City Youth Board to work with a teenage gang.

Swallowing my apprehension, I was surprised to learn that I not only enjoyed the work but was quite effective at it. My background in the Pride, plus my important experience as a Supervisor of the Junior Boys, stood me in good stead. It was a valuable and significant year for me, in this, my first real job after college.

My successful year's work with the Stogies, and two powerful recommendations from Charlie Vladimer and Sam Arcus, both successful alumni, enabled me to gain admission, in September, 1957, to the New York School of Social Work of Columbia University. Habits of frugality, nurtured in the Home, helped keep my living expenses down, and with the help of money saved from my Youth Board salary, I was able to get by. Occasionally, however, I sold my blood to a blood bank when I needed money badly. When my therapist, Dr. Charles Hewitt, found out about this, he generously offered an interest-free deferred-payment arrangement to enable me to continue in therapy.

My two years in graduate school were brightened by the presence of dedicated and charismatic role-models who inspired me with the nobility of their commitment to helping others, and also by their genuine empathy and concern for their students.

It was my special good fortune to have as my faculty advisor Margaret Williamson, a renowned authority in the area of group work supervision. Always caring and supportive, she projected a unique, gentle wisdom which not only spurred my enthusiastic efforts, but helped me to recognize and appreciate my own assets as an aspiring social worker. She helped me over several rough spots which threatened to derail my continuation, and I am indebted to her for her invaluable support and friendship.

Another valuable experience was my work at the Vacation Camp for the Blind. Two outstanding professors of mine, Irving Miller and Sherman Barr, were directors of this summer camp, and I learned a great deal from the two of them.

In 1959, I also did something that I had wanted to do for a long time. I legally changed my name to Craft, finally bearing my mother's maiden name instead of her husband's surname, which he had given to me with great reluctance since I wasn't really his son. His unceasing rejection had long been an open emotional wound. This simple but important change of name proved to be most therapeutic.

My twenty-four-year social work career has spanned different settings. I worked six productive years at a community center in the Harlem section of New York City. Then, I spent two years at the Grand Street Settlement House in Lower Manhattan where I had a unique and wonderful experience. While working with a gang of delinquent teenagers, I got to know its leader, Rauli Concepcion, and his family quite well. I began to help them in many different ways and it was not long before I became emotionally drawn and deeply attached to the entire family. The bond of friendship and caring ripened into something stronger, a sense of loving and belonging that I never had known before.

As each crisis was handled and an increasing number of problems resolved, what had begun as a professional relationship fostered the revival of strong feelings and emotional needs long repressed and buried under the crushing weight of earlier rejection and childhood trauma. Since the age of twelve, when I had recoiled with intense fear at the prospect of being adopted, I had never envisioned becoming a member of a loving family. I already had accepted that fate as my destiny. But now, in the crucible of battle on behalf of the Concepcion family, the mutual trust and affection that developed assumed a momentum and intensity too powerful to resist or ignore. At that point, for me, some form of mutual adoption not only became acceptable, it was logical, desirable, and virtually inevitable.

Without legal papers or other formalities, it took place, simply and spontaneously, in our own hearts with a brief but moving benediction by Petra, the family's beloved matriarch, who was Rauli's grandmother, living in Puerto Rico. She declared, "Fil, te quiero mucho y desde ahora, tu es mi hijo!" "Phil, I love you very much, and from now on you are my son!" Her warm embrace and the tears in her eyes gave her simple, loving words an indescribable eloquence that easily bridged our differences in language and culture. I unexpectedly had found the loving family that I had never had, and to this day, the Concepcions have been that, and much more. I have continued to help them in every way possible as a loved member of the family, and this relationship, which exists to this day, has become an invaluable part of my life.

In 1967, I moved on to a regular casework position with the Wiltwyck School for Boys, a residential facility serving and treating emotionally troubled boys referred by the Family Court. Once again I was privileged and fortunate enough to have as my supervisor a great social worker, Mrs. Eugenie ("Jenni") Stay, who became my mentor and cherished friend.

As a virtual beginner in a regular casework setting, I was in great need of someone on which to model, and no one was better than Jenni! In one basic value, we were in sync from the beginning: namely, the placement of the needs and best interests of our clients above all other considerations.

I was elated when, after my first year at Wiltwyck, Jenni took a similar position at the Graham Home for Children and invited me to join her there. At Graham, which had both boys and girls, my experiences at the Pride again served me quite well in being able to empathize with what my clients were going through and helping to meet those needs effectively.

Working with Jenni was a pleasure, and under her wise and caring tutelage, I grew steadily in judgment, confidence, and skill, and drew increased satisfaction and stature as a respected social worker. My dream of helping others, which had taken root at the Pride so many years before, now had become a highly satisfying reality.

Another bonus for me at this time was my bonding with another family, which became my second personal family. They were a Turkish family, and I actively participated in the growth and maturation of their children, developing a warm, vibrant relationship which continues to this day. I'm fortunate enough to be a part of two loving families.

In the mid-seventies, Graham merged with Windham Child Care and became a larger organization known as Graham-Windham. I continued to work there, productively and happily, and to maintain my close friendship with Jenni Stay, even though, by mutual agreement, we now were in different units. As my skills increased, I was pleased to make important contributions to clients reflective of being a competent caseworker. I felt that my work was valued, and was gaining genuine appreciation and respect, both from clients and colleagues. I enjoyed working with my new supervisor, a fine professional named Gene Kaufman.

But in the eighties, things took a turn for the worse, much worse. The city moved headlong into a push to move kids out of foster homes and into adoptive placements, offering financial grants as the main incentive. Graham-Windham, mainly financed by the city, and always struggling with deficits, brought in a new supervisor to ride herd on the staff to move their kids into adoptive homes. Many of our kids had become quite attached to their foster parents, who, for a variety of compelling reasons, could not opt to adopt them. In pushing for forced adoption, we would be going against the best interests of our kids.

I resisted this pressure in the early stages, as did many of my colleagues. But Gene Kaufman, our understanding and supportive supervisor, had gone, and had been replaced by a new person, considerably less informed about or committed to our young clients. The conflict and tension increased, and there also was a pronounced surge in the volume of paperwork. Always a slow worker, this created a severe time burden for me, but I refused to minimize my time commitment to my clients and their families.

As a result of these added pressures, I gradually was approaching a condition of burn-out, in which sleeplessness, asthma attacks, and episodes of lethargy and depression interrupted my work efforts. I long before had planned an early retirement because other interests were beckoning. However, in 1983 Graham-Windham accelerated the process by replacing me and other senior workers with sociology majors just out of college, whom they paid about half of our salaries, and who could be expected to be far more compliant in pursuing agency objectives, particularly adoptions. My social work career had come to the end of its line. Since there were other things that I wanted to do, I decided, after an initial, unsuccessful search, to retire.

Retirement, of course, is a misnomer for active people, and I've been busier than ever with varied pursuits. I embarked on a long-desired book idea pertaining to a twenty-five-year chronicle of the Israeli's Army's famed 7th Armored Brigade, which played a pivotal role in transforming the Israeli Army into the single most formidable military force in the Middle East. Though the book was never published, the effort was not totally in vain. Because of extensive research, I had become so knowledgeable about tactics and weapons systems that I invented new adaptations for armored vehicles and warships, forwarding these to the Israeli Army's research and development unit.

Since then, I've continued to write, publishing a short story in a national magazine about Brooklyn Dodger great Peewee Reese, and writing many articles for the Pride's Alumni Newsletter. Needless to say, being with my families and friends also continues to occupy my time most happily.

In looking back at where I began, whom I've helped, and what I've achieved, my mental handicaps no longer seem a cause for embarrassment or shame. With devoted help and constant encouragement, the legendary Helen Keller made her mute, soundless, and sightless existence only the starting point for a glorious, inspiring journey to a rewarding life. With the active nurturance, support and encouragement of a long list of caring and devoted friends, mental retardation became merely my own starting point toward ultimate usefulness, productivity, and fulfillment.

I sometimes glow at the comforting thought that if my mother could survey all that has taken place and all that I have achieved, she might smile and perhaps feel that in sacrificing her life to give birth to me, her death was not in vain!

Chapter 21

The Supervisors' Perspective

The supervisors who worked in the Pride were the day-to-day parents of their charges. Some better, some worse, they affected our lives as readily, and as forcefully, as any parent in a regular home setting. This book focuses on four of them.

A Supervisor's Perspective

Sam G. Arcus, M.S.W.

I came to the Pride of Judea Children's Home on September 3, 1942, after completing my first summer as a counselor at the Delaware Cliff Camps in New Jersey, and after a frustrating year in Baltimore. Charlie Vladimer and I, good friends and fellow alumni of the Hebrew National Orphans' Home in Yonkers, had moved to Baltimore after hearing about the great job opportunities in the war industries there. We shared a room in the home of a nice Jewish family and began the frustrating experience of finding work, but did not have much success. Just as our money was running out, Charlie was hired as a plumber's assistant at the shipyard, although he knew absolutely nothing about plumbing. In desperation, I took a job as a repairman with the Electrolux Company, although I knew nothing about vacuum cleaners. Later on, I got a job with the Bureau of Engraving, where I literally began to "make" some real money.

When the summer of 1942 rolled around, we'd both had it and decided that we wanted to work in our main area of interest: children. We took the camp job, had a good summer, and when it ended, we came to the Pride of Judea.

Charlie was hired first by Sam Arano, to be the supervisor for the Senior Boys group. I was hired to be the relief supervisor, taking over when others had days off. The pay wasn't much, $45 to $50 per month, but with room and board. That helped!

In a short time, however, Charlie was drafted into the Army, and I took over his responsibilities with the Senior Boys. Because of my 4-F draft status (due to childhood osteomyelitis) the Pride could count on my staying put if I wanted to. I wanted to, because my experiences in Baltimore had confirmed for me that a higher education was an absolute necessity.

For several years after our departure from HNOH, Charlie and I had talked about the possibility of going to college, but it had never seemed feasible for one reason or another. The head supervisor, Sam Arano, had agreed to my one condition for taking the job, some evening time to attend classes at CCNY. And he honored that agreement, as did his successor when Arano himself was drafted into the Army and left the Pride. So, twice a week, on Tuesdays and Thursdays, I left at 5:00 p.m. for the two-hour subway ride uptown to CCNY, where I had two-plus hours of classes before the two-hour ride back to the Pride. It would be after 11:00 when I "came home" to the Pride, rather exhausted.

Although not easy, working and attending school was a productive symbiotic relationship, as was recognized by some of the older boys who were, in turn, influenced by it. I was setting an example of the importance of a higher education and making the necessary sacrifices to achieve it.

When I arrived at the Pride in 1942, I found an institution quite different from what I had known during the twelve years I had lived there. The Hebrew National Orphans' Home, on the outskirts of Yonkers, New York, was isolated and insulated from the nearest villages, which were three miles away. It accepted only boys, ages five through sixteen, with the upper limits extended later, through high school graduation. It consisted of a massive four-story building on a twenty-acre site containing playgrounds, ballfields, farmland, chicken coops, a barn, and some cottages for employees. It was a fully self-contained community with its own bakery, laundry, shoe-shop, seamstress rooms, three massive dormitories, and everything else. We even went to school there, on the fourth floor. Only when we finished the eighth grade did we leave the fenced-in property to attend outside high schools, and thus, for the first time, be exposed to the outside world!

The HNOH's philosophy of child-rearing was rooted in a system of strict discipline with heavy reliance on corporal punishment and collective punishment, such as detention and standing on line. The caliber of supervisory personnel often left much to be desired. Only in 1939, a year before I was to leave, did things change for the better with the arrival of Reuben Koftoff, who formerly had worked at the Brooklyn Hebrew Orphans' Asylum (BHOA).

In pleasant contrast, the Pride of Judea, although also housed in a massive, imposing building, occupied an entire block right in the heart of its Brownsville–East New York neighborhood and community. It cared for both boys and girls, ages five though eighteen, who left daily to attend the local public school (P.S. 202) and different high schools farther away. Therefore, it was considerably easier for relatives to visit the children, and for the children to visit their families in the community. In short, it was not isolated.

Just as importantly, the Pride had little tolerance for a system of inhumane discipline. Although Sam Arano attempted to impose some of its tenets, it never took hold, because he was drafted before he could implement it, and because the board of directors didn't believe in it. There was no systemized corporal punishment, no detention, no standing on line. This pleased me considerably, since, because of my own painful experiences in the HNOH, I had vowed that should I ever be in a position of authority over kids, I would avoid using such methods, relying on reason and persuasion instead. Thus, when reprimands or punishment were in order, I would assemble my charges in the large playroom and lecture and scold and plead and cajole. This method very quickly led Philly Weinberg Craft to label me "the Judge." But on the whole, despite this characterization, and subsequent caricatures, the method worked!

I found the food at the Home to be quite good, compared to what we had received at HNOH. Edith Loewenthal (a waitress in the staff dining room and wife of our head chef, Fritz, both refugees from Nazi Germany) were continually in awe of my healthy appetite.

Having been raised in an all-boys' institution for twelve years, I found the presence of girls to be pleasing and puzzling. It was pleasing because it was a more natural condition. At HNOH, once a month, girls from the neighboring communities would be invited in for a social evening, such as a dance, even though few of us knew how to dance. It was puzzling because the older boys at the Pride continually were devising strategies to maximize and fulfill the "naturalness" of the situation, above and beyond the frequent and closely supervised socials that the Pride provided.

It also was pleasing to note brothers and sisters in the same place, though, of course, in different dorms, on different floors. Many of us from HNOH, including my older brother and I, had sisters in other institutions, and our relationships with them were distant and meager. For years it had bothered me that the powers that be could not devise a better plan to avoid the painful separation of siblings, particularly those of the opposite sex. Some of my friends from HNOH had sisters in the Pride when I was there, and I felt a special affinity for these girls because my friends had asked me to protect them.

It pleased me greatly to see Pride boys together with their sisters, and I would think to myself, "Why couldn't Al and I have had such luck with our kid-sister, Henny?"

Sam Arano was the head supervisor when I was hired, and George Goldenberg was the executive director during my two-year stint at the Pride. It's interesting to note that he had been superintendent of the HNOH during my early years there, but he did not remember me or my brother. At first, that bothered me, but then I realized that there were over 350 kids there at the time. How could he possibly be expected to remember two out of hundreds?

As it turned out, I didn't see much of him anyway because he was out of the building most of the time—raising funds, I imagine, because that always was a prime need. The day-to-day running of the place was left to the supervisors and support staff. And we did a good job. I remember the ever-present Mrs. Braverman with the youngest boys; Mrs. Weingust with the Junior Boys, and I succeeded Charlie Vladimer with the Inters and Seniors. I don't recall the names of those in charge of the girls' dorms, other than one of the older girl monitors by the name of Adele Rosenthal. I remember her name because she was later to become my wife of over fifty years! There were other memorable people as well, including Fritz and Edith, who were to become our very dear friends, our "family" after we all left this memorable institution.

The essence of my time at the Pride was, of course, working with the boys. The title of this book, *An Orphan Has Many Parents*, alludes to how the supervisors and other personnel (including members of the board) filled the void left by departed parents. And that included me. But I feel uncomfortable with the appellation of parent. The fact is that I only was four or five years older than my oldest charges when I first came to the Pride. And I must admit, I had some trepidation about that. But fortunately a number of the older boys were very decent fellows, and we hit it off at once. I'm sure that was due to my own institutional background and also because we understood each other so well. For me it was more of being an older brother than a parent. Yes, that's what I felt like, and I'm certain that's how the older guys perceived me.

In working with the boys, I tried to clue into their feelings and interests, and to share as much of myself as I could. For example, I've always loved classical music, and the small radio in my room would always be playing Mozart, Beethoven, or Tchaikovsky, and I'd leave the door to my room open. Some of the friendlier boys would ask to enter in order to be more comfortable while listening, and pretty soon the room would be full.

One day someone commented that it was too bad that our dorm didn't have a phonograph so that we could listen to selections of our own choice. Louie Horowitz, a genius in making such things, volunteered to build one if we could get the parts. Another boy volunteered to do the shopping for the records. Suddenly, I felt a dozen sets of puppy-eyes all focused on me. I put up the money from my meager salary, and the phonograph was made in record time (no pun intended).

On his first expedition, our record-shopper went overboard with his purchases, eating up too big a chunk of my monthly salary. We put him on a budget of only two records per month, selections to be made by popular choice. The reason why I did not seek to have the Pride take up the cost was that I wanted to keep the records and build up my own personal library, which I had acknowledged to the boys beforehand.

My favorite activity at the Pride was to talk, one on one, with as many of the boys as I could. I pumped them for information about their family backgrounds, their present feelings, and their dreams about the future. Many of them came from sad backgrounds not unlike my own. In these discussions, I found out that many of the boys were watching me and my efforts to obtain an education, so that when I verbalized positive feelings about my own future, it was not only believed, but they could identify with it.

That connection was made because the boys frequently asked me about my institutional background and family, and whether this or that was possible. And I delighted in telling them about an anecdote I had recently learned about Archimedes, the Greek father of physics: "Give me a place to stand, a long enough pole, and a fulcrum, and I will change the world!"

I enjoyed sharing with the boys all the wonderful things I was learning at CCNY. I felt like a veritable fountain of knowledge; as fast as it poured into me, I would try to pour it out to them, especially to those who showed a gift for school. One of the boys, Roy Lachman, would sit in my room, listen to me, and then sometimes challenge something that sounded far-fetched. My standard reply would be, "Hey, I'll show you the book it came from." It's very satisfying to note that today Dr. Roy Lachman is a distinguished professor of psychology at the University of Houston, and a leading national authority on artificial intelligence. Many of the other boys went on to college and had illustrious careers of their own, all of which makes me very proud and happy.

Even though my daily time was totally full, what with the demands of the job, going to school, doing my assignments and homework, I was not totally unaware of the presence of some pretty attractive girls in the vicinity. Since I was in my very early twenties, some of the older girls tried to fix me up with a girl who recently had left the Pride, Sylvia "Berky" Berkowitz.

Berky was attractive, perky, and interested in me. But I found myself attracted to one of the matchmakers, a girl named Adele Rosenthal, only five years my junior. And it was Berky who recognized this, even before I did, and told Adele, "He's not interested in me. He's interested in you!"

When Adele asked her how she knew this, Berky replied that the few times we went out together, all my questions were about Adele. And so Berky bowed out gracefully (although we remained good friends for years afterwards) and I began dating Adele, though very discreetly. We'd go across the street to the candy store for ice-cream sodas or to an occasional movie. And my good friends Fritz and Edith would invite us to their small apartment nearby for refreshments and talk.

Edith, especially, was encouraging of the relationship, since she and Fritz liked us both very much, and we became family for them. Years later, Adele confided to me that Edith had told her many times, "You'll never be hungry with him!" And to me Edith would say, "Sam, you'll never do better than Adele." And time has proved her very right!

I left the Pride on June 30, 1944, as did Adele. I went to live with my aunt in Manhattan not too far from CCNY, which I now would be attending full-time. Adele went to live with an aunt in the Bronx, traveling daily to Manhattan for her job with Kayser Gloves. Our courtship continued over the next year and a half, culminating in our marriage in January, 1946. My older sister made the wedding in her small home on Legion Street in Brooklyn, not far from the Pride. It was supposed to be a small affair, but it turned out to be a delightful mob scene as word spread to the Pride, and the kids and staff turned out en masse to participate in and enjoy this important day.

So, what kind of place was the Pride of Judea Children's Home? As the preceding narrative has illustrated it was different from the Hebrew National Orphans' Home, where I was raised. But it also was different from all of the other Jewish orphanages, such as the Hebrew Orphan Asylum in Manhattan, the Brooklyn Hebrew Orphan Asylum, the Israel Orphan Asylum of New York City, and even the Hebrew Sheltering Guardian Society, located in nearby Pleasantville, New York. The Pride marched to its own drummer, avoiding sharp shifts in philosophy and methods, steadfastly providing a secure, moderate orthodox environment, with tender loving care for dependent Jewish boys and girls. They did it for almost forty years, and they did it well!

In retrospect, I'm pleased to believe that I made some worthwhile contributions to some of my young charges at the Pride during the period of 1942 to 1944. But serious retrospection also convinces me that I received far more than I gave. The Pride made it possible for me to begin my pursuit of higher education at CCNY by providing me with the setting and income I needed for this purpose. It offered me an important network of supportive people, heretofore lacking in my life, in the persons of my future wife, Adele, my good friends Fritz and Edith, and my young charges. The boys were me just a few years before, and I wanted to be the role-model for them that Morris Plotnick had been for me at the HNOH when he attended CCNY at night. I delight in thinking that I was, as evidenced by the comments of Roy Lachman and others over the years.

This means a lot to me.

Most importantly, the Pride provided me with Adele, my wife of over fifty years. And through her, our son and daughter, and three granddaughters and a grandson. To add to my gifts, the Pride has provided me with years of meaningful and treasured relation-ships with my Pride kids, now grown, with families of their own. I grew up in the Hebrew National Orphans' Home, but I became a mensch at the Pride of Judea Children's Home! Both institutions will forever have a special place in my heart and soul!

The Pride in My Life

Charlie Vladimer, M.S.W.

I came to the Pride of Judea Children's Home completely by acci-dent. Yet if one believes in destiny, there is reason to believe that I was destined to be there all along.

I had an institutional background myself. My mother con-tracted Parkinson's disease when I was a child, and my father sim-ply couldn't work and care for my sister and me at the same time. So he put my sister in the Brooklyn Hebrew Orphan Asylum and me in the Hebrew National Orphans' Home. I was eight when this happened, and I stayed there for about eight years. When I was six-teen, I left HNOH without even graduating from high school.

I supported myself with various jobs for about six years, until one summer I took a job as a counselor at the Delaware Cliff Camps with my good friend Sam Arcus. We would get $25 for the summer if we finished the full season. Well, I loved it! Not only was I good with kids, but they gave me a small bonus and invited me back for the following summer as a division head for the grand salary of $75. It was my first experience supervising kids, and I enjoyed it immensely.

Sam and I kicked around that year in low-level jobs and both looked forward to the summer (1942), when we would return to camp. We had a good summer again and agreed that working with children should become our life's work. After the summer, I found a job as a clerk with the MGM organization in New York City and Sam resumed looking for work.

One weekend, Sam was invited to an interview after responding to an ad for a supervisor's position at a Brooklyn orphanage called the Pride of Judea Children's Home. We had never heard of it before. Not knowing Brooklyn and being a little nervous, he asked me to accompany him. Since I didn't have anything better to do, I went along.

When we got there, I sat in the lobby outside the main office, while Sam was interviewed by the head supervisor, a small, well-built man named Sam Arano. When we were introduced to him, he said, "My name is Sam, but everyone calls me Tony."

I got up, ready to leave, when Sam's interview ended and he came out, but Mr. Arano suddenly asked me if I'd be interested in a job also, because they had two openings to fill. I told him that I already had a position but might be interested in this one because it would involve working with kids. With that, he took me into his office while Sam waited outside.

Two days later, much to my surprise, he called me and offered me a job. When I asked about Sam, he said, "We filled the other position, but another is going to open up very soon, and Sam will get that one." I felt very guilty about this and told Mr. Arano that I'd get back to him shortly.

When I informed Sam and asked his opinion, he strongly encouraged me to take the job and not give his candidacy a second thought. After all, I wanted to work with children and here was a perfect opportunity. Anyway, he'd likely join me before too long if Arano was being truthful. (It did work out that way.)

But I had some reservations. I'd be working with the Senior Boys, some of whom were eighteen years old. I was only twenty-four, and I expressed my apprehensions to Sam. "What if these guys give me a hard time? What if they get physical?"

Sam replied, "Don't worry about it. You'll do fine. You know the score. Be yourself and do the things you did so well at camp."

Duly encouraged, I packed my single suitcase and left for a new chapter in my life at the Pride of Judea Children's Home.

I arrived there late on a Friday evening, at Mr. Arano's request, and waited to see him so that he could get me settled. He figured that with all the kids around on Saturday, that would be a good day for me to start. As I sat outside his office, waiting for him, I was startled to see a bedraggled figure coming slowly down the steps. I suddenly recognized him, and my heart stopped beating! It was Tony Arano! His forehead and face were bleeding; his shirt was torn and bloody; he was a mess! My worst fears were before me and I said to myself, "Oh shit, this is going to be a nightmare!"

Mr. Arano, upon seeing me, smiled weakly and said, "Don't worry. I just took a bad fall, but I'm okay." My life at the Pride was about to begin, and on a very fearsome note.

Later, after I had developed a good rapport with my group, I found out just what had happened that night. The Leibowitz brothers, Petey and Max, both very tough kids, and another youngster with similar tendencies, had been roughed up pretty badly by Arano and had decided to get even. When he made his rounds that night, they jumped him in a dark hallway, knocked him down, and began to beat the daylights out of him. When they realized that he knew who they were, they allowed him to retaliate, knowing that he would get them soon anyway. Everyone was a bloody mess, but the perpetrators were given a hero's welcome by the rest of the kids because everyone had suffered at Arano's hands at one time or another.

Sam Arano would play an interesting role for me. He had come to the Pride with prior experience working in orphanages. He had worked at the nearby Brooklyn Hebrew Orphan Asylum for one year, and he firmly believed in corporal punishment as an effective means of discipline. He didn't hesitate to use his hands and wanted the kids to be afraid of him. His nickname "Tony" was part of this persona. He was a Sephardic Jew, dark and swarthy, and enjoyed his tough-guy image. Later, after leaving the Pride and returning from the military, he began a career running reform schools for juvenile delinquents. It suited him well.

I was the total opposite of Arano in every respect. I learned later that he had hired me over Sam Arcus because I was taller and older, and he thought I'd be able to handle older boys better than

Sam. But did that mean he would expect me to be like him? I dreaded the thought.

So I set out to establish myself on my own terms. I had responsibility for two full groups of boys, the Intermediates and the Seniors, about forty-five in number and having a four-year age range. What could I do to make a positive impact on them? I did two things.

The first was to give them a two-item questionnaire, asking, "What do you most like about the Home?" and "What do you dislike most about the Home?" This was the very first time that any of them had been asked for their views, and I had to assure them that I would treat their responses confidentially and would use the information for their benefit. I did. I made a few changes, based on their answers, and the boys were pleased.

Then, for my second move, I started a social club, so that they could choose, plan, and run fun activities for themselves. This had a magical effect. Suddenly, the aggressive tendencies of kids like the Leibowitz brothers were channeled into more constructive leadership behavior. Petey Leibowitz, for example, was elected the first president of the social club, and he gave it instant importance. When I accidentally ran into him years later, he told me that this experience had been a turning point in his life. The comment delighted me no end!

The kids formed a social club for each of the two groups and made them into an active organization. Philly was involved in the Inter Boys club, and it helped him considerably. I was quite pleased by it all.

To his credit, Arano, seeing how well things were going, left me pretty much alone. However, that didn't mean that he stopped his corporal approach to the kids. In addition to physical punishment, he occasionally used the line-up method of discipline. If a group misbehaved, he would have them stand in line for a very long time, often preaching to them and smacking anyone who breathed too hard. Once, he was angrily yelling at a kid before belting him. When he paused, I rushed over to the kid, began yelling at him also and told him to get up to his room, where he'd be grounded for a week!

I did this to spare a frail kid a sound beating at the hands of Arano, and my good acting job disguised my intentions so that

Arano thanked me later on for getting into the act. I was relieved, but happy to have succeeded.

As this shows, part of my success at the Pride was ironically due to the menacing presence of Sam Arano. I was so different that I was like a breath of fresh air to my kids, as they themselves would tell me later. On one memorable occasion, Arano said to me, "Charlie, I don't mind being the bastard and you being the good guy. It works better this way." Well, it certainly worked for me, and it seemed to have made a positive impression on the kids.

On this, the first of my two stints at the Pride, I was only there for maybe four months before I was drafted into the Army. Those months, however, may have been the most pivotal time in my life. They were so emotionally rewarding that I decided, with great certainty, to make social work, working with kids and people, my life's work. I even did something about it. Two nights a week, I quietly left the Pride to take the courses needed to get my high school diploma. Next stop for me was going to be college! But there was a war on. Uncle Sam reached out his long arm for me, and I was drafted.

I was in the Army for four years, but never lost contact with my Pride kids. Many carried on lengthy correspondence with me, especially Philly Weinberg Craft, whose letters were long, detailed, and from the heart. When I went back to visit on many of my furloughs, the kids would always give me a hero's welcome.

In 1946, upon my discharge, I came back to the Pride for what was to be almost a four-year stay. However, it was not a regular stint. I worked there only the first year on a regular basis. Then, having decided to attend college, I worked at the Pride for the next three years only on a part-time basis, but they were memorable years. I first met Harry Koval during that period and was so impressed by him that he became a valued lifelong friend. Harry came to the Pride in 1946, also after a stint in the service, and I immediately knew that his kids, the Senior Boys, were in great hands. We worked well together, not only enjoying each other personally, but teaming up to become better advocates for our kids when we had to take on higher-ups who had different priorities.

When I came back to the Pride in January of 1946, I was a regular group supervisor for most of the year. Then a power struggle ensued between the head supervisor and the board chairman, Jacob

H. Cohen. Whenever that happened, and it rarely did, the person taking on Jacob H. would find himself "out on the highway."

In this instance, much to my surprise, Mr. Cohen asked me to become acting head supervisor until a replacement could be found. I accepted. But after several months, I began to realize that I was putting in long hours and it was interfering with my work at college, which I was attending on a part-time basis. I went to Mr. Cohen and told him that I had to resign because I couldn't do both, and college was important to me.

Again to my surprise, he offered me the position full-time, but much to my own amazement, I turned it down, citing college once again. He tried to talk me out of it, and he could be very persuasive. He finally relented when I asked him if I could be a relief supervisor on a part-time basis, which would permit continuing at the Pride and sufficient time for school.

This arrangement worked out to everyone's benefit. Later, people would ask me if I ever regretted not assuming the full-time position of executive director. My answer, then and now, is no. My college degree and subsequent M.S.W. degree put me on a path to a full and enjoyable career in social work. The position of executive director required one to work very closely with Jacob H., and I doubt that I would have lasted too long.

Jacob H. Cohen was a formidable and interesting man. He had been hand-picked by Max Blumberg, the Pride's chief founder, to be his successor, and he ruled with an iron hand as board chairman for over twenty years. Jacob H. could be quite ruthless, and stepped on a lot of people when he didn't get his way. As a result, he wasn't well liked, but he was highly respected because he made sure that the Pride would get the budget it needed each year, and that all of its operational problems would be solved sooner rather than later.

I happened to like him and thought that he was a good man, with the kids' best interests at heart. He, in turn, liked me, which probably explains why he didn't fire me outright when I turned down his offer of the director's position. Instead, he was happy to have me stay—and on my terms, no less! This rarely happened with others.

I remember one time when, as acting director, I interviewed an excellent candidate for a supervisor's position. Before sending him to Cohen, who always had the final say, I told the man, "Look,

Mr. Cohen is sure to bargain you down in salary. But stick to your guns, because I'm going to recommend you highly." Sure enough, the man sees him and I get a call from Mr. Cohen. "Charlie, this man was willing to work for us for $50 less than our advertised salary, and that's what we agreed upon." My heart sank. Then Jacob H. went on. "But I know that you want him. So when you call him, tell him that you got the $50 back for him, because I want him to be indebted to you. and he'll be loyal to you as a result."

I couldn't help but laugh out loud, as if to say, "Jacob H., you're up to your tricks again." He knew what my laughter meant, because he chuckled himself. Not too many ever got one up on him. But I liked him because I felt that he genuinely cared for the Home's kids.

When I was in the HNOH, I remember seeing our chairman once a year, usually at Passover. He'd walk in with his entourage and behave like a pompous ass each time. We all hated him. Cohen, on the other hand, was at the Pride frequently. He'd come to different functions and really show some interest in the kids, their talents, and their activities.

Of course, he loved those pictures of himself with each year's class of bar mitzvah boys because that was a prime fund-raising tool, and he loved being seen as the benevolent papa. Considering all the time and effort he devoted to the Pride, the description was more accurate than not.

The Pride of Judea played a pivotal role for me. When I first came there in 1942, I was at a difficult stage in my life; no satisfactory job, no family to speak of, and little reason for much self-satisfaction. The Pride changed all of that. When I was able to inject some hope into the lives of my kids and save them from the iron-fisted oppression of Sam Arano, they responded with such an outpouring of affection that I found it to be the most emotionally gratifying feeling I had ever experienced up to that point!

Small wonder that I returned to the Pride on my first few leaves from the Army. The kids would drop whatever they were doing and just flock to me. It was such a magnificent feeling to know how much they cared for me, and that it was based on what I had done for them. On one such occasion, Jacob H. Cohen had been meeting with his board of directors. When they heard a big commotion outside in the yard, Cohen went to the window to investigate, then began to laugh, thus piquing the curiosity of his colleagues. When they asked him what was going on, he said, "Don't worry. Charlie's back!"

It was this wonderful rapport that I had with the kids that later made him offer the director's position to me. But by the same token, it also solidified my desire to get my collegiate degrees and go on to a full career of helping people.

I am indebted to the Pride for many things. After the war, I came back and met Harry Koval, the finest of people, who became a lifelong friend. I very much enjoyed working with Harry. We were quite different in our personalities but both cared for our kids with great passion, and their welfare was our top priority.

I fondly remember our good-natured competitions with each other, which I always seemed to lose. We'd take the two Senior Boys groups out to play, and Harry would let me have first picks. I'd load up on the best players, but it rarely helped. My kids laughed more than his because I was into humor while he was into quiet coaching. My kids did well but his kids did better. We had a good time, though, and that was emphasized, plus good sportsmanship.

Harry was the epitome of the good sportsman, and he set the tone in terms of compliments, encouragement, and the like. At the end of each game, the handshakes between teams were without rancor, and the smiles on the faces of most of the kids indicated that everyone had won! It was Harry's influence and example; he was a great person with whom to work. I learned so much from him!

I am indebted to the Pride for the wonderful affection and love I received there at a time when it was missing in my own life. It has endured throughout my life. For example, after being drafted, I thought, "Well, that was nice, but now it's over. What next?"

But it wasn't over. Far from it. A number of kids began to write to me, and their letters touched and moved me. As stated earlier, Philly's letters often were thirty or more pages long and very sensitive. I tried to respond in kind to him and to others. In doing so, I became closer to all of them, and I began to realize that my Pride experience would be an ongoing one that would touch my life forever. And it has!

What made the Pride of Judea different? I have the unique perspective of having been raised by the HNOH and also having worked at the Pride. They were totally different. Recently, I went to one of the yearly reunions of my HNOH friends, and one thing struck me. There wasn't one former supervisor there, and when I began to think about it, I couldn't recall any of us having maintained contact with a former supervisor over an extended period of time.

The Pride alumni meetings are totally different. Former supervisors such as myself and Harry not only are invited, but are affectionately prodded into attendance. Sam Arcus and Lou Feigelson are telephoned regularly and written about in the Newsletter. The alumni give us the reverence they would have given their parents. Why?

I can only believe that it was due to the intimacy we shared with the kids when we were there. It became more than a job to us. We cared about the kids within and without those walls, and they knew it. How valuable that was to them and, ultimately, to all of us! My period of service at the Pride may have been in bits and pieces, but during my time in the Army, in my correspondence with people like Philly and others, we really opened up and got to know each other better than before. We not only kept our relationships alive, they were deepened and made more meaningful. This helped the kids immeasurably, and it helped me too. It enabled our relationships to remain uninterrupted and to provide the opportunity to express regard and affection for each other. When that correspondence flowered, we became family, and indeed, I have had close contacts with many of the same people, and other Pride alumni, through the years.

Another unique quality of the Pride was its location right in the middle of a community. The kids went out each day, went to school, and related to community kids who often played with them on the Pride's ballfield. Many of the kids had relatives living nearby, and this interaction and exchange helped maintain a normalcy for them, so that they were more ready to leave and make a good adjustment to the outside than I had been in the HNOH. Remember, the latter was isolated. Kids stayed there for school and for everything else. The Pride kids were encouraged to pass into the community for various reasons, and this had to be helpful for them.

I'm probably the only person to have worked with all three of the other supervisors that the Pride Boys loved so much, Sam Arcus, Lou Feigelson, and Harry Koval. These three men and I had one major thing in common: we were dedicated to our kids. Their welfare was uppermost in our minds, and our actions were determined by that standard. It's really not surprising that all four of us have had sustained contacts with our former Pride kids at such a warm and affectionate level. The HNOH alumni get together yearly, and we talk on the phone occasionally. Oddly enough, I don't know of anyone who has kept up contact with a former supervisor for any length of time. The Pride succeeded in developing a more intimate connection between certain supervisors and their kids, and this intimacy has made the difference!

The Harry Koval Story

Harry Koval

I was tall for my age and well coordinated. I ran track and played basketball in high school, and was a good athlete. I loved sports and games, and so it was a natural choice for me to major in Physical Education at the University of Illinois, where I did quite well.

I always was a very quiet and serious person. I attribute that to my strained home life, where love and lively conversation were in short supply. Perhaps that's why I gravitated to organizing and leading games for people, which always have been so enjoyable for me.

Upon my graduation, I took the test for a teaching position in Chicago. It was the time of the Depression, however, and jobs were scarce. I was told that unless I had some good political connections, it was unlikely that I'd get a job. Then I learned of a position for a recreation director in a Jewish community center in Atlanta. I went there and really learned my trade. I had to organize and run teams, leagues, clubs, competitions, special events; you name it, I ran it! I wrote newsletters, officiated at everything, handled complaints and human relations problems, and even directed the summer camp program. This position taught me organizational and leadership skills that I've put to good use ever since.

I remained in Atlanta for six years until I was drafted into the Army in 1942. Upon my discharge from the Army in 1946, I was invited back to my former position in Atlanta. They were about to build a new community center and wanted me to run its recreation program. However, I had been away from my New York based family for a long time. They prevailed on me not to take the Atlanta position, but to find work in the New York area. I agreed.

Soon thereafter, I noticed an ad in the newspaper from a Brooklyn orphanage called the Pride of Judea. I went down for an interview and was hired. I was made supervisor of the Senior Boys group, which had twenty-eight boys. I immediately was impressed by the niceness of the boys. There was very little profanity, and there may have been only one boy who smoked—on the sly, of course. Coming from the Army, where bad language and smoking were the norm, and not the exception, this level of conduct was impressive.

The first thing I knew I had to do was to keep these boys very busy. I organized all sorts of games, activities, and hobbies for them, made sure that there was something for everyone, and monitored the activities each step of the way. Soon, I found myself in the unfamiliar area of dramatics and performing. Some of the kids were quite good, and I put their talents to good use.

For example, all the kids in the Pride would come down to the dining hall for a meal and the food wouldn't be ready. They'd have to wait ten or twenty minutes, or more, and the noise level and restlessness would become an ordeal for everyone. When this became too frequent, I decided to do something about it. I had the kids perform. We did skits, sketches, solo songs, group songs, and even instrumentals. To this day, the alumni will remind me about those sessions. Not only did it solve the problem of the unpleasant wait, but it gave the kids a showcase to perform their talents and have fun as well.

We had supply problems at the Pride. Mrs. Gatner, director of operations, who had been there for a very long time, liked to do things her own way and could not be dissuaded. For example, she'd give out one bottle of ketchup and one of mustard per group for each meal. I'd find myself running around my five tables each meal, relaying the bottles from one table to another. When I asked her for more bottles, she looked at me as if I were crazy. I couldn't convince her otherwise.

But the kids were good. Charlie Vladimer had the Junior Boys when I arrived, and we immediately hit it off. Working together, we kept things positive, busy, and as fun-filled as possible. Charlie remarked how comparatively tension-free these kids were as compared to the infamous Arano era, when he had done his first stint at the Pride some years earlier. Indeed, most of the photos of the kids from the 1946–47 era show smiling, happy faces. We did many activities and things that turned out well and provided good experiences for the kids. That was important to us. Not the winning or losing, but the participation and getting something out of the activity.

In addition to the conventional games and sports that kids usually play, I had them into other things. For example, we did magic. I'd walk out of the room while the twenty-eight boys in the group picked someone. Then I'd walk back in and pick that person on the first try. They were flabbergasted! "How'd you do that, Harry?" I'd say, "Magic." Later on, I promised, I might let them in on the secret. I had an accomplice who would signal me one way or another. I wanted all of their senses to be activated, and we did a wide range of things that were fun for them and made for good learning as well.

The kids at the Pride loved to eat. They were voracious eaters who could never get enough. We had one youngster in the group who was so skinny that he was called "Bones." Yet he was our biggest eater. I constantly had to cajole the kitchen people into ordering the quantity of food needed to fill up some of my kids. Thank God for Abie Nagel, who worked in the kitchen. A Pride kid himself, he always was there for us when we needed extra food.

He was terrific on the weekends as well. That's when the alumni would visit, play ball, and needed some food and drink. Abie would always supply them with bottles of cold milk, cookies, peanut butter and jelly, and the like. Fortunately, Mrs. Gatner and Mr. Nierow were off then, and Charlie and I were left in charge. The availability of food and drink made a big difference and enabled the alumni to feel really welcome.

The kitchen generally had enough food for every meal, but not always. There was once a bad stretch when food was in meager supply. I recall one meal which kept popping up: matzoh brei. When I asked what was for dessert, the cook said, "matzoh brei!" The same meal was repeated once a week for awhile: matzoh brei and syrup. That was it. Fortunately for me, since we had to eat the same food as the kids, if we didn't like the meal, we could leave later, go to Schneider's deli and get some good hot dogs.

While most kids didn't leave the dining room hungry, some did. There were more instances of food theft than of any other kind of theft. Kids would try to sneak into the kitchen and steal whatever food they could find. Whenever the executive director asked me to look into it, I'd say that I would, but I'd point out that what this theft meant was that the kids weren't getting enough to eat. In general, though, the meals were satisfactory, both in quantity and quality.

I had problems with Mrs. Gatner throughout my four years at the Pride. She was well entrenched there, and you had to do things her way or not at all. She'd take in new supplies, put them in the back of the rotation, and use up the old first. This was tough in the area of clothing. The kids changed clothes three times a week. Mrs. Gatner decreed that supervisors would only get as many clothing items as there were children in their groups. For me, that was impossible. I had twenty-eight kids of varying shapes and sizes. I needed like thirty-five shirts and trousers, etc., to clothe my kids so that their outfits would fit well.

I solved this problem by going to Mrs. Silver, who was in charge of clothing, when Mrs. Gatner wasn't around. She was a nice lady who immediately understood my needs and gave me the quantity that I needed. I very much appreciated her presence, and we worked well together.

I also was frustrated in getting game supplies and equipment for my kids. I remember being on duty on Sunday afternoons and sometimes community residents would stop in and ask if they could make a donation to the Home. If money was given, it would go into the general fund and the kids wouldn't benefit. So I'd always say, "If you really want to help the kids, buy a record player, or some baseball gloves, or some new books, etc." I named specific items and told them to ask for me when they delivered them. In that way, I knew that my kids would directly benefit from their generosity.

We were poorly paid at the Pride. Our salaries were minimal and we had few health benefits. We had to live in a room near the kids and were on twenty-four-hour call, with only one day off a week. We didn't even get normal vacation time, just irregular days here and there.

We just couldn't seem to make any inroads despite our frequent requests for improvements. Things were very tight for me because I had married one of my female colleagues, who, upon our marriage, left the Pride for a more lucrative job elsewhere. Yet I wanted to remain, if at all possible, because of my attachment to the kids. They were near and dear to me.

It wasn't surprising when my colleagues came to me in 1950 and suggested that we form a union, affiliate with a nearby local, and see if we couldn't force the issue for improved pay and other benefits. They asked me to serve as president. I asked if they were prepared to lose their jobs on this issue, because that was a real possibility. When they said that they were, I accepted, and we unionized.

When I went to Jacob H. Cohen to inform him of our changed status, he fired all of us on the spot! Stating that he didn't want Communists working at the Home, he directed us to leave. That was it. We were gone. The union told us to picket the Pride, and we did so for about a week. Jacob H. wrote some letters to the local papers and even sent out his own account to the surrounding residents. They were amazed at the turn of events, and several approached us on the picket line. They had assumed that we were like teachers or social workers and were getting remunerated similarly. When we told them our salaries, they were amazed. Nonetheless, Jacob H. stood firm and all of us were out of there. Fired with us was the dedicated Mrs. Braverman, who had worked at the Pride for some twenty years.

This marked the beginning of the Pride of Judea's last decade as a residential orphanage.

What was unique about the Pride? The most distinctive thing about the Pride was that its comparatively small size was comfortable for kids, making it possible to respond to their needs, and enabling them to get most of the benefits of a substitute family. The kids were able to develop the socialization skills that would permit them to function well in the outside world. They also had enough competition from peers to prompt them to try harder to develop themselves in all respects.

The Pride was very lucky in its personnel. It paid so poorly that it had too many short-term employees, and their rapid turnover was not good for the kids. Yet we did have the Charlies, Andy Schreiber, Mrs. Braverman, and the like, who held the place together and made it into a better Home for the kids. Maybe that was the influence of its founders, but the Pride did get decent people, for the most part; and everyone involved in running it, from the founding fathers through the supervisory staff to the boards of directors, wanted the kids to develop fully and to succeed in life.

An underlying current of dedication to the kids ran consistently through the place. No matter how frustrated I became, I was never deterred from trying to solve the problems facing me as they related to the kids. I could and did overlook my own discomforts, which were considerable, and never let them get in the way of giving my best efforts to my kids. That was the thrust of the job for me at the Pride.

I had strong beliefs that carried me forward. Those who didn't have such beliefs came and went rather quickly. No matter if the Pride hierarchy treated me poorly, I take more from my experiences there than any sense of injustice. It means far more to me today, and has throughout the years after I left the Pride, that the alumni, all adults now, with their own families, can greet me and remember specific instances of my work with them that made a difference in their lives. Can anything be more important and more valuable? I think not!

Chapter 22

The Pride Today

From Orphanage to Mental Health Center

In the 1950s, two developments occurred that began to shorten the life of the Home as an orphanage.

First and most important was a major shift in the thinking of child-care professionals about the suitability of orphanages as the best placement for indigent children. More and more of the leading authorities began to advocate either foster home placement or adoption for children who would once have been prime candidates for placement in orphanages like the Pride of Judea. Orphanages began to be perceived, as one author put it, "as relics of the nineteenth century."

Indeed, where there had been as many as a half-dozen orphanages of all denominations in the borough of Brooklyn alone at the start of the forties, now, but ten years later, there was only the Pride of Judea Children's Home. It had outlasted the largest Jewish orphanage in the metropolitan area, the Hebrew Orphans' Asylum, located in Manhattan, as well as its other counterpart, the Hebrew National Orphans' Home, in Yonkers, New York.

Quite naturally, a second development occurred—a sharp drop in enrollment at the Pride. When the fifties began, there may have been slightly more than 100 boys and girls, ages six to fifteen, residing in the Home. As the decade progressed, the number dropped dramatically, so that by 1958 there was but one child, a girl, living in the institution. Sometime that year she left, and the Pride of Judea closed its doors forever as an orphanage.

But the Pride was not finished. The formidable Jacob H. Cohen was still president of the board, and he and his colleagues wanted to continue the tradition of tzedakah which had been the Pride's priority ever since its inception in 1915. They engaged leaders in the child-care field to determine how the Pride could still effectively meet the pressing needs of children.

In 1959, the Pride assumed its new identity by opening up the Pride of Judea Child Guidance Clinic and a related Family Aide Service. The stated purpose of the Clinic was to diagnose, treat, and prevent emotional problems in children and their families. The Family Aide and Homemaker Services were designed to provide in-home assistance to families in times of emergency or dire stress so as to keep them together and help them get through their crisis.

Warren Deutsch, C.S.W., was appointed director, and Dr. Melvin A. Scharfman, psychiatrist and psychoanalyst, with considerable expertise in child matters, was called in as consultant to the board. The Clinic, in its first two years of existence, was swamped by an increasing volume of cases and very quickly demonstrated its worth to the community.

With an ever expanding clientele, it became clear that there were many severely disturbed children requiring more intensive services. The question was whether to open a residential facility for autistic children or an outpatient school with more individualized family services. Thanks to a strong recommendation from Dr. Scharfman, the latter course was chosen, and the Pride opened an important third strand, the Day School and Treatment Center for Seriously Disturbed Children. It soon became one of the foremost institutions in this specialized field and was known as perhaps the best school of its kind in New York City.

In 1962, after some twenty-three years of outstanding philanthropic activity, Jacob. H. Cohen stepped down as president of the Pride board and was succeeded by Maurice Bernhardt, then a district court judge. In recognition of his singular contributions, the Clinic was renamed the Jacob H. Cohen Child Guidance Clinic.

As the sixties progressed, it became clear that a new location was needed. The Pride's Brooklyn neighborhood, once so comfortable and user-friendly, had deteriorated quite badly. Vandalism and break-ins to the building were occurring. Staff members and patients were being mugged, and night services, an essential part of the Center, had to be stopped. It was time to move.

In a market survey for a new location in the metropolitan area, the Pride's board of directors decided that the growing region of northeastern Queens and northwestern Nassau County was lacking in the kinds of outpatient mental health services the Pride could provide. A temporary location was opened in 1969, and within a year, more than 400 children and their family members were being treated there, with an ever-crowded waiting list of over 200 continuing to grow daily.

A prime site, on Northern Boulevard in Douglaston, was purchased in 1971, and construction soon began on a modern, state-of-the-art facility. Eighteen months later, on December 10, 1972, dedication ceremonies were held for the opening of the Pride of Judea Treatment Services. The two-story building had rooms for individual and group therapy, conference rooms, and a large meeting room suitable for seminars, chapter functions, and fund-raising activities.

With the opening of the new center, the Pride's board made another decision that was a quantum jump forward. Henceforth, all of the skilled mental health services offered by the Pride would now be available to everyone, regardless of race, religion, age, or creed. It would continue to be a nonprofit center, meaning that patients would pay sliding-scale fees based on their income and their ability to do so.

As a not-for-profit, nonsectarian clinic, the Pride began to receive some funding from the New York City Department of Mental Health. This enabled it to expand staff and services to meet the increasing needs of its growing clientele. At the dedication dinner marking the opening of the new building, Dr. Melvin A. Scharfman, now the agency's medical director, noted that the growing staff permitted the Pride to do more community outreach work with both schools and hospitals, so as to provide the most integrated and effective approach to helping clients. "The challenge is great," he concluded, "but for those who care about children, a continuing effort must be made!"

The passage of years brought a continuing increase in the Pride's programs, both in quantity and quality. The training of staff to meet the ever changing needs of clients was ongoing and of high priority. By the mid-seventies, under the stewardship of the new board president, Sol Orlinsky, challenging goals had been set, with most being reached. A full range of psychiatric services was now available to all people, regardless of age. Many families with adopted children were being helped to make the appropriate adjustments in their relationships. By the late seventies and early eighties, with a burgeoning divorce rate tearing up families, this problem was to be addressed by new and expanding family treatment.

In the eighties, fueled by the ever-growing problems of a complex society, a sharp growth in applications for service clearly indicated a need for further expansion. Once again a dedicated board responded, and in 1987 a third floor and an elevator were added to the building to enable an increase in programs for young children, the elderly, and the handicapped. The cost of the project would be a financial burden for many years. Whereas the original two-story structure had cost less than $500,000 to build, the new addition would cost well over $1.3 million before its completion. The Pride pushed on.

At the dedication ceremonies for the new addition, Dr. Steven Katz, then New York State Commissioner of Mental Health, referred to the Pride's "extraordinary contributions to the clients being served. In providing these outstanding services, you have brightened the prospects for countless individuals and have provided a model worthy of being replicated statewide."

In 1987, Lawrence Simon became the new board president, inheriting a quarter-million-dollar budget deficit left over from the expansion. He set out to address this problem by bringing to the board a wider network of businessmen and people with financial acumen. Their expertise would be needed more than ever because the cost of running such a comprehensive agency would always be more than its funding from established sources. Government funding accounted for 30 percent of the budget; patient fees brought in 40 percent more, leaving a full third of the budget each year to be funded by private philanthropic sources. The need for successful fund-raising was a persistent concern.

A strong source of leadership and assistance came in the person of Paula Held Sharf, who joined the agency in 1980. Paula, who soon became administrative director, was very effective in the challenging task of fund-raising, as well as in providing the quality of leadership that enabled the agency to meet the varied needs of its diverse clientele. It effectively continued to do so under her stewardship.

Another significant event occurred in the early eighties that was long overdue. The alumni of the Children's Home finally came together as a cohesive organization integrated with the Mental Health Center, as an active and supportive chapter.

This was largely due to the initiative of several alumni. In early 1982, Irv Schneider and his brother Marv (both Pride alumni), and Irv's wife, Joyce, set about convening an alumni reunion at the roller rink that they owned in Commack, Long Island. Enlisting the help of the alumni whom they knew, they slowly but surely widened the network of names and addresses of alumni all over the country and from different eras of residence in the Home. They sent out several hundred invitations to the reunion, which was to be held on a Sunday in June, at the rink. Lo and behold, several hundred people came, and the event turned into a festive and emotional reunion of people who had not seen each other for scores of years.

Prior to that time, smaller alumni organizations had briefly been in existence. Now, here were several hundred former Pride residents under one roof, laughing, crying, and relishing their renewed contacts with friends from the Home. Most had not seen each other in many decades.

As good as it was, it didn't last. No alumni organization was formed right away. A jump-start was needed, and it came, regrettably, in the untimely death of Rose Nadler Schefer in 1984. Rose, who had lived in the Home for sixteen years of her childhood, had become an active volunteer at the Mental Health Clinic. She had dreamed of the formation of an active alumni organization that would assist the Pride in its important work. When she lost her battle with cancer, her Pride friends, both old and new, decided that an alumni chapter, in her name, would be a fitting memorial.

In February of 1985, a letter of intent to form an alumni chapter in Rose Schefer's name was sent to all the alumni. Manny Fineberg, an alumnus, and himself a licensed psychologist, offered to lead the movement. Subsequently, the alumni were invited to a luncheon meeting in October at the Mental Health Center, and the response was outstanding. Manny was elected president of the fledgling chapter, dues were set, and the Rose Nadler Schefer Alumni Chapter of the Pride of Judea was underway.

Since then, the chapter has been very active. It holds two planned events yearly, sends out some six newsletters per year to its members, and helps the Mental Health Center with its fund-raising efforts. In 1991, when the Pride celebrated seventy-five years of existence, the alumni raised over $5,000. As one chapter officer was heard to say, "The Children's Home was there for us when we needed it. Now it's give-back time, and we'd like to do what we can to help our namesake carry on its important work!"

And the Mental Health Center has carried on, becoming one of the finest agencies of its kind in the country, albeit with considerable trials and tribulations, most of them monetary. To shore up its financial base and widen still further its important umbrella of services, the Pride, in the summer of 1997, merged with a premier mental health and human services agency, the Jewish Board of Family and Children's Services.

As a result of the merger, the name of the Pride of Judea continues stronger than ever, with all eleven programs of both agencies now located in Queens, New York, under the aegis of the Pride of Judea division. Paula Held Sharf, continuing as director of the division, had this to say about the eighty-two-year legacy of the name and organization:

> From its inception, the Pride of Judea always was known for its professionalism, flexibility, and strong ability to respond to the needs of its clients. This was the case when it was an orphanage and certainly has held true right up to the present time. Since its very first day, many years ago, when that small but dedicated group first broke ground for a new orphans' home in Brooklyn, the Pride has not stood still when its services were needed by so many. It has not, it cannot, it will not. We must continue to meet the needs of individuals who are crying for help, and we cannot remain passive while that need exists. With the support of those committed to being their "brother's keeper," we will continue to strive for the day when such help may no longer be needed!

Amen! The tzedakah tradition of the Pride continues. From orphanage to still-expanding mental health center, it has not missed a beat in maintaining its eighty-plus-year, singular tradition of being its brother's keeper!

Chapter 23

The Home: Its Full Meaning

There are three pertinent questions to be addressed in this concluding chapter. Was the Pride of Judea Children's Home a successful institution, and if so, why? Is an orphanage like the Pride a viable option today as a residence for needy children? Finally, what impact did the Pride have on our total lives?

In answering the first question as succinctly and accurately as possible, the adage that springs to mind is: "The proof is in the pudding." In its thirty-six-year history as an orphanage, the Pride of Judea Children's Home, according to our best estimates, cared for approximately 2,000 children. What became of them and what their own evaluations and views of the Home are, constitute probably the most accurate indicators of success for this orphanage.

Our Alumni organization has been an active one. We have a mailing list of close to two hundred names and we send out about six newsletters each year to them. We involve them in the newsletter by printing their letters, announcing family and other news, and by generally making them the main substance of the newsletter itself. We actively search for alumni not on the mailing list and make a big deal out of it when "new" alumni are found and added to the list. We run two lively events each year; one a festive pre-Hannukah Brunch at the Pride building, and the other, an equally delightful picnic in June. In the former, our program generally centers about a discussion by the entire assemblage relating to our personal memories of the Pride. With family members present, these have been animated, emotional, strongly nostalgic, and always, very powerful.

The overwhelming majority of alumni feel that the Pride was an extremely successful orphanage. Most of them came out of it with a better foundation for their lives, as compared to what might have been the case had they remained in their own personal circumstances, or had they been placed in foster care. In the Pride, they received the stability and security of an environment that they could trust for consistency, longevity, and protection.

Since education was stressed and made a focal point of every day, we know of no Pride alumnus who didn't graduate from high school, with many getting college and post-graduate degrees. With the parallel emphasis on preparing us to earn a living, virtually every alumnus developed a strong work ethic which has enabled almost all of us to have sound and successful careers in our chosen vocations. Many alumni contend that their childhood in the orphanage did more to "toughen" them up for their adult lives than a more conventional background.

We know of no alumnus who has had difficulty with the law. Virtually all of us have been involved, either through career choice or community activity, with many pro-social, helping activities. There is a pronounced sense of helping others that runs through many of our lives.

A strong sense of family is a central value of all alumni. Most have been in long-term marriages and have raised families. Others have developed family situations of their own. All willingly assume and fulfill their family obligations, many quite generously.

Was the Home successful? Both, from the narrative of this book, as well as from all of the data and reactions of alumni, the only conclusion to be reached is that the Pride of Judea was indeed a most successful children's home. It provided its residents with all of the ingredients necessary for them to become successful, well adjusted adults, and contributing members to society. The body of information from alumni, former supervisors, and from everyone connected with the Home, strongly affirms this conclusion.

This does not mean, however, that the Pride of Judea was per-fect, or that it did not have flaws. It wasn't and it did. Many alumni have indicated that immediately upon leaving the Pride, they were unprepared for the initial adjustment into the next phase of their lives, and could have benefited from better preparation and coun-seling. Another major dissatisfaction was the frequent turnover of supervisors as they came and went at the Pride. With a generally poor rate of pay and 24-hour-a-day responsibilities, many able peo-ple would make this a short-term stop, early in their careers, per-haps to pick up valuable experience in the child-care field. It resulted in a revolving door cycle of short stays and new adjustments which, generally, were not easy on the kids. Fortunately, as indicated clearly in the body of the book, some high-quality, dedicated people were a good part of that mix and they made major contributions to our lives.

Both authors of this book have had active leadership roles in our alumni organization. During its thirteen years of existence, we've compiled many data, some verbal and some in writing, from the alumni about their experiences in the Pride. While this information is steeped in nostalgia, nonetheless, it also has the singular force of first hand experience and the clarity of time and maturity. Given our advanced ages and long-term perspectives, our view of the Pride is rooted in the reality of our lives.

As orphans, the Pride indeed gave us many "parents"; many average, some poor, some extraordinary. In their entirety, they probably ran the range of effect of our own parents, were they alive or able to care for us in the more conventional setting of our own would-be homes. That was their value, because we all need parents, or parent substitutes, to nurture us, to nourish us, to discipline us, to relate and react to us, to do all of the myriad things that push and pull and prod us into adulthood. Spending our formative years in this orphanage, we indeed had many parents and many siblings in a total environment that truly met our varying and important needs. This was our good fortune and our lives are much better because of it!

Is an orphanage like the Pride a viable option today for the residential placement of needy children?

The plight of children today is as problematic as ever, and perhaps, even more so. Over a million runaway children are reported to the nation's police departments each year. Close to 150,000 children are institutionalized yearly for mental disabilities. The incidence of child abuse remains at epidemic levels. The incidence of drug and alcohol abuse among the young increases each year. So does every other problem category. All of the above reflect the serious dysfunction of families, which is the main reason why so many young people are removed from their homes each year and placed elsewhere. At present, most of them are placed in foster care.

As of May, 1997, over a half million children were in foster homes in this country. The federal government funds and determines much of foster care policy, which is finalized and carried out by the states. Originally intended to provide safe, temporary homes for abused or homeless children, the $12 billion foster care system, according to the U.S. Department of Health and Human Services, has an average stay per child of 3.5 to 5.5 years in a foster home, at an average annual cost of $17,500 per child per year.

In a recent study of youth who leave foster care at 18, it was found that within four years, 40% of them had either been on public assistance or incarcerated. A recent Bureau of Justice study found 17% of the total jail population had once been in foster homes.

Adoption, as another important option for children in need of home placement, accounts for some 60,000 children each year. Bringing up the distant rear as a residential placement category for children, is orphanages and small group homes. Some 10,000 children fall into this category each year.

Why are orphanages still held in such low esteem by the ruling authorities that they are a distant last as a viable placement option for needy children? Were comprehensive studies ever done, in the past or present, to warrant such a conclusion? There are few, if any, to be found. Have people who actually lived or even worked in orphanages ever been surveyed by child care authorities so as to provide a first hand evaluation of their respective institutions? The answer appears to be a resounding no!

When decisions were made in the forties to phase out orphanage referrals in favor of foster care placement, the prevalent thinking of that era concluded that a more normal home atmosphere would better serve the growth needs of young children than an orphanage. This was a decision based, not so much on research data, but on the age-old assumption that a good foster home is better than a good orphanage. Hence, let's go in that direction. Given the need to use public funds as effectively as possible, let's use them for the placement of children in good foster homes.

This historical shift appears to have been made by the leaders in the child-care field based on their observations and feelings. However, there appears to have been little or no information gathered from the hundreds of people who have experienced childhood life in an orphanage, or, for that matter, even from those who have been in foster care. The dominant thinking at that time, as reflected in the writings of several leading authorities, was that orphanages were "relics of the 19th century" and that the needs of indigent children could be served best, mainly in foster care.

Right or wrong, this thinking has held sway for the past fifty years and is still in vogue, reflected by the vast numbers of children in foster homes today. But, there are at least two significant factors, not present fifty years ago, that may compel different conclusions to be drawn about favorable residential placements for needy children.

The first is the increasing deficiencies of the foster care system; its very mixed results, swelling costs, and its most major indictment, that it frequently fails to provide essential security and stability for its children. There is an increasing body of data to substantiate these deficiencies, as well as mounting criticism from many observers of the foster care scene.

The second factor is the increased amount of commentary, research and observations from those who have lived in orphanages, particularly in the last decade, which provide a very different perspective of their worth as compared to their depiction fifty years ago. While these data may not be sizable as yet, they are quite significant and central to a more accurate assessment of orphanages, which will help determine their truer worth today as a possible placement option for children in need of a home.

This new, valuable, and increasing body of data, about orphans and orphanages, does not, to our knowledge, have a specific name, defining it as a separate social science category. Therefore, we'd like to embody the study of orphans and orphanages as "orphanology", and have it be known as such.

Orphanology is most pertinent to our central question raised earlier: Is a small, quality orphanage a viable option as a residence for needy children today? The following, pertinent excerpts from some of the recent literature in this area speak directly to this question.

In his book, The Luckiest Orphans (1992), Hy Bogen chronicles the history of one of the oldest and largest Jewish orphanages, the Hebrew Orphan Asylum of New York. The primary emphasis of the book is on the 100 year history of this institution, but he does make reference to the value of orphanages. "The lives of our alumni offer strong evidence that the HOA had a lasting effect. Many have done remarkably well in their lives."

As for foster care, Bogen had this to say.

> The social work profession's dependence on only one form of care in
> the last fifty years was a smug, narrow and short-sighted approach.
> There will never be enough good foster homes for all the children
> who need them. Many of our alumni who had been in foster care,
> preferred the HOA by far, over their foster homes. Art Buchwald, one
> of our alumni, who had lived in three foster homes, said, in a televi-
> sion interview, "Neither the child or the people who take you in ever
> make an emotional commitment. A foster child senses this very early
> and he doesn't want to get too close because he knows that these peo-
> ple are not for real."

Rick Safran was in the Israel Orphan Asylum and in the
Hebrew National Orphan Home (HNOH) for a total of eleven
years. A former New York City high school teacher of English and a
school administrator, with a very successful career in education, he
now is the editor of the Alumnus, the alumni newspaper of the
HNOH. In his own written pieces, Rick speaks candidly about the
rough and tumble existence of his life in these orphanages. He also
contends that "we survived. We not only survived, we flourished.
We became tough and self-sufficient." He believes that because of
his upbringing, he has been much more appreciative of the things
in his life, such as family, education, etc. than those from more
conventional backgrounds. As is the case with most other HNOH
alumni, he speaks fondly of the former HNOH Executive Director,
Reuben Koftoff, who impacted this orphanage with his credo,
"Survive, grow, flourish!"

Karl Fleming entered the Methodist Orphanage in Raleigh
North Carolina at the age of eight and left, nine years later, at 17, to
join the Navy. A former Newsweek and CBS journalist, with a successful career in communications, he had the following comments
about his orphanage in a May, 1995 article in Newsweek, entitled,
"Please Sir, Let's Have Some More, Orphanages can be a positive
source for a good life."

> Despite its shortcomings, the Methodist Orphanage was a good place
> in which to grow up, given its alternatives, and a valuable incubator
> for adulthood and good citizenship. We learned honesty, loyalty, self-
> discipline, self-sufficiency. We learned to take pride in working hard
> and doing well, even in the most menial jobs. We learned to keep our
> word. We learned fair play and how to live with others. We learned

respect for our elders and how to take our medicine when we did wrong.

The results speak for themselves. Of the 2700 children who came and stayed during the eight decades that the orphanage existed, as I knew it, only one, as far as I heard, ever went to prison. There was not a single unwed teenage mother. Though there is no official data, I know firsthand that the divorce rate is extremely low, as are alcoholism, addiction and joblessness.

There's an alumni reunion every year and I go back, always with mixed memories of pleasure and pain. Like my "brothers and sisters", I am much more grateful than not, because the orphanage gave me the home, the stability, the family and the tools for life that I could not otherwise have had.

Dr. Charles D. Aring, M.D. is a distinguished professor emeritus of neurology at the University of Cincinnati and the author of the book, *The Understanding Physician*, and other articles. He also was an orphan and resided in an orphanage from the age of seven through fifteen and a half. His article, "In Defense of Orphanages", (The American Scholar, Fall, 1991) makes several pertinent points in this discussion.

First, he decries the "Dickensian cloud" that has been hung over orphanages, contributing to their negative reputation and ultimate disuse. Virtually every piece written by a former orphan also protests this characterization as being inaccurate and generally held by those with no first hand or substantive contact with any reputable children's institution.

Secondly, Dr. Aring records the "debits and credits" of his orphanage, discussing discipline, education, religious training, work, and play. Standout features for him included "the camaraderie amongst the children, particularly the older boys. If not a family, we were a clan and would close ranks in competition with children outside the walls."

Another highlight was expressed as follows:

The superlative merit of the institution was the great good health that prevailed among us during my entire tenure. This was the major benefit of my stay there; it set a pattern and perhaps influenced my eventual choice of occupation as well. I had come from an unhealthy environment: my mother had been an invalid since my birth, and her mother and sister required frequent hospital care. But in the orphanage, everyone was expected to be healthy, and usually we were. Except for the usual assortment of contagious diseases and cuts and bruises, there was little illness. During my entire stay, there were no deaths and nothing serious. Had I derived nothing more from my orphan life (and I did) than the reversal of my family legacy of poor health, the experience would have been worth it.

The third important point made by Dr. Aring is his claim that good orphanages do exist today and he introduces us to one, Girard College, located in Philadelphia, Pennsylvania. This institution, now over 150 years old, contains more than 500 boys and girls between the ages of three and eleven. Its central emphasis is on education, "with every opportunity afforded by a large enthusiastic faculty for students to develop to the extent of their capacity. From the day of admission, it is expected that the student will go on to a university, and practically all of them do so on scholarships underwritten by the Girard endowment, with similar arrangements for graduate school."

Dr. Aring regards Girard as one of the "outstanding orphanages in the United States", and believes that it should serve as a model for other orphanages, which he strongly recommends as a beneficial environment for children in need of a home.

The most famous orphanage in our country is Boys Town, Nebraska, probably due to the memorable 1938 movie of the same name. Prominently mentioned in the 1994 Congressional debates about welfare reform, it was visited by author Brian Jendryka for his article which appeared in the Summer, 1994 issue of the Heritage Foundation's journal, *Policy Review*. In it, he states, "As illegitimacy mounts and more and more American families fall apart, Boys Town is a model for a foster care system in crisis, and an attractive alternative to a welfare system that undermines parental responsibility."

Why is Boys Town a model orphanage? Jendryka explains as follows:

> The number one thing that Boys Town does is, it keeps kids safe, it keeps them out of trouble. What both the boys and girls say they most appreciate is that they're off the streets, away from gangs and violence. They're also out of their family environment where they used to be beaten regularly and even molested. Now they're in a small family environment with parent figures who are much needed role models.

Jendryka describes the current picture of Boys Town:

Kids live in single family homes where highly trained married cou-
ples, serving as "family-teachers" function as 24 hour per day parents
to only eight boys or girls, who become like brothers or sisters to
each other. These family-teachers, working in close alliance with Boys
Town school teachers, use a motivational approach to get the kids to
learn by doing the behaviors that are appropriate and pay off in the
long run; skills they missed in their previous dysfunctional environ-
ments.

Believing that religion is "absolutely crucial" for transforming
troubled children into well adjusted adults, every child is required
to learn how to pray and worship in his or her own faith. Though
run by a Roman Catholic priest, the children are directed to a faith
of their own choice. There is a Catholic and a Protestant church on
campus and Jewish children attend an off-campus synagogue, with
similar arrangements made for children from other religious tradi-
tions.

Jendryka concludes by saying, "Boys Town's success has been
amazing. Most children arriving there are two or three grade levels
behind academically. Three quarters come from one parent families.
A majority of the girls and 40% of the boys have been sexually
abused, many have tried drugs and alcohol, 20% have attempted
suicide and 40% have been on probation or parole. Nevertheless,
80% graduate from their family cottage style program and high
school, stay out of trouble with the law, remain in a job and off
welfare, and many go on to college and beyond."

The current director of Boys' Town Father Val J. Peter, in his
own fine article, appropriately entitled, "What's Best for the Children?" (*USA Today Magazine*, November, 1995), adds several more
pertinent and important thoughts to the discussion.

Says Father Peter,

What Boys Town and other institutions like it do is part of the solution, not the entire solution. "Orphanage" has been redefined so that,
in its place, there is a substitute family to love and teach boys and girls
what their own family should have if it were not disabled in some
severe way.

There are five essential characteristics of any arrangement to help
children. It must be safe. Procedures need to be in place that minimize any possibility of abuse and give early warning signs of any
breach of this covenant of loyalty with children. Second, the children
must be happy. Given their choices in a less than ideal world, they

need to want to be there. Third, the kids have to get better. So many children in need of help today have multiple behavioral and mental health problems. Substitute care must assure that they get better. Fourth, the format has to be family-style and family-based. Children cannot learn family skills and values unless they are in a family. Family life is role-modeled; it is every moment of every day. It is not an academic pursuit. Lastly, the program has to be replicable. It must be able to be copied effectively over and over again. (This model currently is being used in fourteen different metropolitan areas in this country.)

In conceding that this contemporary model of an effective orphanage is expensive, Father Peter calls on governmental leaders at every level to not politicize this issue; to provide adequate funding as an authentic, needed investment in our children, one that not only will pay off in better results, but also will be cheaper in the long run, given the staggering costs of today's ineffectual social systems.

Probably the most extensive research in orphanology has been done by Dr. Richard McKenzie, a professor of Economics at the University of California at Irvine. Dr. McKenzie, himself, spent eight years of his childhood in a North Carolina orphanage, which he recounted in a recent book, *The Home*. In 1995, he sent an eight-page, detailed questionnaire to each of 1,200 alumni of three different orphanages; his former one in North Carolina, which was Presbyterian, a non-sectarian one in rural Ohio, and a Jewish one in urban Ohio. He received 600 responses back, a very high return, with the following results:

The respondents, all white, surpassed all of the national norms, educationally, at all levels.

Their rate of unemployment was 1% as compared to the national norm of 6%. Their median income averaged 16% higher than their counterpart group. Their poverty rate was half that of their counterparts. Only 3% of them ever had been on public assistance, as compared to 19% for the general population. Less than 1% of them ever had served prison time, far lower than the norm. 13% of them reported the need for some counseling in their lives, as compared to 24% of the regular population. Of this group, only 2% felt that it was connected to their stay in an orphanage.

Their attitudes toward life were far better than the average population, as well. Each year, in a variety of public opinion polls, Americans are asked, "Taking all things together, how would you say things are going these days?" In 1994, 29% of the respondents indicated they were "very happy"; 59% said, "somewhat happy"; and 12% responded, "not too happy". The former orphans, on the other hand, were far more positive in their general outlook. 58% were "very happy"; 37% were "somewhat happy"; and only 5% were "not too happy".

Most significant was their strongly stated preference for their institutional care. When asked if they preferred growing up in their orphanages, or in foster care, over 92% chose their orphanages, less than 2% chose foster care, and the remaining 6% did not make either choice. When asked to choose between growing up in their orphanages, or with available members of their own families, 75% of the respondents chose their orphanages, and only 16% chose their families.

From this extensive survey, which appears to be the largest one ever done on an orphan population, Dr. McKenzie makes the following qualifications and draws the following conclusions.

> Clearly this survey has limitations, the most important of which is that the respondents were not drawn randomly from the national population of all former orphans. The alumni who had good experiences might be more likely to be on their alumni mailing lists and more likely to respond. Tracking down all residents of any given home for children is simply not possible.
>
> However, even after allowing for some upward bias, the survey results do seriously undermine some of the critics' most sweeping, negative assessments applied to all orphanages. The findings also indicate that while institutional care may not be desirable for all disadvantaged children, it was helpful for many. The study strongly suggests that at least some, if not many, orphanages in this country appear to have known how to break the cycles of poverty, neglect and abuse for large numbers of children, and they did it, often with much gratitude from a majority of alumni.
>
> The evidence also suggests that partisans in the current child-care debate would be well advised to revisit some strategically important questions, not the least of which are: What types of orphanages were successful? Did not homes for children have a higher ratio of successes to failures than the current foster care system? To what extent can the attributes of the successful homes of yesterday be duplicated today?

Based on the mounting evidence in the young field of orphanology, as described in part above, there appears to be sufficient data to respond to Dr. McKenzie's very pertinent questions. Orphanages of the past were far more successful in their child rearing efforts than they ever were given credit for. They indeed do appear to have had a much higher ratio of successes to failures, a ratio attested to by the very people who had first hand experiences in these institutions.

There indeed are successful orphanages out there today, modified in design and format to meet the myriad problems of today's troubled children. While they may vary in size and design, Boys Town and Girard College, the central experience and main environment for each child is the family unit. Their results already have produced data that are substantive, reliable and impressive. These institutions, whether they're called orphanages or children's homes, are most worthy of center-stage placement today in the important discussion of "what's best for our children?"

Nor are the answers to this worthy question subject to a "one size fits all " solution. Our own beloved, former supervisor, Sam Arcus makes this point in an unpublished piece, entitled "Is There a Place for the Home (Institution) in the 21st Century?" He has been a prolific writer and thinker across the spectrum of the entire social work field. As he considers the value of different placement options for needy children, he writes, "Assuming the presence of emotionally balanced and loving parents, then remaining in one's home obviously is most desirable. Second best, would be foster care but only if constant transfers can be avoided and only if genuinely caring foster parents are available, preferrably in the child's own community. If these conditions are not present, then a well monitored institution, focusing on the best attributes of congregate group living can be very beneficial. Thus, it is not a simple one or the other selection. Each case, each child must be assessed in terms of his particular and special needs. It is important for our society to have available alternatives which can meet the wide variety of child welfare needs. We must stop seeking the "one size fits all" panacea to this social problem. In the light of all the foregoing: is there a place for the "Home" (Institution) in the 21st Century? I should hope so!"

It has been said that if "we always do what we've always done, then, we'll always get what we've always got!" With respect to the best care for those unfortunate children who need a different home than their own, it is time to cast an informed and accurate spotlight on the value of orphanages; to recast them in modern styles, to fund them accordingly, and to place many of our needy children in them for the best possible care.

Just as the Pride of Judea Children's Home was an invaluable and indispensable part of the lives of its residents, today's orphanage of like quality, can make that same essential contribution to many needy children. We orphans from the Home were fortunate enough to have "many parents" in a relatively healthy, protective environment. We hope that today's generation of "orphans" can say the same fifty years from now.

The Impact of the Pride on My Total Life

Phil Craft

All of us in the Pride came from poor families, who, for one reason or another, could not support us. Nevertheless, we grew up at the Pride learning and developing middle class attitudes and values. Self-sufficiency, development of one's potential, maximum effort and success in the outside world, always were conscious goals to strive for, and were reflected by the Pride's agenda of activities and policies.

All aspects of our life invited and compelled us to be self-sufficient. There was a minimum of janitorial service at the Home. We made our beds, swept the floors, cleared the tables, changed our linens and clothes, etc. Extra privileges and small material rewards were offered to those who helped out beyond the usual chores and responsibilities common to all of us. Starting in the forties, even outside jobs were encouraged for those who could handle such a demanding daily schedule. The self-direction and discipline required to meet such obligations had a definite maturing effect, and the pride and self-confidence from doing so was satisfying beyond measure.

The Pride provided a vital mantle of protection, comfort and security by its location, its physical stature and by its rules and procedures.

Despite this healthy emphasis on security and safety, we were not kept as isolated and confined as were children from other orphanages. We frequently had field trips to museums, the zoo, children's productions, amusement parks, and the like. Week-end trips to the local movies were a regular item. We often were taken to Ebbets Field, that wonderful ballpark that was home to the Brooklyn Dodgers. We even were permitted to visit the homes of outside school friends, as long as we notified our supervisors in advance. Such frequent interaction with our outside age peers did much to build our social skills and sense of "normalcy" and self-confidence.

Such privileges and opportunities often were at the hub of a generally healthy disciplinary system. While almost everyone, at one time or another, got smacked by a supervisor, such actions were, by far, the exception rather than the rule. Misbehave, etc. and you lose some valued privilege or trip opportunity. Not many relished missing a weekend movie trip, or an excursion to Ebbets Field to see the "Beloved Bums" play.

Within our close knit community, where we lived in such close proximity to each other, a heightened sense of social behavior was encouraged that made for a more pleasurable living environment. Most of us have fond memories of our dorm life because we really did enjoy our dorm-mates, as well as the activities that went on there. While some bullying and thievery did take place, this was looked down upon, and while we maintained the normal code of silence in turning the perpetrators in, we usually did a number on them ourselves that discouraged repeat activity. Such attitudes, unbeknownst to us at the time, fostered integrity, pro-social values and a sound sense of morality, contributing much to the development of a stronger character in each of us. It is no surprise that we cannot think of a single alumnus who ever was incarcerated for any illegal activity, or had any difficulty with the law.

The Home always placed a high value on school effort and educational achievement which even was reflected in our attitudes towards one other. The brightest and most successful among us were not regarded as "nerds", but often were looked up to and respected. Nobody wanted to be regarded as a "dumbell" with weak prospects for the future. Our report cards were monitored closely and remedial help was offered, if needed.

Virtually every Pride child graduated from high school. Those who had gone to a vocational or commercial high school generally were equipped to earn a living. Those who went to an academic high school were prepared to go on to college. Even those of us who went to a trade school, but who were inspired and encouraged by caring supervisors, were able to retrack ourselves academically and go on to earn college and graduate degrees. Education was THE road we were stimulated to take and many of us did so, thanks to this substantial impetus. It is no wonder that a great majority of Pride alumni had hard working, but successful lives.

Nor was formal education the only way the Home encouraged us to develop our capabilities.

Throughout its long history, the Pride provided special opportunities for individuals to develop their interests and aptitudes within a recreational context. There was a band and a full range of music lessons, a scouting program, a newspaper, photography lessons, arts and crafts sessions, various social clubs, and even dance and drama lessons. Plays were staged, often with elaborate costumes, and often for the outside auxillary chapters, for fundraising. Then, of course, there was a full range of sports and recreational activities. It was like a "Pygmalion effect" with Henry Higgins (the Pride) looking to make "cultured dukes and duchesses" out of us all.

Our religious education and development received priority treatment as well. Weekly participation in Sabbath activities, Hebrew School training for both bar and bat-mitzvah, plus the celebration of all Jewish holidays substantively, made us aware and appreciative of our religion. The bar-mitzvah and bat-mitzvah, occurring in the Pride's shul and then in the lavish St. George Hotel, was a memorable experience for everyone. Whether or not we were religious, we came out of the Home with a healthy sense of our Jewish identity.

It also was our special good fortune to be in a coed institution. Not only did that permit family siblings to remain together, which was an important plus, it also permitted us the opportunities to develop healthy attitudes and relations with the opposite sex. It is not surprising to note the many marriages of Pride residents to each other, virtually all of which lasted for a lifetime.

Of all the services provided by the Home to promote the health and well being of the children, the most important contribution was made by caring staff members: supervisors, kitchen people, seamstresses, medical personnel, and specialty counselors. In varying ways, almost each of them left a special imprint on me during their stay. They came from a variety of backgrounds, were overworked and poorly paid; yet they generally cared about us, and showed it each day in different ways.

It was the supervisors, of course, who made the most enduring impact, and the precious group of them that I describe in this book, have given me a priceless legacy that has done much to brighten my life. Their length of time with me at the Pride was fleeting; yet it was as if they, collectively, were the legendary Merlin, who helped transform a frightened, clumsy runt into a more confident and effective individual with real substance and promise.

Each child who passed through the Home harbors unique memories and tales of their own circumstances and experiences. For many, these simply added up, at least, to a more pleasant and satisfying existence. For a few, like myself, the Home was more than a sheltering presence and sanctuary during a temporary period of dire need. For me, the Pride has been almost the total expanse of my conscious world, providing the only real family that I ever knew as a child. The Pride enabled me to grow as a total person and to be able to fend for myself in an adult world which often had seemed as frightening as any distant continent. I can only imagine the despair and ultimate tragedy that surely would have followed me but for the growing inner strength and confidence which each of these caring parent figures helped to implant and nourish during their time with me at the Pride. I cannot even contemplate how I would have fared in another institution, or in foster care, where my overwhelming needs and difficult problems would have taxed beyond measure, the patience and good will of all but the most dedicated of care-givers. Fortunately, my pathway brought me into contact with just such a premier group and their impact on my life has been nothing short of remarkable!

The Pride's Personal Impact on My Total Life

Stan Friedland

I am sixty-six years old as I write this and I have the luxury of retrospection and the benefits of hindsight. I'd like to use both as I contemplate the pivotal question: "What would my life have been like without my seven years in the Home?"

Losing my father when I was not yet four, and then being severed from my mother barely a year later, my brother and I were set adrift to sail the uncharted waters of orphanages and foster care. Our first orphanage stop was unmemorable, which I attribute to my tender age. Our second stop, a three and a half year stay in a Brooklyn foster home, was only too memorable because it was so bad.

There I was, at age nine, and we had just run away from an abusive foster home.

It most certainly was a pivotal point in my life. Looking back on it now, I'm convinced that if we had had one or two more harmful placements at that time, then both my brother and I would have been scarred permanently. What form that would have taken can only be speculative, but it would not have been in our favor.

Fortunately, we were placed in the Pride of Judea. It literally was our sanctuary, our much-needed port in a storm.

Given my needs at that time, physical, psychological and social, this place was ideal for me. My peers were kids just like me, and they were a good bunch. There was an immediate cameraderie which was sustained throughout my entire stay. The adults in my life, not only didn't hassle me, they even appreciated my abilities, especially my being able to get along well with others. The outstanding supervisors provided the affection, acceptance, and achievement that all young people require for their healthiest development.

Add to the mix the additional pluses of the Pride; its relative smallness (two to three hundred children) which was conducive to a more relaxed and pleasant environment; its emphasis on scholastic success, which suited my own aspirations; its many recreational activities in which I was an active participant; its full summer programs, which we all loved; and its healthy coed contacts, which were valuable to me and everyone else. It's quite easy to see why it was such a good fit for me. I really thrived there. Looking back at that period, I clearly can see the somewhat frightened nine-year-old "Peewee" arriving at the Pride on a cold December day after five years in two horrible residential settings. I also can see the more confident, even somewhat cocky sixteen-year-old, seven years later, angry as hell at his sudden, unwanted departure, but really quite able to face the vagaries of his future in a fairly strong way.

Looking back at my life, I believe that I had three major pillars in my foundation as a human being. The first was having the invaluable presence of a wonderful elder brother during my most vulnerable childhood years. From the age of four-and-a-half, when I was placed in my first orphanage, and then, through the unpleasant three and a half year foster home stay, Bernie was there for me, in every which way. Whether I actually needed him or not, just his presence was a major security blanket for me, and it helped immeasurably.

My second pillar was my seven-year stay in a much needed, positive environment that provided me with the requisites to grow and flourish, the Pride of Judea.

And, of course, probably most important of all, the amazing impact of my mother. It's hard for me to say this, but if I had had a normal home life with her, I don't know whether her effect would have been so profound. It was as if her affliction, which robbed her of her life, was also her strength, enabling her to become such a spiritual force for the two of us. Just as I was blessed by her love while she was alive, so too have I been blessed by her memory throughout my entire life.

The Pride of Judea, then, was indeed an indispensable part of my life; a "safe-haven" when one was needed desperately. It was that and more. It was my home and I look at it now with warmth and gratitude.